The Structure of Technical English

The Structure of Technical English

A. J. Herbert

Longman

LONGMAN GROUP LIMITED
London

Associated companies, branches and representatives throughout the world

First published 1965
First published for E.L.B.S. 1971
*New impressions * 1973 ; * 1975 ;*
** 1976 ; * 1977 ; † 1978*

ISBN 0 582 52523 3

Printed by Koon Wah Lithographers, Singapore.

Preface

This practice book is intended for foreign engineers or students of engineering who have already mastered the elements of English, and who now want to use their knowledge of the language to read books on their own subjects. Readers should understand, however, that the purpose of the book is to teach language, not to teach engineering.

The language in which scientific and technical facts are expressed is certainly not a different language from that of everyday life, but all the same it presents the foreign student with a number of special problems. The most obvious and the most widely recognised of these problems is the vocabulary. Fortunately a number of excellent dictionaries of scientific and technical terms exist. There is, of course, a vast vocabulary of technical words, but the problem is not so frightening as it looks. In the first place, many of these highly technical words are fairly international; and in the second place, they usually have very specialised meanings. In any case, they are not the concern of this book. Much more difficult are the semi-scientific or semi-technical words, which have a whole range of meanings and are frequently used idiomatically. One of the aims of this practice book is to present as many of these words as possible, and as often as possible: words such as ***work*** and ***plant*** and ***load*** and ***feed*** and ***force***. Words like these look harmless, but they can cause a lot of trouble to the student.

And then there is another kind of word which is important: the verbs, adjectives and adverbs which are not specifically scientific, but which belong to the phraseology of science. These are usually formal, dignified and foreign-sounding words, like ***extrude*** and ***propagate*** and ***obviate*** and ***negligible***, which are partly responsible for the slightly fossilised appearance of the typical scientific statement. A wide selection of these words will be found in this book.

But more than anything else, I have tried to describe the technical statement: that is, the completed sentence rather than the individual word. Many of the structures illustrated in the book are found also in ordinary language though not so commonly. But they are essential to the expression of technical facts and ideas – at least for the present. Perhaps in time a more amiable way of writing will emerge, and in fact technical writers are already conscious of the obscurity and pomposity of a great deal of technical writing. But there is a justification for many of their tricks of style, and I have not attempted to criticise them at all, merely to analyse them. The structures and practice sentences in this book are intended to familiarise the foreign student with the kind of writing and the kind of statements he is likely to find in his reading of scientific and technical literature.

In writing technical sentences at all, one is forced to assume that the reader knows a certain amount of the subject. But the knowledge assumed here is not very great. I have taken for granted a knowledge of the terms of elementary mechanics and physics of the kind that would be studied in High Schools. The majority of the sentences in the exercises refer either to common knowledge or to the material contained in the preceding reading sections. This may explain the lack of diversity in the exercise statements, but the only alternative was to assume a wide knowledge of all branches of engineering, which did not seem a good idea. It is expected that the teacher will provide further illustrative material in the subject which his students are taking.

The reading passages which begin each section have been specially written to illustrate features of technical style, and for no other purpose. But I hope that they are reasonably accurate from the engineering point of view, and for this I must express my grateful thanks to a number of lecturers in the University of Birmingham who had read sections of the book and corrected a number of mis-statements: to Dr J. W. R. Griffiths of the Department of Electrical Engineering; to Mr K. E. Porter of the Department of Chemical Engineering; to Mr F. D. Hobbs of the Graduate School in Highway and Traffic Engineering; and above all to Mr P. D. Allen of the Department of Mechanical Engineering, who has given me a great deal of help and answered a layman's questions with endless patience.

A, J. Herbert

Contents

Substitution Tables

Some patterns of English structure are set out in this book as in this example:

<table>
<tr><td rowspan="2">A safety valve is provided</td><td>to
so as to
in order to</td><td>allow</td><td rowspan="2">excess pressure to escape.</td></tr>
<tr><td>for the purpose of
with the object of
with the aim of
with a view to</td><td>allowing</td></tr>
</table>

From this table we can make seven sentences; we may cross vertical lines but not horizontal lines: *to, so as to, in order to* must be followed by *allow* and not by *allowing*. Two of the seven sentences would be:

A safety valve is provided *so as to allow* excess pressure to escape.
A safety valve is provided *with a view to allowing* excess pressure to escape.

Sentences with Common Features

Numbered (in some cases, lettered) sentences are often set out in such a way as to show a common word or phrase, as in:

<table>
<tr><td>1. The work</td><td rowspan="3">} is likely to
} will probably</td><td>{ start early next year.</td></tr>
<tr><td>2. The new engine</td><td>{ be a good one.</td></tr>
<tr><td>3. An explosion</td><td>{ occur at any minute.</td></tr>
</table>

In this case we make only six sentences, since a numbered sentence is continued only on the same line. The first three of our six sentences are:

1. The work *is likely to* start early next year.
2. The work *will probably* start early next year.
3. The new engine *is likely to* be a good one.

Section 1

Reading: Iron and Steel

The earth **contains** a *large number* of metals which are useful to man. One of the most important of these is iron. Modern industry needs *considerable quantities* of this metal, either in the form of iron or in the form of steel. A *certain number* of non-ferrous metals, **including** aluminium and zinc, are also important, but even today *the majority* of our engineering products are of iron or steel. Moreover, iron possesses magnetic properties, which have made the development of electrical power possible.

The iron ore which we find in the earth is not pure. It *contains* some impurities which we must remove by smelting. The process of smelting **consists** of heating the ore in a blast furnace with coke and limestone, and reducing it to metal. Blasts of hot air enter the furnace from the bottom and provide the oxygen which is necessary for the reduction of the ore. The ore becomes molten, and its oxides combine with carbon from the coke. The non-metallic **constituents** of the ore combine with the limestone to form a liquid slag.

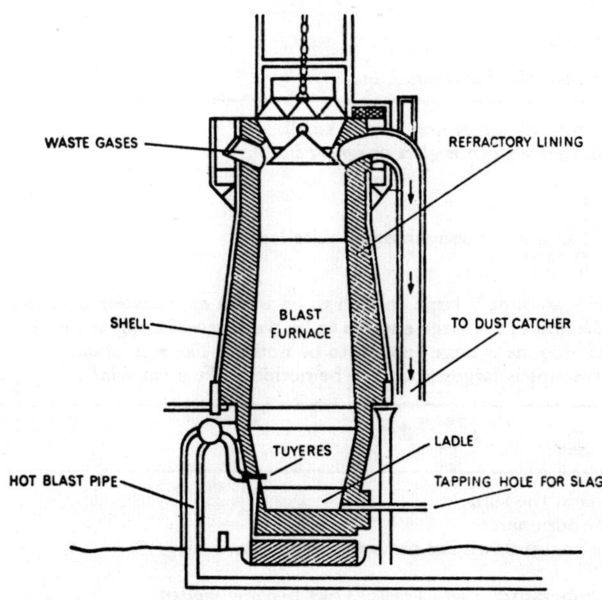

Cross-section of blast furnace

This floats on top of the molten iron, and passes out of the furnace through a tap. The metal which remains is pig-iron.

We can melt this down again in another furnace – a cupola – with more coke and limestone, and tap it out into a ladle or directly into moulds. This is cast-iron. Cast-iron does not have the strength of steel. It is brittle and may fracture under tension. But it possesses certain properties which make it very useful in the manufacture of machinery. In the molten state it is very fluid, and therefore it is easy to cast it into intricate shapes. Also it is easy to machine it. Cast-iron **contains** *small proportions* of other substances. These non-metallic **constituents** of cast-iron **include** carbon, silicon and sulphur, and the presence of these substances affects the behaviour of the metal. Iron which **contains** a *negligible quantity* of carbon, for example wrought-iron, behaves differently from iron which **contains** a lot of carbon.

The carbon in cast-iron is present partly as free graphite and partly as a chemical combination of iron and carbon which we call cementite. This is a very hard substance, and it makes the iron hard too. However, iron can only hold about 1½% of cementite. Any carbon **content** above that *percentage* is present in the form of a flaky graphite. Steel **contains** no free graphite, and its carbon **content** ranges from almost nothing to 1½%. We make wire and tubing from mild steel with a very low carbon **content**, and drills and cutting tools from high carbon steel.

WORD STUDY

Negligible, Considerable, Substantial, etc.

A *negligible* amount of something is very small.
It is so small that we can *neglect* or *ignore* it.

A *considerable* / An *appreciable* / A *substantial* / A *material* } amount of something is quite large.

An *appreciable* amount is large enough to be worth *appreciating* or *noticing*.
A *considerable* amount is large enough to be worth *considering* or *noticing*.
A *substantial* amount is large enough to be noticed, like a *substance*.
A *material* amount is large enough to be noticed, like a *material*.

Melt, Molten, Smelt

Ice-cream *melts* in the sun.
Ice *melts* in the summer.
The *melted* ice comes down the mountain in rivers.

At a certain temperature, metals *melt*. They become *molten*.
The *molten* iron passes out of the furnace into moulds.

We *smelt* iron ore by heat, and change the ore into its metal state:
During *smelting*, the temperature in the furnace is raised and the iron *melts*.
When the ore is *smelted*, it becomes pig-iron.

Property

Every metal possesses certain *properties*, or *characteristics* or *qualities* which we can find by experiment; these *properties* may make the metal suitable or unsuitable for any particular purpose. Designers of high-speed aircraft need new materials with special *properties* such as heat resistance and strength at high temperatures.

Here are some of the *properties* which metals may have:

The metal is *fluid.*	It has *fluidity.*	It flows easily when it melts.
plastic.	*plasticity.*	It pulls out of shape without breaking.
elastic.	*elasticity.*	It always returns to its original shape.
ductile.	*ductility.*	It can be stretched without breaking.
malleable.	*malleability.*	It can be hammered out of shape without breaking.

PATTERNS

1. Make + *Noun* + *Adjective*

<table>
<tr><td rowspan="2">This</td><td>makes</td><td>the problem</td><td colspan="5">easy.[1]
difficult.
interesting.</td></tr>
<tr><td>makes
renders</td><td>the metal</td><td colspan="5">hard.
soft.
strong.
tough.</td></tr>
<tr><td rowspan="2">This</td><td rowspan="2">makes
renders</td><td rowspan="2">the metal</td><td rowspan="2">harder.
softer.
stronger.
weaker.</td><td rowspan="5">=</td><td colspan="3">WITH A FEW COMPARATIVES, ANOTHER STRUCTURE IS POSSIBLE</td></tr>
<tr><td>This</td><td>hardens
softens
strengthens
weakens</td><td>the metal.</td></tr>
<tr><td rowspan="3">This</td><td rowspan="3">makes</td><td>the metal</td><td>longer.
shorter.</td><td rowspan="3">This</td><td>lengthens
shortens</td><td>the metal.</td></tr>
<tr><td>the screw</td><td>tighter.
looser.
flatter.</td><td>tightens
loosens
flattens</td><td>the screw.</td></tr>
<tr><td>the hole</td><td>wider.
deeper.
broader.</td><td>widens
deepens
broadens</td><td>the hole.</td></tr>
</table>

[1] Students unfamiliar with this form of substitution table will find an explanation on page xii.

2. Quantity

<table>
<tr><td rowspan="4">The earth contains</td><td colspan="3">few
not many
a few
some</td><td rowspan="2">precious metals.</td></tr>
<tr><td rowspan="2">a</td><td>small
moderate
certain</td><td rowspan="2">number of</td></tr>
<tr><td>large
great
considerable</td><td rowspan="2">useful substances.</td></tr>
<tr><td colspan="3">a great many
a lot of
plenty of</td></tr>
</table>

<table>
<tr><td rowspan="4">The earth contains</td><td colspan="3">little
not much
a little
some</td><td rowspan="2">uranium.</td></tr>
<tr><td rowspan="2">a</td><td>small
moderate
certain</td><td rowspan="2">amount of</td></tr>
<tr><td>large
great
considerable</td><td rowspan="2">iron ore.</td></tr>
<tr><td colspan="3">a great deal of
a lot of
plenty of</td></tr>
</table>

<table>
<tr><td>The engine
The motor</td><td>produces</td><td>a</td><td>certain
negligible
small
moderate
considerable
large
great</td><td>amount of</td><td>power.</td></tr>
</table>

<table>
<tr><td>A</td><td>certain
moderate
considerable
large</td><td>percentage
proportion
part
amount</td><td>of the world's coal lies in this country.</td></tr>
</table>

EXERCISE

Answer these questions, using an appropriate phrase from the table above.

1. How many substances are present in iron ore?
2. What proportion of countries use electricity from nuclear power stations?
3. How much carbon does wrought-iron contain?
4. How much power do you need to drive a large liner through the water?
5. Are there many gold-fields in the world?
6. How much petroleum is pumped out of the ground every year?
7. What percentage of people in your country work in factories?
8. Are any metals besides ferrous metals used in industry?
9. How much oxygen is needed to burn a ton of coal?
10. How much soil do the rivers carry down to the sea in a year?
11. What proportion of passengers flying in aircraft are killed in crashes?
12. How much of your country's electrical supply is derived from water power?

3. Contents

Contain, Consist, Comprise, Constitute, Include

---

1. The packet	*contains*	20 cigarettes.[1]
2. The gas		about 5½% of carbon monoxide.
3. The alloy		5% nickel and 5% iron.
4. The tank		100 gallons of oil.

5. The carbon monoxide	*content*	was about 5%.
6. The moisture		of the cylinder increased.
7. Part of the heat		of the gases is lost.

8. He emptied out the *contents* of the box.
9. A tank is a large *container* for holding liquids.

10. The class *consists of* twenty-four students.
11. The atmosphere *comprises* a number of gases.
12. The machine *is composed of* several different parts.
13. Cast-iron *is made up of* about six different substances.

14. The factory produces *components* for aircraft.
15. The resultant force acting on an aircraft wing may be resolved into a vertical *component* and a horizontal *component.*
16. The *composition* of cast-iron is different for different purposes.

17. Twenty-four students *constitute* the class.
18. A number of gases *form* the atmosphere.
19. Ferrite and carbon *make up* mild steel.
20. Ferrite and carbon are the *constituents* of mild steel.

---

[1] Students unfamiliar with this way of presenting alternatives will find an explanation on page xii.

21. The students in the class *include* three from Germany and four from France.
22. The gases in the atmosphere *include* oxygen and nitrogen.
23. The mixture in the furnace *includes* a certain amount of limestone.

EXERCISE

Complete these statements with the proper 'Content' word:

1. The metals which we find in the earth ...... iron, lead and copper.
2. The carbon ...... of wrought-iron is very low.
3. We know the chemical ...... of the liquid from previous analysis.
4. Smelting ...... of heating the iron ore in a furnace and removing the slag.
5. The ...... of moulding sand ...... quartz, felspar and mica.
6. The atom ...... a nucleus, and electrons moving round it in space.
7. All matter ...... of atoms.
8. Metals which we use widely in industry ...... aluminium and steel.
9. We can discover the ...... gases of a fuel by chemical analysis.
10. The total floor space of the factory ...... 20,000 square feet on two floors.
11. The moisture ...... of the gas can be reduced by condensation.
12. Chromium is a necessary ...... of stainless steels.
13. This concrete ...... 1 part lime, 2 parts sand and 4 parts aggregate.
14. Most fuels ...... a mixture of different substances.
15. This company does not manufacture the engine itself, but only certain ...... of it.
16. The compound strip ...... two strips riveted together, one of iron and the other of copper.
17. It is easy for any faulty ...... to be taken out of the machine and replaced.
18. A flask of water, a glass rod and a rubber bung ...... the only equipment which we need for the experiment.
19. The flask ...... a very small amount of water.
20. The 30,000 books in the library ...... a substantial number of books on engineering.

Section 2

Reading: Heat Treatment of Steel

We can alter the characteristics of steel in various ways. In the first place, steel which contains very little carbon will be *milder than* steel which contains a higher percentage of carbon, up to the limit of about $1\frac{1}{2}\%$. Secondly, we can heat the steel above a certain critical temperature, and then **allow** it **to** cool at different rates. At this critical temperature, changes begin to take place in the molecular structure of the metal. In the process known as annealing, we heat the steel above the critical temperature and **permit** it **to** cool very slowly. This **causes** the metal **to** become softer than before, and *much easier to machine*. Annealing has a second advantage. It helps to relieve any internal stresses which exist in the metal. These stresses are liable to occur through hammering or working the metal, or through rapid cooling. Metal which we **cause to** cool rapidly contracts *more rapidly* on the outside *than* on the inside. This produces unequal contractions, which may give rise to distortion or cracking. Metal which cools slowly is *less liable* to have these internal stresses *than* metal which cools quickly.

On the other hand, we can make steel harder by rapid cooling. We heat it up beyond the critical temperature, and then quench it in water or some other liquid. The rapid temperature drop fixes the structural change in the steel which occurred at the critical temperature, and makes it very hard. But a bar of this hardened steel is *more liable to fracture than* normal steel. We therefore heat it again to a temperature below the critical temperature, and cool it slowly. This treatment is called tempering. It helps to relieve the internal stresses, and makes the steel *less brittle than* before. The properties of tempered steel **enable** us **to** use it in the manufacture of tools which need a fairly hard steel. High carbon steel is *harder than* tempered steel, but it is *much more difficult to work.*

These heat treatments take place during the various shaping operations. We can obtain bars and sheets of steel by rolling the metal through huge rolls in a rolling-mill. The roll pressures must be *much greater* for cold rolling *than* for hot rolling, but cold rolling **enables** the operators **to** produce rolls of great accuracy and uniformity, and with a better surface finish. Other shaping operations include drawing into wire, casting in moulds, and forging.

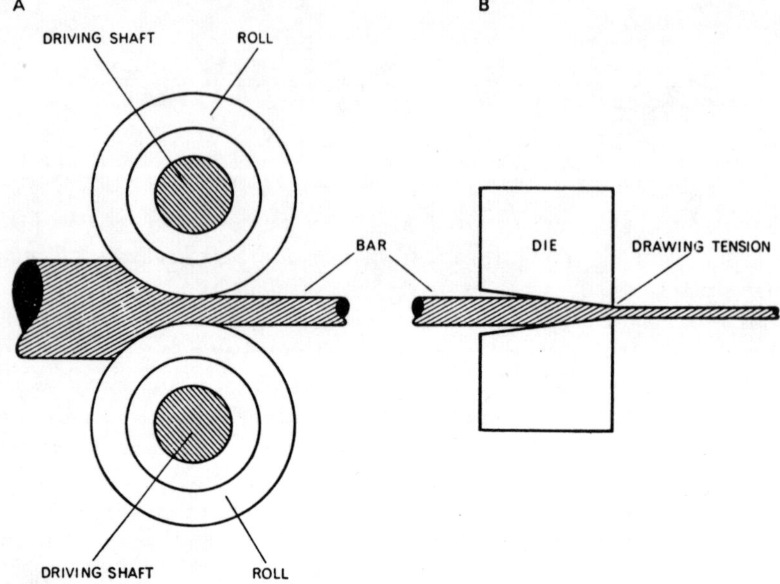

(A) Roller-mill with rolls
(B) Drawing-bench

WORD STUDY

Likely, Liable, Susceptible

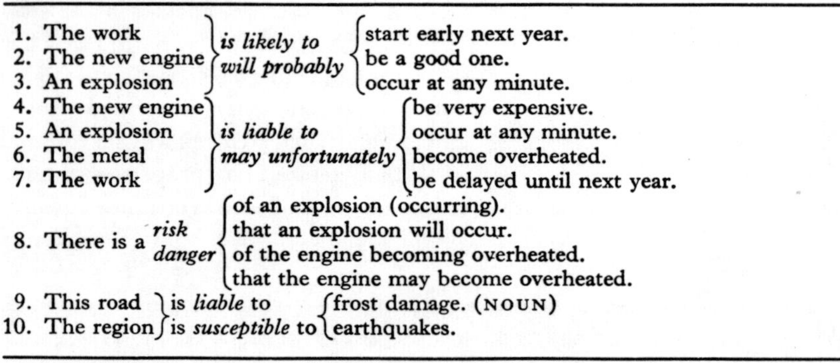

1. The work 2. The new engine 3. An explosion	*is likely to* *will probably*	start early next year. be a good one. occur at any minute.
4. The new engine 5. An explosion 6. The metal 7. The work	*is liable to* *may unfortunately*	be very expensive. occur at any minute. become overheated. be delayed until next year.
8. There is a	*risk* *danger*	of an explosion (occurring). that an explosion will occur. of the engine becoming overheated. that the engine may become overheated.
9. This road 10. The region	is *liable* to is *susceptible* to	frost damage. (NOUN) earthquakes.

Bring about, Produce, Cause, Give Rise to

1. Changes in temperature 2. The high temperature 3. These experiments 4. A drop in pressure 5. Automation	may will can	*bring about* *produce* *give rise to* *cause*	changes in the length of the bar. cracks in the furnace walls. new methods of construction. cylinder condensation. a lot of unemployment.

Expand, Contract

Most substances *expand* when they are heated. = They grow bigger or longer.
Most substances *contract* when they are cooled. = They grow smaller or shorter.

When substances are heated, *expansion* takes place.
When substances are cooled, *contraction* takes place.

The *coefficient of expansion*, which tells us how much a substance will *expand* for each degree rise in temperature, is different for different substances.

Relieve (= to make less severe)

When the pressure in a boiler becomes too great, we can *relieve* it by allowing some of the steam to escape.
We can *relieve* the stresses in a steel bar by tempering it.

Critical

1. = decisive (point or stage) and therefore important or serious.
   The sick man is going through a *crisis*. He is in a *critical* condition.
   There is a political *crisis*. The political situation is *critical*.

2. = a decisive point in temperature, pressure or angle at which something is about to happen.
   The *critical* temperature of steel: above or below this temperature the molecular structure changes.
   The *critical* temperature of a gas: above this temperature it cannot be liquefied by pressure.
   The *critical* pressure: the pressure at which a gas can be liquefied.

Help, Assist, Facilitate

1. Annealing *helps to remove* (*helps or assists in removing*) internal stresses from the metal.
2. Safety devices *help to prevent* (*help or assist in preventing*) accidents in the machine shop.

3. A good transport system	*facilitates* (*makes easier*)	the distribution of goods.
4. Prefabrication of the walls		rapid erection of houses.
5. The use of standard components		replacement when they are worn.

Conducive

1. Regular maintenance is	*conducive to* (*helpful to*)	better performance of the machine.
2. Good labour relations are		improved production.
3. Turbulence in the cylinder is		more efficient burning of the gases.

PATTERNS

1. Enable, Allow, Make, etc. + Infinitive

Note: *Enable* really means to *make possible*, but it is often used in the same sense as *allow* and *permit*. *Let* is spoken, but not often written in this sense. With *let* and *make*, the word 'to' is not used before the infinitive.

1. The microscope 2. A thermometer	*enables*	scientists the doctor	*to*	examine very small objects. measure body temperature.
3. Helicopters 4. Good production methods	*enable*	passengers the factory	*to*	land in the city centre. manufacture more cars.
5. Expansion joints 6. Safety valves 7. We	*permit* *allow*	the pipes the steam the metal	*to*	expand or contract. escape from the boiler. cool slowly.
8. The heat 9. Weakness in the metal	*caused*	the metal it	*to*	melt. fracture under tension.
10. The heat 11. Weakness in the metal	*made*	the metal melt. it fracture under tension.		

EXERCISE

Complete these statements using the verbs shown above:

1. The rise in temperature ...... the mercury ...... rise up the tube.
2. The motorway ...... motorists ...... travel from London to Birmingham much more quickly than before.
3. The use of tractors ...... more food ...... be produced more cheaply.
4. The presence of oxygen ...... the mixture ...... burn rapidly.
5. The failure of both engines ...... the aircraft ...... crash.
6. The increase in exports ...... the country ...... import more raw materials.
7. The risk of an explosion ...... the workers ...... leave the factory.
8. The speed of the train ...... it ...... leave the rails on the curve.
9. The fluidity of cast-iron ...... it ...... be cast into intricate shapes.
10. The use of a pressure gauge ...... the engineer ...... read the boiler pressure.
11. The sharp rise in temperature ...... the engine ...... overheat.
12. The presence of non-metallic constituents in iron ...... it ...... behave in various ways.
13. Rapid cooling ...... unequal contractions ...... occur in the metal.
14. The growth of industrial towns ...... many people ...... leave the countryside.
15. The differential gear ...... the two rear wheels ...... turn at different speeds.

2. Comparative

Here are some of the most useful patterns for comparing two things:

Steel	is	stronger far stronger slightly stronger more expensive much more expensive a much more expensive material a much more expensive material to produce	than	cast-iron.
Cast-iron	is	weaker less expensive much less expensive a much less expensive material a much less expensive material to produce	than	steel.
Cast-iron	is	not so expensive not quite so expensive not quite such an expensive material not quite such an expensive material to produce	as	steel.
Cast-iron	is	as useful almost as useful almost as useful a material	as	steel.

EXERCISE

Join the two statements in each line, by comparing one with the other. Turn the comparison round both ways:

e.g. *A is larger than B*
B is not so large as A, etc.

1. The carbon content of mild steel is 0·2%; the carbon content of cast-steel is 1·2%.
2. Wrought-iron contains 0·02% of carbon; it contains 0·02% of manganese.
3. The British engine weighs 3 tons; the French engine weighs 3½ tons.
4. The electric heater costs a penny an hour to run; the gas heater costs twopence an hour.
5. Cast iron-contains up to 3·0% of silicon; it contains up to 1·5% of phosphorus.
6. The temperature in this room is 28° C; the temperature outside the room is 22° C.
7. My radio works very well; my brother's radio works very badly.
8. The journey takes four hours by day; it takes five hours at night.

9. Alcohol is not often used in thermometers; mercury is used very often in thermometers.
10. Alcohol boils at 78° C; water boils at 100° C.
11. The new car does 35 miles per gallon; the old car did only 30 miles per gallon.
12. Aluminium has a coefficient of expansion of 0·000025; copper has a coefficient of expansion of 0·000017.
13. The steel workers receive 30 shillings per shift; the coal miners receive 30 shillings per shift too.
14. This engine needs servicing every 3 months; the latest engine needs servicing every 5 months.

3. Maximum and Minimum

---

1. *a.* The ***maximum*** temperature The ***upper*** temperature ***limit***	in this country is about	35° Centigrade.
b. The ***minimum*** temperature The ***lower*** temperature ***limit***		0° Centigrade.
c. The ***average*** / ***mean*** temperature		$17\frac{1}{2}$° C.
d. The temperature ***range***		35° C.

e. The temperature in this country *ranges* / *varies* from 35° C to 0° C.

---

2. *a.* In summer the temperature *rises.* / *increases.* There is *a rise* / *an increase* in temperature.

b. In winter the temperature *falls.* / *drops.* / *decreases.* There is a *fall* / *drop* / *decrease* in temperature.

c. By *heating* / *cooling* a substance, we can *raise* / *lower* its temperature to *boiling* / *freezing* point.

---

3. *a.* The maximum ***pressure*** in the boiler is 500 lb/in^2.

b. The maximum ***speed*** of the aircraft is 800 m.p.h. (miles per hour).

c. The maximum ***fuel consumption*** of the engine is 30 m.p.g. (miles per gallon).

d. The maximum ***speed*** of the turbine is 8000 r.p.m. (revolutions per minute).

e. The maximum ***diameter*** of the tube is $\frac{9}{16}$ inch.

Section 3

Reading: Lubrication of Bearings

The machine tools in a workshop sometimes have their own electric motors, or they may take the power they need from a motor which feeds several machines. The shafts which carry the power from the motor to the machines need some kind of support to *keep them steady*. We call these supports bearings. There are different types of bearings for different purposes. We can classify them according to whether they take the load on the

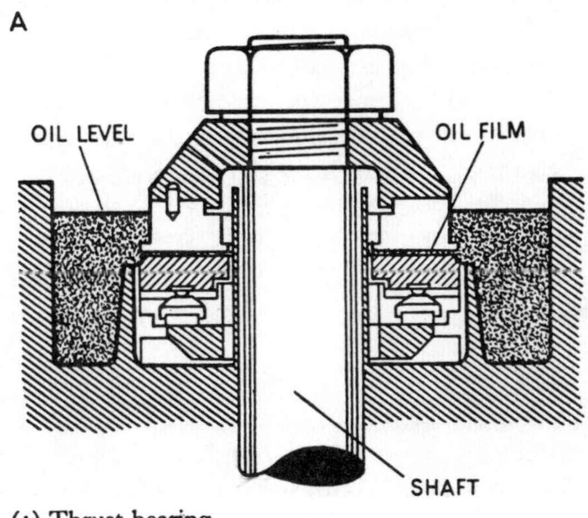

(A) Thrust bearing

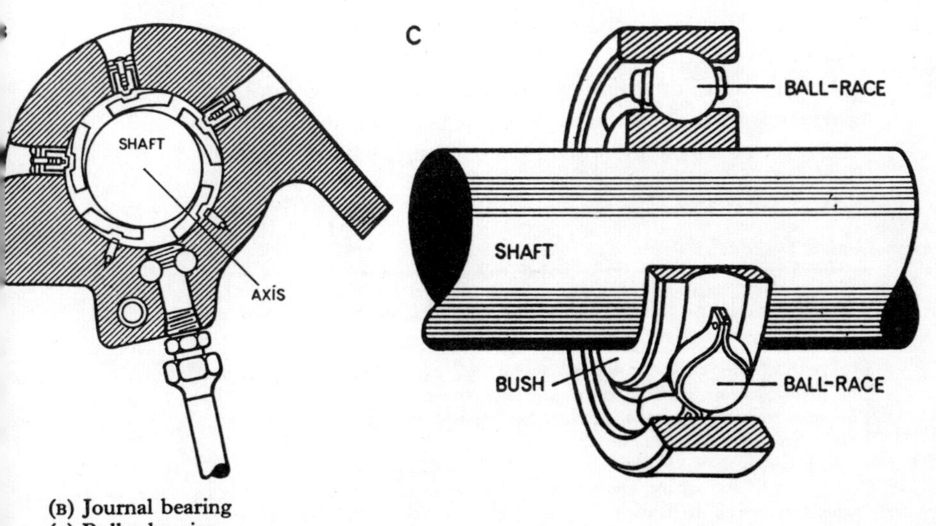

(B) Journal bearing
(C) Roller bearing

shaft or the thrust along the axis of the shaft. The former type is known as a journal bearing, and the latter type as a thrust bearing.

The rotating shaft bears on a stationary bush or tube. We therefore have two metal surfaces in close contact with each other, and sliding over each other often at high speed. This will cause friction and the bearing will become heated. So we have to *protect* the metal surfaces *from* overheating and damage. First of all, we *avoid* making the shaft and the bush of the same material. The shafting itself is generally of steel, but we use another metal such as cast-iron or bronze or white metal for the bush. At a certain temperature, the metal in the bush will seize or run, and this will *prevent* damage to the shaft. But of course it will not *prevent* overheating *from* occurring.

However, we can *reduce* the danger of overheating by lubrication. We have a thin film of oil between the two metallic surfaces to *keep them apart*. The internal friction of oil is much less than the friction between two solids, and generates less heat. Lubrication also offers another advantage. A film of oil on the metal surfaces will *prevent* them *from* corroding by *protecting* them *from* the air.

The sort of lubricant which we use depends largely on the running speed of the bearing. We can use grease in low-speed bearings, but grease offers more resistance to the turning movement of the shaft. A lighter oil causes less friction, and so an oily lubricant is better for high-speed bearings. The rotation of the shaft carries the film of oil round the inside of the bearing and *keeps* the shaft *from* contact with the bush which houses it. We can feed the oil into the bearing in several ways. Sometimes we allow it to drip down under the influence of gravity. More commonly, a pump or gun feeds it in under pressure. In motor-car and other engines, we half cover the bearing in an oil-bath, and oil splashes up into it.

We can reduce the amount of friction even more with rolling bearings. The hardened steel balls in this type of bearing roll round in a finely-ground ball race, and make little more than point contact with the race.

WORD STUDY

Contact (= touch)

When the platinum points *are in contact with* / *make contact with* each other, a current flows.

The two moving surfaces are ***in contact with*** each other as little as possible.
The piston does not come ***in contact with*** the cylinder cover.
The water which is ***in close contact with*** the steam will evaporate first.
The various departments are ***in close touch*** with each other all the time.

The leaves of the spring are ***not in contact with*** each other. They are ***separated*** or ***kept apart*** by strips of rubber.

House, Accommodate

---

1. The university *houses* / *accommodates* most of its students in hostels.
2. An aluminium bush *houses* the bearing.

3. The cylinders	*accommodate*	a certain volume of steam.
4. The air cannot	*hold*	any more steam without a rise in temperature.

Resist, Withstand

---

1. High-speed aircraft need metals which can	*resist*	very high temperatures.
2. Turbine blades must be able to	*withstand*	creep and corrosion.

3. Curved rails	*offer resistance to*	the movement of the train.
4. Some materials		the passage of electric current.
5. Silicones		moisture and heat.

6. Thick grease *offers more resistance to* motion than thin oils.

7. Silicones are *resistant to* moisture and heat.

Advantages

The *advantage of* rolling bearings *is that* they cause less friction.

This type of bearing *has* / *offers* / *possesses* several *advantages over* the sliding bearing.

Its low cost *confers* a great *advantage on* this type of engine.

The earlier type of engine *has* / *suffers from* *the disadvantage of* being expensive to run.

PATTERNS

1. The Use of Will, Can and May

These are the most important uses of these three words:

1. *Futurity* (*Will*)

   Note: We do not often use the form *is going to* in technical writing or speech to show the future.

Production of the new machine *will* commence next year.
Work *will* shortly begin on the new motorway.
The new aircraft *will* fly for the first time on Monday.

---

2. *Capability* (*Will, Can, Capable, Are able to*)

These planes	*will fly* *can fly* *are capable of flying* *are able to fly*	at 800 miles per hour.

3. *What always happens* (*Will*)

This solid *will* vaporise when we heat it.
Friction *will* cause the bearings to become heated.
Good lubrication *will* reduce the friction.

4. *What sometimes happens* (*May, Can*)

Metal which cools rapidly Unguarded belts or chains The testing of new planes	*may* *can*	fracture. cause accidents. take a long time.

5. *Ability* (*Can*)

Work on the new engine *can* start in a few weeks.
We *can* easily calculate the frictional losses.

Note: The uses shown above can have both active and passive forms (see Section 5) But the use which follows is nearly always in the passive form.

6. *Possibility* (*Can, May*)

Low-speed bearings This problem The steel Thermo-couples	*can be* *may be*	lubricated with grease. approached in several ways. quenched in either water or oil. used to measure high temperatures.

EXERCISE

Decide on the meaning of these statements, and add *will*, *can*, etc. Where there is more than one possibility, show whether there is a difference of meaning or not:

1. This type of disease (...... cause) death.
2. A number of metals (...... carry) electric current.
3. The tank (...... hold) ten gallons of petrol.
4. The drive to a machine (...... obtain) from a shaft.
5. The bridge (...... take) about eighteen months to complete.
6. The docks (...... handle) more than twenty ships at a time.
7. Severe storms (...... occur) in the Atlantic during winter.
8. The winds in the centre of the storm (...... be) up to 130 miles per hour.

9. Heat-treated steel (...... give) strengths as high as 120 tons per square inch.
10. A flexible belt (...... twist) in more than one plane.
11. The new motorway (...... have) three traffic lanes in each direction.
12. An error of judgement on the part of the pilot (...... be) disastrous.
13. A magnetic needle (...... point) towards the magnetic north pole.
14. Castings (...... contract) slightly as they cool.
15. Iron and steel at a high temperature (...... oxidise) in the air.
16. A bright surface (...... reflect) sunlight, but a dull surface (...... absorb) it.
17. This metal (...... resist) temperatures of 600° Centigrade.
18. The factory (...... take on) a number of skilled workmen in the autumn.
19. The boiler (...... feed) with any type of solid fuel.
20. Above a certain critical temperature, the structure of the steel (...... change).

2. Prevention, Protection, etc.

Good lubrication	*prevents*	overheating. damage to the bearings.	
	prevents *keeps*	the bearings from	becoming overheated. being damaged.

This *keeps* the	water	in.	=	This	*prevents* *keeps*	the	water from	escaping.
		out.						entering.
	pressure	up.					pressure from	falling.
		down.						rising.
	screws tight. air clean.						screws from working loose. air from getting dirty.	

A thin film of oil *protects* the bearings from corrosion.
A guard on the machine *protects* the workers from injury.

Workers should *avoid*	wearing loose overalls in the factory. using these materials wastefully.

By taking precautions in the factory we can	*reduce* *prevent* *avoid* *obviate* *eliminate*	the	risk danger possibility	of accidents.

EXERCISE

Complete these statements with a suitable verb from those used above, or the corresponding noun:

1. Coal miners wear safety helmets to ...... them from falling rock.
2. The lock on the door ...... the thieves from entering the office.
3. The noise from the street ...... him from sleeping.
4. The doctors ...... the patient alive with drugs.
5. Lack of capital ...... the company from buying the new machinery.
6. We have to ...... the steel from contact with air when we heat or cool it. This ...... oxidation from taking place.
7. These drugs do not afford complete ...... from the disease, but they ...... the likelihood of catching it.
8. We normally ...... having two similar metals sliding over each other.
9. The non-return valve ...... the steam from escaping.
10. A refrigerator ...... food fresh for a long time.
11. The filter ...... grit from getting into the engine.
12. The use of helium rather than hydrogen ...... the possibility of explosion.
13. Good planning ...... the production costs down.
14. The ...... of fire in a mine is of the greatest importance.
15. Working in shifts ...... shutting down the boilers at night.
16. Cooling the metal in oil rather than water ...... the risk of cracking.

3. Classification

There are	two three several many	*types* *kinds* *sorts* *classes* *varieties*	of bearings.	
Bearings are	*of*	two, etc.	*types*, etc.	(*of* = belonging to).
We can *classify*	bearings	according to	their position on the shaft. whether they take the load on the shaft or the end thrust.	
We can *divide*	bearings	into several	*classes* *categories* *groups*	according to . . . (as above).

EXERCISE

Try to classify the following in the same way:

1. Engineering (e.g. mechanical, electrical, chemical).
2. Schools (e.g. primary, secondary, technical).
3. Bridges (e.g. suspension, cantilever).
4. Disease.
5. Metals.
6. Iron.
7. Words.
8. Fuel.
9. Waves.
10. Engines.

Section 4

Reading: The Lathe

The lathe is one of the most useful and versatile machines in the workshop, and is capable of carrying out a wide variety of machining operations. The main components of the lathe are the headstock and tailstock at opposite ends of a bed, and a tool-post between them which holds the cutting tool. The tool-post stands on a cross-slide which enables it to move *sidewards* across the saddle or carriage as well as along it, **depending on** the kind of job it is doing. The ordinary centre lathe can accommodate only one tool at a time on the tool-post, but a turret lathe is capable of holding five or more tools on the *revolving* turret. The lathe bed must be very solid to prevent the machine from bending or twisting under stress.

The headstock incorporates the driving and gear mechanism, and a spindle which holds the workpiece and causes it to *rotate* at a speed which **depends** largely **on** the diameter of the workpiece. A bar of large diameter should naturally *rotate* more slowly than a very thin bar; the cutting speed of the tool is what matters. Tapered centres in the hollow nose of the spindle and of the tailstock hold the work firmly between them. A feed-shaft from the headstock *drives* the tool-post along the saddle, either *forwards* or *backwards*, at a fixed and uniform speed. This enables the operator to make accurate cuts and to give the work a good finish. Gears between the spindle and the feed-shaft control the speed of *rotation* of the shaft, and therefore the *forward* or *backward* movement of the tool-post. The gear which the operator will select **depends on** the type of metal which he is cutting and the amount of metal he has to cut off. For a deep or roughing cut the *forward* movement of the tool should be less than for a finishing cut.

Centres are not suitable for every job on the lathe. The operator can replace them by various types of chucks, which hold the work between jaws, or by a front-plate, **depending on** the shape of the work and the particular cutting operation. He will use a chuck, for example, to hold a short piece of work, or work for drilling, boring or screw-cutting. A *transverse* movement of the tool-post across the saddle enables the tool to cut across the face of the workpiece and give it a flat surface. For screw-cutting, the operator engages the lead-screw, a long screwed shaft which runs along in front of the bed and which *rotates* with the spindle. The lead-screw *drives* the tool-post *forwards* along the carriage at the correct speed, and this ensures that the threads on the screw are of exactly the right pitch. The operator can select different gear speeds, and

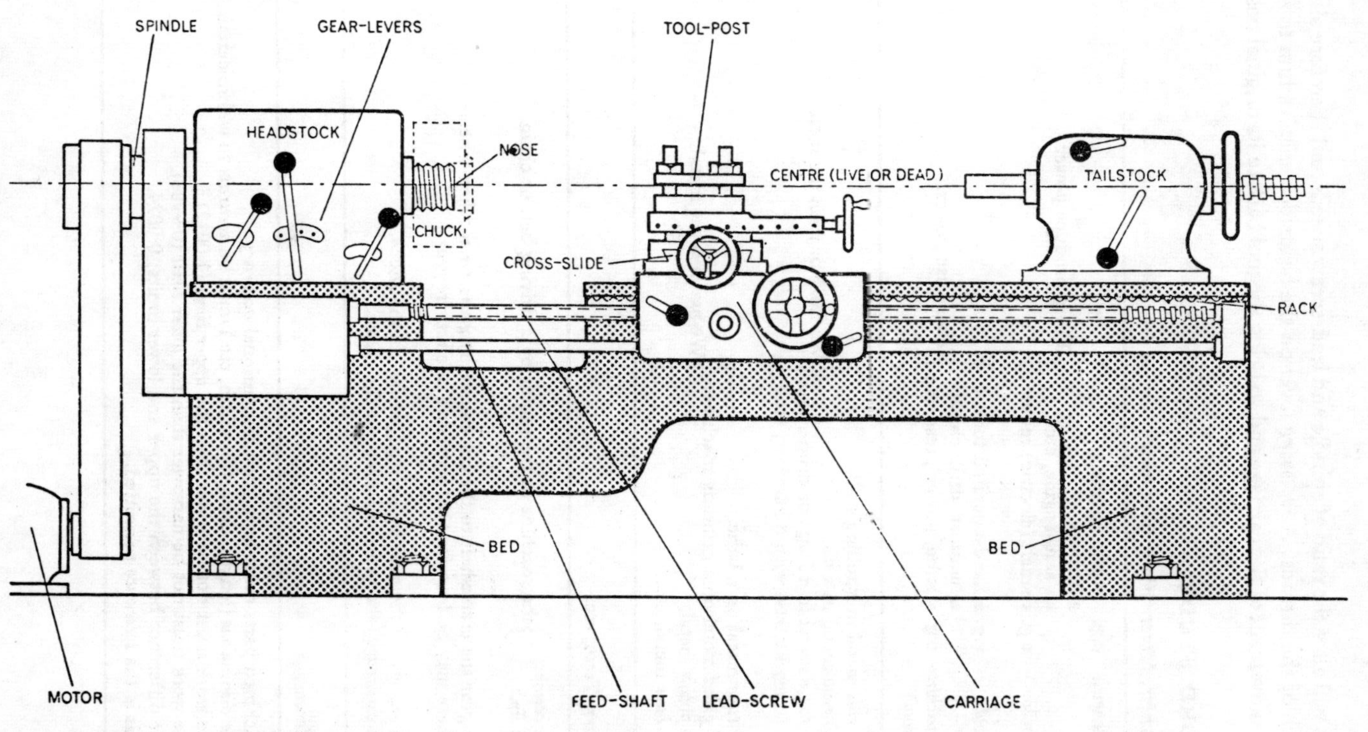

Centre lathe

this will alter the ratio of spindle and lead-screw speeds and therefore alter the pitch of the threads. A *reversing* lever on the headstock enables him to *reverse* the movement of the carriage and so bring the tool back to its original position.

WORD STUDY

Machine, Motor, Work, Tool, etc.

An *engine*	e.g. a steam engine a turbine an aero-engine, etc.	These produce power.
A *motor*	e.g. a small (electric) motor	
A *tool*	e.g. a hand-operated tool, a hammer, drill, chisel	These use power.
A *machine-* (*tool*)	e.g. a lathe, power press, etc.	

We *roll* metal in a rolling-mill. We *draw* metal in a die. We *forge* metal in a forge or drop-forge. We *hammer* metal with a hammer, etc.	We *work* or *form* the metal.
We *turn* metal on a lathe. We *grind* metal on a grinding machine. We *polish* metal. We *bore* metal, etc.	We *machine* the metal.

Gears, Teeth, etc.

We *connect* / We *link* } the machine to the motor by a driving belt or chain.

We *gear* the crankshaft to the car engine by *gears,* or toothed wheels. (There may be four *forward gears* and one *reverse gear.*)

We *engage* the gear by *letting* (*putting*) *in* the *clutch.*
We *disengage* the gear by *letting out* the *clutch.*

Tolerance

Machined parts must have great dimensional *accuracy.*
The *dimensions* (length, diameter, width, etc.) must be *accurate* to within certain limits.
The work must not be wider than the *upper limit* (1·0012).
The work must not be narrower than the *lower limit* (0·9988).
The difference between the upper and lower limits: 0·0024.
This is the *tolerance* permitted.

Incorporate

The pulley *incorporates* (has) a brake.
The headstock *incorporates* (contains) the gears and driving mechanism.
The solder *incorporates* (includes) a fluxing material.
The vessel *incorporates* (has) a number of new constructional features.

PATTERNS

1. Dependence

You should pay special attention to the contructions used with this word. Notice that the first meaning (1*a*) is slightly different from the rest.

---

1. *a.* The aircraft is *dependable* (*reliable*). You can *depend on* (*rely on*) it. It will not break down.
   b. The aircraft *depends on* its wings and engines to provide lift.
   c. Sweden *is dependent on* her hydro-electric resources for power.
   d. Our customers *rely on* our completing their order by the agreed date.

2.

a. The size of the motor	*depends on* / *is dependent on*	the amount of power it has to produce.
b. The rise in pressure		the speed of rotation of the pump.
c. The hardness of the steel		the proportion of carbon it contains.

3.

a. The steel will be mild or hard	*depending on* / *according to*	the proportion of carbon it contains.
b. The metal will expand or contract		whether the temperature rises or falls.

4. The climate remains the same, *independent of* (*irrespective of*) the season of the year.

EXERCISE

Complete these statements with the appropriate word or words.

1. The amount of expansion which takes place ...... the coefficient of expansion of the metal.
2. The saturation pressure of a vapour ...... its temperature.
3. The building work will start this month or next, ... how soon enough labour is available.
4. The depth of the road surface will ...... the volume of traffic it carries.
5. This country ...... imports from abroad for more than half its food.
6. The motor may be large or small ...... the amount of power it has to give.
7. The research programme will continue ...... the cost.
8. The angle of refraction of light ...... the angle of incidence.
9. The value of a metal ...... whether it is rare or abundant.

10. He teaches all the children of the neighbourhood, ... whether they are rich or poor.
11. The passengers ...... the pilot and navigator for their safety.
12. Progress with nuclear reactors will ...... solving many engineering problems.
13. The velocity of the liquid flow ...... the diameter of the pipe it flows through.
14. A number of different tools are available ...... the amount of money you can spend on them.
15. The number of tools which you can buy ...... the amount of money you can spend.

2. Movements

1. *a.*	A trip-lever	*actuates* *operates*	the valve.		(= makes it move).
b.	A flexible belt	*drives*	the motor.		(= makes it {move / turn / work}).
2. *a.*	The piston	*moves* *travels* *slides* *runs*	forwards. backwards. up. down.	=	A(n) *forward* / *backward* / *upward* / *downward* movement of the piston The *travel* of the piston is the *distance* it travels.
	The piston	*reciprocates*, or *moves*, etc.			A *reciprocating* movement. / engine.
b.	The pendulum	*oscillates*, or *swings*.			An *oscillating* / *oscillatory* movement
c.	The cross-slide	*traverses* *crosses*	the carriage.		A *sideward* / *transverse* movement.
d.	The wheels	*rotate.* *turn.* *revolve.*			A *rotational* / *rotary* movement.
e.	The liquid The steam The air	*circulates*	through the pipes.		A *circulating* movement through a *circuit.*

3.	The machine is	*at rest.* *stationary.*
	The machine is	*in motion.* *moving.*

3. Velocity

The	*velocity* *speed*	of the	aircraft fluid gas, etc.	*increases.* *rises.* *decreases.* *falls.*

The aircraft	*increases speed.* *speeds up.* *accelerates.*	There is an	*increase*	in speed.
	decreases speed. *reduces speed.* *slows down.* *decelerates.*		*decrease* *reduction*	

Opening the throttle of a car	makes it go faster. *accelerates it.*
Applying the brake of a car	makes it go slower. *retards it.*

Section 5

Reading: Welding

There are a number of **methods** of joining metal articles together, depending on the type of metal and the strength of the joint which *is required.* Soldering gives a satisfactory joint for light articles of steel, copper or brass, but the strength of a soldered joint is rather less than a joint which *is brazed, riveted* or *welded.* These **methods** of joining metal *are normally adopted* for strong permanent joints.

The simplest **method** of welding two pieces of metal together *is known* as pressure welding. The ends of metal *are heated* to a white heat – for iron, the welding temperature should be about 1300° C – in a flame. At this temperature the metal becomes plastic. The ends *are then pressed* or *hammered* together, and the joint *is smoothed off.* Care *must be taken* to ensure that the surfaces are thoroughly clean first, for dirt will weaken the weld. Moreover, the heating of iron or steel to a high temperature causes oxidation, and a film of oxide *is formed* on the heated surfaces. For this reason, a flux *is applied* to the heated metal. At welding heat, the flux melts, and the oxide particles *are dissolved* in it together with any other impurities which may be present. The metal surfaces *are pressed* together, and the flux *is squeezed out* from the centre of the weld. A number of different types of weld *may be used,* but for fairly thick bars of metal, a vee-shaped weld *should normally be employed.* It is rather stronger than the ordinary butt weld.

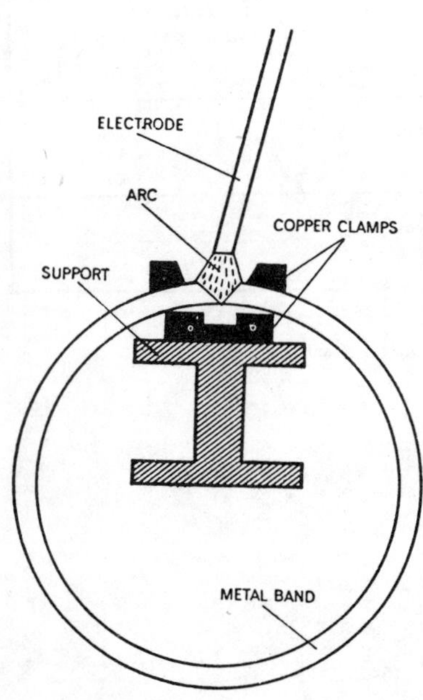

Electric arc welding

The heat for fusion welding *is generated* in several **ways,** depending on the sort of metal which *is being welded* and on its shape. An extremely hot flame *can be produced* from an oxy-acetylene torch. For certain welds an electric arc *is used.* In this **method,** an electric current *is passed* across two electrodes, and the metal surfaces *are placed* between them. The electrodes *are sometimes made* of carbon, but more frequently they are metallic. The work itself constitutes one of them and the other is an insulated filler rod. An arc *is struck* between the two, and the heat which *is generated* melts the metal at the weld. A different **method** *is usually employed* for welding sheets or plates of metal together. This *is known* as spot welding. Two sheets or plates *are placed* together with a slight overlap, and a current *is passed* between the electrodes. At welding temperature, a strong pressure *is applied* to the metal sheets. The oxide film, and any impurities which *are trapped* between the sheets, *are squeezed* out, and the weld *is made.*

WORD STUDY

Adopt (= take over, accept, put into use)

1. Various methods can be	*adopted*	to keep the temperature down.
2. We have		the conclusions reached in the report.
3. Paraffin is now		as a fuel because it is easily atomised.
4. Great Britain recently		the Centigrade scale for temperatures.
5. The designers		a more compact form of construction for the machine.

Apply (= put on)

1. A pressure of x lb./in² is	*applied*	to the piston.
2. When pressure is		to the ice, some of it will melt.
3. Insulation should be		to the wire in the form of a paste.
4. Grease may be		to the bearings with a grease gun.
5. This principle was successfully		to the design of high-speed aircraft.

Exploit, Utilise, Employ

1. The government intends to	*exploit*	the natural resources of the country.
2. It will be difficult to	*make use of*	this invention commercially.
3. This country failed to		its five-year lead over other countries in jet-engines.

1. The properties of uranium are	*used*	in nuclear reactors.
2. Electrical power from the generator is	*utilised*	in the motor.
3. Steam at boiler pressure is	*employed*	to produce draughts of air in the boiler.
4. Different types of electric arc are		for various purposes.

Fairly, Rather, Slightly

1. The temperature in the boiler is	*normal* (500° C).
	slightly high (505° C).
	fairly high (= this is an advantage).
	rather high (= this is a disadvantage).

2. (Comparative)

The temperature in the boiler is	*slightly above normal* (505° C).
	rather above normal (520° C).
	slightly higher than it should be.
	rather higher than it should be.

Note: *rather*, not *fairly*, is used with comparatives, whether they indicate an advantage or a disadvantage.

PATTERNS

1. The Impersonal Passive

In the first four sections, we avoided using the passive type of statement, and concentrated on the types of statement which are frequently made in the active form. But you must remember that the majority of statements in technical writing are in the passive form, because the technical writer wants to be objective and impersonal. He does not usually start a sentence with *I* or *you* or *the operator*, etc. From this section on, we shall be using the passive form very often.

Here are a few examples of the change from active into passive.

Active	*Passive*
The driver starts the engine. He welds the plates together.	The engine is started. The plates are welded together.
The furnace smelts the ore. The man sharpened his tool. He welded the plates together.	The ore is smelted in the furnace. His tool was sharpened. The plates were welded together.
They will start the work soon. We must lubricate bearings. A lathe can cut screws.	The work will soon be started. Bearings must be lubricated. Screws can be cut on a lathe.

As you see, Passive constructions require this pattern:

(PRO)NOUN + a form of *be* + PAST PARTICIPLE

EXERCISE

Change these active statements into impersonal passive statements.

1. We can cast this type of metal into very complicated shapes.
2. We smelt the ore in a blast furnace and reduce it to pig iron.
3. A skilled operator can carry out many operations on a lathe.
4. We clamp the two metal plates together.
5. Coal miners produce millions of tons of coal every week.
6. The company marketed several new products every year.
7. They will start production on the new type of reactor soon.
8. We can generate heat for welding in several ways.
9. We pass an electric current across the electrodes.

10. Welders normally prefer a vee-shaped weld.
11. That country does not produce any heavy industrial machinery.
12. This allows the cross-slide to move across the saddle.
13. The operator selects the appropriate gear for the job.
14. We call these supports bearings.
15. This will prevent damage to the shaft.
16. This will prevent the metal surfaces from coming into contact.
17. We can use a thin grease as a lubricant in rolling bearings.
18. We can alter the characteristics of steel in various ways.
19. We must heat the steel above its critical temperature.
20. You must take care not to damage the machinery.

2. Methods

1. *a.* Welding is one *means* / *method* / *way* of joining pieces of metal together.

   b. There are many *methods* / *ways* / *means* of joining pieces of metal together.

   c. One of the best *methods* / *ways* / *means* of joining pieces of metal together is to weld them.

Note. *Means,* as a noun, is the same in both singular and plural (see Section 8). Without the 's', *mean* is an adjective (see Section 2).

2. New *methods* of production were *adopted* / *put into practice* / *employed* / *introduced* a few years ago.

3. Should

This word is used very often in technical writing, with several slightly different meanings.

1. *Instructions to operators, employees,* etc.

These machines *should be handled* with great care.
Safety precautions *should be observed* at all times.
The results of the experiment *should be plotted* on a graph.

N.B. This is sometimes used for politeness when *must be* is really meant.

2. *Specifications* (what is required of something)

The steel *should not contain* more than 0·5% of carbon.
The maximum internal diameter *should be* 40 thousandths of an inch.

---

3. *Expectations* (what is expected to happen)

The process of cooling *should continue* for several hours.
This building *should be completed* by the end of next year.

EXERCISE

Decide on the exact meaning of *should* in these statements, and complete them. Some examples are in the passive. Occasionally more than one meaning is possible.

1. This experiment (...... *give*) us the answer to the problem.
2. The mould (...... *make*) slightly larger than the casting we want.
3. Smoking (...... *permit*) within fifty yards of the store.
4. High tensile steels (...... *temper*) up to 600° C.
5. The new reactor (...... *be*) in operation by 1968.
6. A flux (...... *apply*) to the heated metal to prevent oxidation.
7. The motorway (...... *have*) three lanes in each direction with a reservation in the middle.
8. The results of the experiment (...... *write*) up carefully.
9. Wear on the bearings (...... *reduce*) considerably with good lubrication.
10. The heated metal (...... *allow*) to cool slowly over a long period.
11. Construction workers (...... *wear*) safety helmets at all times.
12. The road surface (...... *be*) capable of withstanding very heavy traffic loads.
13. The material we are looking for (...... *be*) capable of withstanding very high temperatures.
14. All cutting-tools (...... *keep*) sharp and in good condition.
15. Delivery of the engines (...... *start*) by the middle of next year.

Section 6

Reading: Steam Boilers

Large quantities of steam *are used by* modern industry in the generation of power. It is therefore necessary to design boilers which will produce high-pressure steam as efficiently as possible. Modern boilers are frequently very large, and are sometimes capable of generating 300,000 lb of steam per hour. To achieve this rate of steam production, the boilers should operate at very high temperatures. In some boilers, temperatures of over 1650° C may be attained. The fuels which are burned in the furnace are selected for their high calorific value, and give the maximum amount of heat. They are often *pulverised by* crushers outside the furnace and forced in under pressure.

Modern boilers which employ solid fuels are usually **too large to** be hand-stoked, and stoking is then *carried out by* mechanical stokers, which ensure that an **adequate** quantity of fuel is conveyed into the furnace at the proper speed. The air which *is needed by* the fuel for combustion *is blown* across the firegrate *by* steam jets or fans. The amount of air which is allowed to enter is just more than **sufficient for** complete combustion of the fuel. An **insufficient** supply of air will prevent complete combustion, but any air **in excess of** the minimum merely reduces the temperature of combustion. The hot gases which *are produced by* the combustion of the fuel are circulated round banks of water-tubes. These are inclined at an angle over the furnace, and connect the upper and lower steam drums. A large proportion of the heat *is absorbed by* the water in the boiler. The remainder may be used to heat up the incoming air-supply through an air-heater. The water and steam in the boiler should circulate freely. The water and steam circuits are designed to allow the greatest possible fluid velocity to be attained, and rapid movement of the fluid *is achieved by* forced circulation. This assists rapid heating and also prevents the formation of steam pockets in the tubes.

Loss of efficiency in the boiler will *be caused by* the dissipation of heat through the walls of the combustion chamber. This heat loss can be considerably reduced by the use of firebricks round the walls of the chamber. This helps to insulate the chamber and to conserve the heat which is generated. However, at the temperatures which are attainable in modern boilers, the solid walls of the furnace are liable *to be damaged by* **excessive** heat. To avoid this, they are often lined with water-tubes, and some of the heat of combustion *is absorbed by* the water.

The steam from the boiler is passed through a superheater and out past a

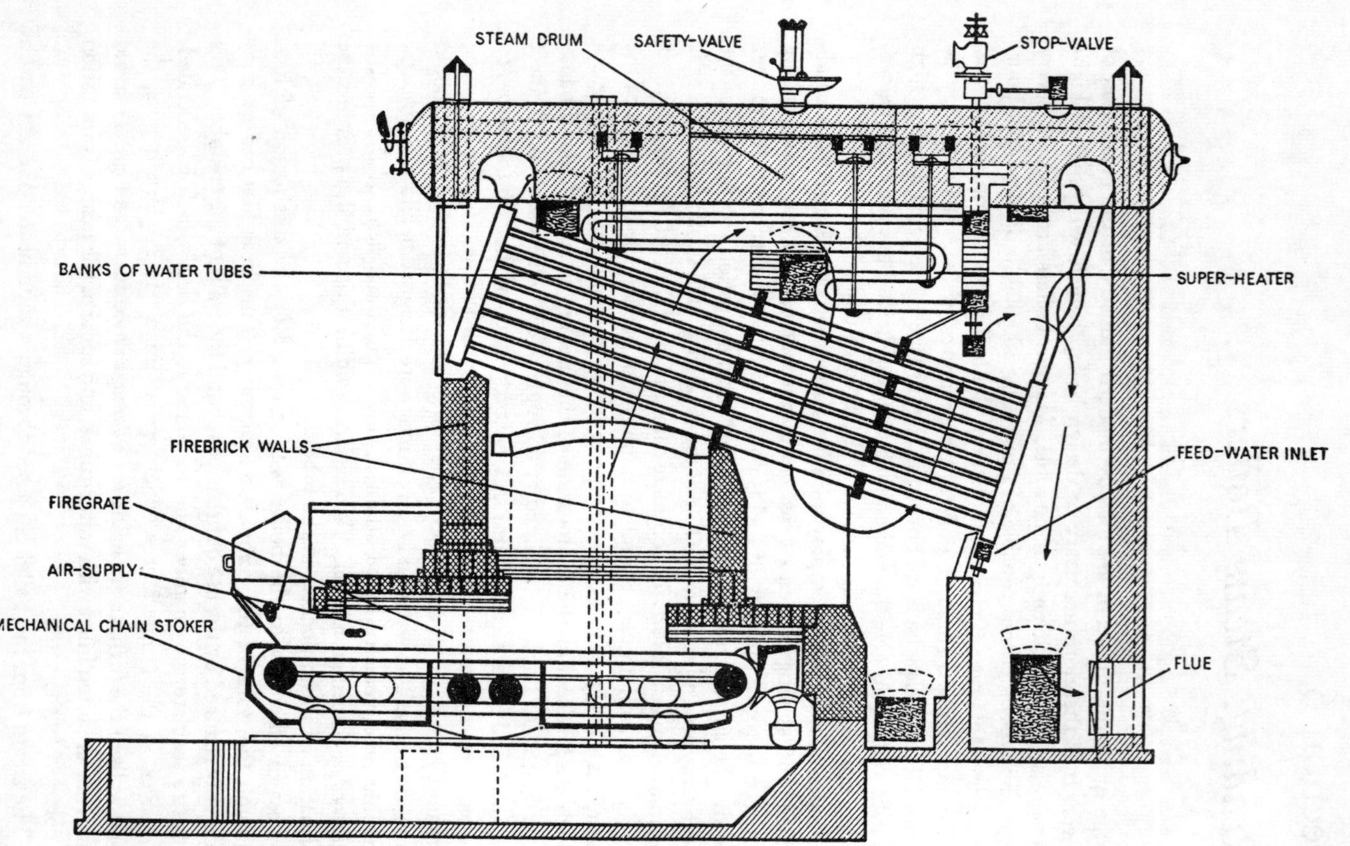

Cross-section of boiler with mechanical stoker

stop-valve at high pressure. A fresh supply of water *is fed by pumps* into the boiler to replace it. The feed-water should be pure, and free from dissolved salts which will cause deposits on the tubes and lead to overheating.

WORD STUDY

Attain, Achieve (= reach)

The aircraft is capable of	*reaching* *attaining* *achieving*	a speed of 4000 miles per hour.

1. Pressures of up to 300 lb/in² were 2. An efficiency of only 4% or 5% was 3. A high degree of accuracy can be	*reached* *attained* *achieved*	in the boiler. by the engine. by cold-working the metal.

A greater efficiency should be	*attainable* *achievable*	with certain modifications.

Absorb (= take in)

1. A sponge will 2. The spring must 3. The water will 4. Dark surfaces	*absorb*	water. most of the shock. a large proportion of the heat from the furnace. heat more than bright surfaces.

Sponges are *absorbent*. They have	great *absorptive* power. a great power of *absorption*.

Conserve – Dissipate

The law of the *conservation* of energy states that energy cannot be lost or created. It can only be changed into different forms. Energy is always *conserved*, or *kept*.
The refractory linings of the furnace *conserve* the heat (= keep it in).
The government tries *to conserve* the natural resources of the country (= to use sparingly).
But in many countries, the natural resources are being *dissipated* (= used wastefully).
60% of the heat which the engine produces *is dissipated* through the cylinder walls (= escapes).
Firebricks are used in a furnace to prevent undue *dissipation* of useful heat to the atmosphere.

Efficiency

1. The *efficiency* of a machine is the ratio of the work which is done to the energy which is supplied.
2. The *efficiency* of a jet engine at great speeds and altitudes is greater than that of a piston-engine.

3. An ideally *efficient* machine is one which has an efficiency of 100%.
4. An *efficient* water circulation in the boiler is necessary for rapid production of steam.

Deposit (= put down)

1. *a.*	The money was	*deposited*	in the bank.
b.	The copper ions are		on the cathode as metallic copper.
c.	Condensed steam is		on the cold surfaces of the cylinder.
d.	The scale which is		in the water-tubes must be removed.

2. *a.* A fairly small *deposit* of soot on boiler tubes may be beneficial.
   b. There are large coal *deposits* in the north of the country.

PATTERNS

1. Passive Verb + by + *Noun* (agent)

'*The postman delivered the letters*' could be written in the passive as '*The letters were delivered by the postman*'. *By the postman* is simply the grammatical *agent* in the passive sentence.
In technical writing, it is not usual to add the name of the agent to a sentence of this kind, *if the agent is a person.* But very often the agent is not a person, and it may be necessary to add it. For example:

Large quantities of steam are required by modern industry.

Note: This agent only occurs in passive sentences.

EXERCISE

Complete these sentences in the same way, using the Present tense, and where possible the Past and Future tenses.

1. The bridge (...... build ......) the Know-all Construction Company.
2. Heat (...... generate ......) friction.
3. Many engineering scholarships (...... give ......) the government.
4. The machine (...... power ......) a small electric motor.
5. Loss of efficiency (...... cause ......) dissipation of heat through the furnace walls.
6. Unequal contractions (...... produce ......) rapid cooling of the metal.
7. Blow holes in castings (...... cause ......) bubbles of trapped air.
8. The bronze plates can (...... replace ......) soft rubber discs.
9. The steam (...... carry along ......) a jet of water.
10. A large proportion of the heat (...... absorb ......) the water.
11. The heat (...... provide ......) an oxy-acetylene torch.
12. Three machines can (...... control ......) a single operator.
13. The light (...... refract ......) the surface of the glass.
14. Coal (...... form ......) the decay of vegetable matter.
15. All responsibility for the accident must (...... accept ......) the designers.

16. A very strong joint (...... produce ......) a vee-shaped weld.
17. Some of the heat (...... absorb ......) the water-tubes round the boiler.
18. The work (...... grip firmly ......) the jaws of the chuck.
19. The heat (...... provide ......) the combustion of pulverised fuel.
20. The damage to the machine last week (...... cause ......) carelessness.

2. Too Much or Too Little

<table>
<tr><td colspan="2">The boiler</td><td>consumes</td><td>an excessive
undue</td><td>amount of</td><td>fuel.</td></tr>
<tr><td colspan="2">Too much air
An excessive amount of air</td><td>enters</td><td colspan="3">the furnace.</td></tr>
<tr><td colspan="2">The excess air</td><td>reduces</td><td colspan="3">the temperature of combustion.</td></tr>
<tr><td colspan="2" rowspan="2">The temperature</td><td rowspan="2">was</td><td colspan="3">excessive.
excessively high.
too high.</td></tr>
<tr><td>too high</td><td colspan="2">for the boiler to withstand.</td></tr>
<tr><td colspan="2">The metal</td><td>was</td><td>too hard</td><td colspan="2">to machine.
to be machined.</td></tr>
<tr><td colspan="2">The temperature in the combustion chamber</td><td>exceeded
was greater than
was in excess of</td><td colspan="3">2000 C. degrees.</td></tr>
<tr><td colspan="2">The temperature</td><td>was</td><td colspan="2">high enough
sufficiently high</td><td rowspan="2">to melt the metal.
for the metal to melt.
for the metal to be melted.</td></tr>
<tr><td>Enough
Sufficient
Adequate
An adequate amount of</td><td>heat</td><td>must be</td><td colspan="2">supplied</td></tr>
<tr><td colspan="2">The heat</td><td>was</td><td colspan="2">not enough
inadequate
insufficient</td><td>to melt the metal, etc.</td></tr>
<tr><td colspan="2">Nuclei which</td><td>are deficient in
have a deficiency of
do not have enough</td><td colspan="3">neutrons are unstable.</td></tr>
</table>

EXERCISE

Complete these statements, as shown above.

1. The boiler should be strong ...... to withstand the pressure inside it.
2. The sand should be ...... porous to permit the air to escape.
3. The heat which is generated is ...... to raise the steam to a high temperature.
4. Heavy water was ...... expensive to be used as a coolant in the reactor.
5. The quantity of oil which is delivered ...... the quantity which is needed for lubrication.
6. An ...... overflow pipe should be fitted to carry away the ...... water.
7. The diet of many undernourished people is ...... protein.
8. The fall in speed is ...... rapid ...... this method of testing to be adopted.
9. The fall in speed is ...... rapid ...... adopt this method of testing.
10. ...... little grease may cause bearing failure because of ...... lubrication.
11. Vehicles are not permitted to ...... a speed of 30 m.p.h. in built-up areas.
12. When supply ...... demand for any product, the prices are liable to fall.
13. The motor should not be run at an ...... speed.
14. Efficient heat removal at an ...... high temperature is necessary for the economic working of the reactor.
15. ...... surveys must be carried out before the construction of the dam can begin.
16. The world supply of petroleum is ...... for all foreseeable demands.
17. This load is ...... heavy ...... be carried by the motor.
18. This load is ...... heavy ...... the motor to carry.
19. The load is ...... for the motor.
20. To avoid ...... frictional losses, the bearings must be efficiently lubricated.

3. Instructions (*Imperative*)

In Section 5, we noted that *should* is often used to give impersonal instructions to operators, etc. on the correct method of doing something, or on what is wanted. A more *direct* form of instruction is given by the *imperative* form of the verb. It is often used for *experimental* or *handling* instructions, and in *hypotheses* or *calculations*.

---

1. *Allow* the water to cool for ten minutes and then *take* the temperature.
   Hold the convex lens in front of the white paper.

2. *Calculate* the amount of expansion which will take place.

3. *Consider* a steam chamber of high pressure and *imagine* its pressure to be x lb/in^2.
Let x equal the number of revolutions per minute.
Suppose the water is drawn directly from a river.
Assume that there is no loss of heat from the boiler.

EXERCISE

(*should* and *imperative*)

1. Give instructions on how to mend a puncture in a bicycle tyre.
2. Give advice on how to prevent burglars from entering houses.
3. Tell a new employee of the safety precautions he should observe in the machine shop.
4. Instruct an apprentice on how to cut screws on a lathe.
5. Rewrite this passage, using *should* with passive forms instead of the imperative form.

   Fill a test-tube half full of water and heat it nearly to boiling point. Support the tube on a stand and allow it to cool. Take the temperature every minute. Stir carefully with a glass rod. Record the readings you obtain, and plot them on a graph of temperature against time. Repeat this with a tube half-full of crystals. Allow the solid to melt. Heat the liquid to 100° C, fix the tube on the stand and allow it to cool. Record the results as before and plot them.
6. Rewrite this passage, using the *imperative* instead of *should.*

   The ends of the metal articles should be thoroughly cleaned. No dirt should be left on them. The ends should then be heated to a white heat. An oxy-acetylene torch should be used for this. A flux should then be applied to the weld. The surfaces should be pressed together. Care should be taken to squeeze out the whole of the flux. The joint should then be smoothed off.

Section 7

Reading: Steam Locomotives

From the date of the introduction of the steam locomotive about 130 years ago, there was a continuing increase in the size and weight of trains. This **necessitated** engines of greater and greater power. *In order to achieve* this increase in power, much higher steam pressures were **required.** The modern steam locomotive is capable of generating steam pressures often in excess of 300 lb/in^2, against the 50 lb/in^2 pressure of Stevenson's 'Rocket'. Normally the demand for increased steam capacity is met by increasing the size of the boiler. However the boiler of a steam locomotive is strictly limited in size by the dimensions and load capacity of the railway track which it works on. It is therefore **necessary to** have a very large heating surface within the boiler.

There are two fire-boxes inside the boiler, an inner one and an outer one, which extend a long way forward. The inner fire-box is linked by tubes to the fire-plate at the front of the boiler. Practically the whole of the heating surface, which includes these fire-tubes, is surrounded by water. A high rate of evaporation in the boiler is **essential,** *in order to generate* the large quantities of steam which are **required.** *For this purpose* a powerful draught of air is blown over the fire. The steam which is evolved is passed through a superheater, which raises its temperature and makes it as dry as possible. Rapid evaporation at the heating surface tends to make the steam wet. The use of wet steam **necessitates** excessively high pressures in the cylinder. Superheating the steam enables the **requisite** power to be obtained with considerably lower pressures.

The superheated steam is passed to the steam-chest which is attached to the cylinder. From the steam-chest it is introduced into the cylinder at the appropriate moments through ports. These ports are opened and closed by slide valves, which are actuated by the rotation of the locomotive crankshaft. The steam is admitted under pressure to one side of the cylinder, and drives the piston forwards. The inlet port is then closed, and a second charge of steam is admitted at the other side of the cylinder *to drive* the piston in the reverse direction. The exhaust steam from the first charge is driven out into the atmosphere through a blast pipe. This is done *in order to increase* the draught over the fire. The reciprocating action of the piston is changed into a rotational movement of the wheels by a connecting rod and crank.

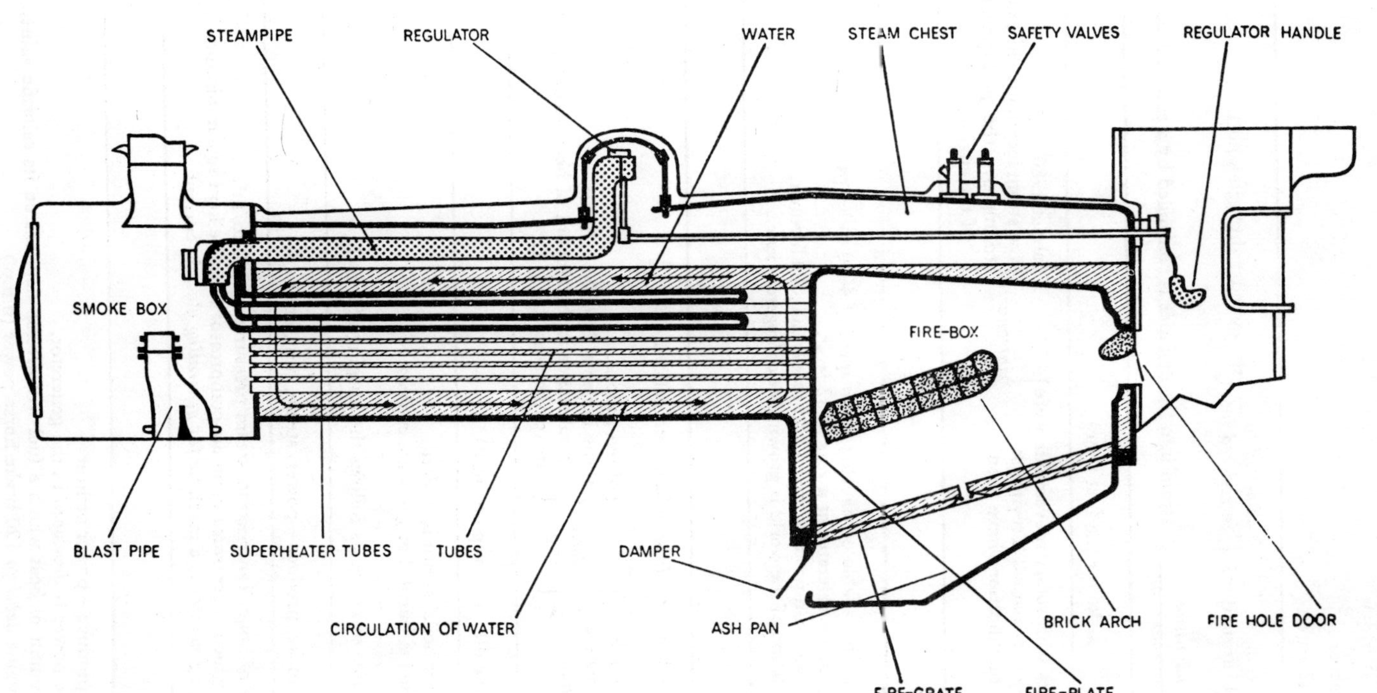

Cross-section of steam locomotive

WORD STUDY

Admit, Introduce

1. = allow to enter

a. The steam is	*admitted to*	the cylinder through a port.
b. A fuel/air mixture is	*introduced into*	

c. The *admission* / *introduction* of steam into the cylinder is controlled by a slide-valve.

2. *Introduce* (= make for the first time)

a. Engines with rotary movements were	*introduced*	about 1780.
b. An engineer named Trevithick		the steam locomotive in 1804.
c. Many modifications have been		to improve the performance of the engine.

Speed, Rate

1. The aircraft is capable of travelling *at a speed of* 4000 miles per hour.
2. A falling body accelerates *at a rate of* 32 ft/s^2.
3. This generator can produce steam *at a rate of* 200,000 lb/hour.
4. The population of the world is growing *at a dangerous rate.*

Capacity

1. This oil tank *is capable of* holding ten gallons.

2. This oil tank has a	*capacity*	of ten gallons.
3. The evaporative		of the boiler is 200,000 lb/hour.
4. The thermal		of a substance is the amount of heat needed to raise its temperature by 1° C.

Evolve (= give off – gas, vapour, heat)

1. When water boils, steam is *evolved.*
2. When a fuel is burnt, hot gases are *evolved.*

3. The *evolution* of hot gases follows the burning of a fuel.

Generate (= make, produce – power, steam, heat, etc.)

1. This type of boiler can *generate* steam pressures of 300 lb/in^2.
2. The heat which is *generated* in an air-compressor must be kept to a minimum.
3. An electric *generator* is a machine for *generating* electric current.

Develop

1. = make, produce – power or heat
   - *a.* Electric power is *developed* in the generator.
   - *b.* The amount of heat which a fuel will *develop* depends on its calorific value.
   - *c.* This engine *develops* 120 brake horse power (b.h.p.).

2. = improve, as a result of research
   a. New types of steam generators have recently been *developed.*
   b. A new method of fuel injection was *developed* during the war.
   c. A long period of *development* is necessary for these new rockets.

3. = start
   a. There is a possibility of leaks *developing* in steam pipes.
   b. Trouble *develops* in the engine when pressures are too high.

PATTERNS

1. Purpose

These are the commonest ways of expressing the purpose for which we do something

1. The *purpose* / *aim* / *object* of the safety valve *is to* allow excess pressure to escape.			
2. A safety valve is provided	*to* *so as to* *in order to*	allow	excess pressure to escape.
	for the purpose of *with the object of* *with the aim of* *with a view to*	allowing	

EXERCISE ONE

For practice, read these sentences using *purpose*, *aim* and *object* in front.

1. The purpose of	fitting water-tubes in a boiler is to absorb some of the heat.
2. etc.	annealing the metal is to relieve some of the stresses.
3.	lubricating bearings is to reduce the friction.
4.	superheating the steam is to ensure that it is fairly dry.
5.	working the metal cold is to obtain a more accurate finish.
6.	using firebricks is to minimise heat losses in the boiler.
7.	incorporating a gauge is to measure the pressure in the boiler.
8.	using pure feed-water is to prevent the formation of deposits.
9.	the test is to calculate the total temperature rise.
10.	forced circulation is to prevent the formation of steam pockets.
11.	a large heating surface is to increase the amount of steam which is produced.

EXERCISE TWO

Change each of the sentences in Exercise One into the patterns shown in (2) above.

N.B. For the last three sentences, you will have to add a verb. e.g.: The purpose of the test is to calculate the total temperature rise = *The test is made for the purpose of* .... etc.

2. Requirements and Necessity

<table>
<tr><td>The bearings</td><td>need
require</td><td>lubricating.
to be lubricated.
some lubrication.</td></tr>
<tr><td>The machine</td><td rowspan="3">needs
requires</td><td>repairing.
to be repaired.
a new clutch.</td></tr>
<tr><td>The tool</td><td>re-grinding.
to be re-ground.
a re-grind.</td></tr>
<tr><td>The scale in the tube</td><td>removing.
to be removed.
removal.</td></tr>
</table>

The bearings *must be* lubricated.

It is *necessary* / *essential* *for* the bearings *to be* lubricated.

<table>
<tr><td>Friction</td><td rowspan="2">makes necessary
necessitates</td><td>a good lubrication system.</td></tr>
<tr><td>Increased wages</td><td>an increase in prices.</td></tr>
<tr><td>The use of plastic pipes</td><td rowspan="2">makes unnecessary
obviates the need for
dispenses with the need for
does away with the need for</td><td>protection against corrosion.</td></tr>
<tr><td>Superheating the steam</td><td>very high pressures in the boiler.</td></tr>
</table>

The furnace rapidly reaches the	*required* *requisite* *necessary*	temperature.

EXERCISE

Complete these statements, as shown above.

1. Increased speeds ...... improved cooling systems in the engines.
2. This type of engine has the advantage that it ...... very little maintenance.
3. It is ...... for the feed-water to the boiler ...... pure.
4. The crude ore ...... purifying before it can be of any industrial use.
5. Clear diagrams ...... the need for lengthy explanations.
6. The production of this new model will ...... complete re-tooling of the factory.
7. By placing the engines in the tail of the aircraft, we ...... with the need for very thick wings.
8. To ensure freedom from distortion, it is necessary ...... the metal bar ...... cooled slowly.
9. The use of the auto-lathe dispenses ...... continual removal and replacement of tools.
10. A large area of heating surface ...... to produce the ...... weight of steam.
11. A nuclear reactor ...... large quantities of water for cooling, and this ...... siting it near a river or on the coast.
12. The metal is heated up to the ...... welding temperature.
13. The demand for low-cost power ...... engines of greater efficiency and with a low fuel consumption.
14. With vehicles which will run on a cushion of air, the need for wheels can be ......
15. 10% of the total power developed will be ...... to drive the supercharger.
16. Radiation is the most efficient form of transmission for heat which ...... to be transmitted in all directions.
17. Steel with the ...... properties is ...... for this special purpose.

REVISION (SECTIONS 1–7)

Read these statements, choosing the correct word from the alternatives in brackets.

1. The clinical thermometer is used (*for*, *to*) measuring (*body's*, *body*) temperature. It (*contains*, *includes*, *consists of*) a tube made (*of*, *from*, *with*) glass, which (*contains*, *consists of*, *comprises*) a certain (*amount*, *number*) of mercury. When the mercury is (*hot*, *heated*), it (*expands*, *extends*, *increases*) and (*raises*, *rises*) up the tube, which is graduated in degrees Fahrenheit or Centigrade (*according*, *depending*) on the country of manufacture.
2. The temperature in the furnace is (*great*, *high*, *hot*), so that the maximum

amount of steam may be (*generated, evolved, given off*). For (*this, that*) reason, the furnace must be built of (*substance, material*) which is (*able, capable*) to (*restrain, restrict, withstand*) extreme temperatures. In order to (*prevent, avoid*) heat losses through the furnace walls, they are lined (*by, with*) bricks. By this (*mean, means, way*) the heat is (*preserved, conserved*) inside the furnace.

3. The crew of the aircraft (*is, are*) (*comprised, composed, constituted*) of two pilots, a navigator and a radio operator. They have all been flying (*since, for*) (*a number, numbers*) of years, and are all (*largely, greatly, highly*) qualified men.
4. Coal production has been (*fairly, rather*) higher this year (*as, than*) last year. (*That, This*) is because of the (*employment, exploitation*) of new automatic (*machinery, mechanism, engines*) capable (*to cut, of cutting*) far more coal (*as, than, that*) can be cut (*with, by*) hand.
5. Mercury (*provides, produces, offers*) a (*number, quantity*) of advantages (*on, over*) alcohol in measuring (*heat, temperature*). It has a (*rather, fairly*) constant rate of expansion (*in respect, irrespective*) of temperature, and remains liquid over a (*big, large, wide*) range of temperatures. It can be employed up to about 350° C. (*under, in*) normal atmospheric pressure, and even higher when the pressure is (*bigger, larger, greater*) than atmospheric.
6. In (*the most of, most*) countries, the Centigrade scale has been (*adopted adapted, applied*) for all temperature measurements. (*On, in, by*) this scale 0° is the temperature (*with, on, at*) which pure ice melts, and 100° is the boiling (*point, level*) of pure water under (*usual, normal, normally*) atmospheric pressure.
7. Ferrous metals are very (*apt, liable, possible*) to corrosion by oxidation or by some other (*chemic, chemical*) (*act, action*), and they have therefore to be (*prevented, avoided, protected*) in some (*method, way*). One (*mean, means*) which is often employed to (*achieve, obtain, acquire*) this is to give the metal a (*coat, jacket, clothing*) of zinc by a process which is (*known, called, termed*) as galvanising.
8. The lathe is a (*machine, tool, mechanism*) which enables (*works, work, jobs*) to be (*worked, machined*) to a (*great, high, exact*) degree of accuracy. The (*food, feed*) is controlled automatically by (*means, way*) of a shaft which is (*revolved, impelled, driven*) by a system of gears which are (*incorporated, accommodated*) in the headstock.
9. An (*enough, adequate*) supply of air is necessary (*to, for*) the combustion of the fuel in the furnace. If (*too, excessive*) much air is present, the temperature of the furnace will (*reduce, fall, lower*). There should be just enough air to (*ensure, enable, let*) (*complete, thorough*) combustion to take place.

10. An (*intensely, intensively*) hot flame is produced in an (*electric, electrical*) arc by passing a current (*through, across, between*) two electrodes and placing the metal plates which are (*to weld, to be welded*) (*between, among, through*) them.
11. A (*rise, raise*) in temperature will (*make, cause*) the steam pipe to (*extend, expand, increase*) in length, and in order to (*prevent, resist, eliminate*) stresses from being set up in the metal, expansion joints are fitted which (*relieve, reduce, release*) the stresses by (*allowing, permitting, letting*) the pipe to expand or contract freely.
12. A country which possesses (*few, a few, little*) natural (*reserves, resources, deposits*) is dependent (*on, of*) the import of (*natural, crude, raw*) materials, and must pay (*them, for them*) by exporting the manufactured goods.
13. These (*experiences, experiments*) began a few months (*ago, since*), and some progress (*has, have*) already been (*done, performed, made*) It is unfortunate that, owing to (*lack, absence, short*) of money, they must now be (*culminated, terminated*) before the real (*object, subject*) has been (*accomplished, achieved, resulted*).
14. The dam which is now being (*erected, constructed*) will (*bring, cause, make*) many benefits to the country. It will (*at first, first of all*) (*dispense, prevent, obstruct*) the danger of flooding, and also (*enable, ensure*) that there is plenty of water for irrigation. It will also (*enable, ensure*) the water to be used to provide hydro-electric (*power, force, energy*).
15. Dr Smith has (*devoted, concentrated*) many years to (*carrying, carry*) out (*research, researches*) (*on, in, into*) the (*characters, properties*) of this (*matter, material*). The results of his work have appeared as (*articles, essays, papers*) in a number of learned (*journals, magazines, papers*), and have (*roused, aroused, raised*) much interest.

Section 8

Reading: Condensation and Condensers

Steam which is admitted to a cold engine cylinder is liable to be partially condensed by contact with the cylinder walls. That part of the steam nearest to the walls is cooled and condenses as a film of water. The volume of steam in the cylinder is *thereby* considerably reduced, and more steam must be admitted **in order that** the pressure is sufficiently high to drive the piston along the cylinder. Condensation in a cylinder therefore raises the steam consumption of the engine and *thereby* lowers its efficiency. It is therefore necessary to devise means of getting rid of this condensation as far as possible, and in modern reciprocating steam engines, condensation problems have been practically eliminated.

This is effected *by superheating* the steam in the boiler and also *by fitting* steam jackets round the cylinder. These are fitted into the annular space between the cylinder and the cylinder liner, and are connected to the steam supply. *By raising* the temperature of the cylinder walls in this way, the outward flow of heat is greatly reduced.

Steam which is exhausted from the cylinder still has a considerable heat content, and **in order that** this heat energy should not be wasted, the steam is condensed and passed back to the boiler as hot feed water. Rapid condensation is accomplished *by means of a condenser*. In this condenser, a liquid coolant is circulated through banks of metal tubes. *By flowing* over these tubes, the steam is caused to transmit some of its heat to the liquid, and a rapid drop in temperature occurs. The steam condenses, and is collected at the bottom of the condenser as condensate. *By ensuring* that there is no contact between the condensate and the coolant, a pure distilled water can be produced which is ideal for boiler feed water. This type of condenser is commonly used where pure water is not plentiful. The condensate is usually re-heated, **so that** it may be circulated back to the boiler at an adequate temperature.

In other types of condensers, which are known as jet condensers, the steam is cooled *by allowing* it to mix intimately with jets of cold water which are injected into the condenser. *By this means*, rapid condensation takes place, and the mixture of condensate and coolant is withdrawn *by means of an extraction pump*. The water which is normally used as a coolant cannot usually be utilised in the boiler, and cannot therefore be re-circulated. It is either pumped up to a cooling tower or it gravitates into a cooling pond, and is stored for later use in the condenser.

A

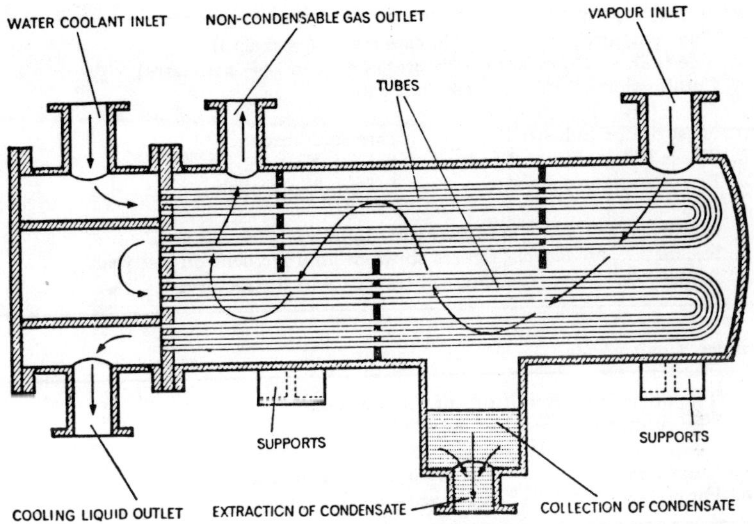

B

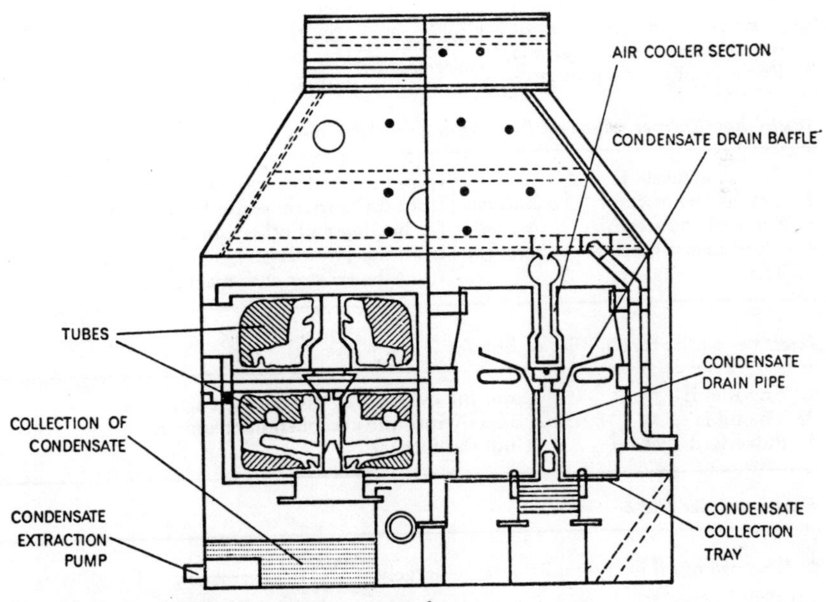

Cross-sections of (A) horizontal-process condenser
(B) steam surface condenser

WORD STUDY

Produce, Product, Production

1. *a.* The company		1000 cars a day. (= makes)
b. The boiler	*produces*	high-pressure steam. (= generates)
c. Combustion		very hot gases.

2. *a.* Most of our industrial		are sold abroad.
b. These hot gases are the	*products*	of combustion.
c. Petrol and kerosene are		of crude petroleum.

3. *a* Motor-car		is increasing rapidly.
b. Recent	*production*	figures show an improvement on last year.
c. A new		line will be set up in the factory.

Consume, Consumption

1. *a.* The boiler *consumes* 3 tons of fuel per hour.
   b. The reactor *consumes* less material than it produces.

2. *a.* Engine efficiency may be measured by steam *consumption.*
   b. Family cars are designed for low fuel *consumption.*

Achieve, Obtain, Effect, Accomplish (= bring about)

1. A reduction in condensation is	*achieved*	by the use of steam-jackets.
2. Control of the power output is	*effected*	by varying the fuel supply.
3. Rapid closing of the valve is	*accomplished*	by fitting a heavy spring.
4. Removal of excess heat is		by means of a radiator.

Withdraw, Extract, Abstract (= take out or draw out)

1. The condensate is		from the condenser by a pump.
2. The molten metal is	*withdrawn*	from the furnace, ready for casting.
3. Some of the steam is	*extracted*	for heating and other purposes.
4. The exhaust gases are	*abstracted*	from the cylinder.
5. The fuel-rods are		from the reactor core mechanically.

Inject (= squirt through jet or nozzle)

1. The fuel is		into the cylinder by compressed air.
2. The oil is	*injected*	directly into the combustion chamber.
3. Pulverised fuel is		into the furnace.

Eliminate, Get Rid of

1. The use of oil in hydraulic systems largely *eliminates* / *gets rid of* corrosion.

2. In the interview, all except one applicant was *eliminated* for one reason or another, and this one man got the job.

PATTERNS

1. Means (by + *noun* or -ing)

In Section 6, we noted that **by** + *an agent* sometimes follows the verb in a *passive* statement

Large quantities of steam are required by modern industry

A second and more important use of **by** is to indicate the *means* or *method* of doing something or achieving some result.
It can occur in both *active* and *passive* statements.
It often occurs with the phrase **by means of.**
Sometimes it is possible to use **with** instead of **by** before a *noun*.
With really means **with the help of,** and there is a slight difference in meaning; it is not advisable to use *with* unless the meaning is truly instrumental.

The road was cleared **by (means of)** *a bulldozer.*
The road was cleared **with (the help of)** *a bulldozer.*

<table>
<tr><td colspan="2">Heat losses can be reduced
We can reduce heat losses</td><td>by</td><td colspan="2">firebricks.
the use of firebricks.
lining the furnace with firebricks.</td></tr>
<tr><td>This can be</td><td>done
effected
achieved
accomplished</td><td colspan="2">by means of</td><td>firebricks.</td></tr>
<tr><td>By</td><td colspan="2">lining the furnace with firebricks,</td><td colspan="2">heat losses can be reduced.</td></tr>
</table>

N.B. You will notice in the last example that a clause or participial phrase may come *before* the main part of the statement.
The word **thereby** means **by means of this.**
By means of cannot be used before a participle; only **by** is possible in such a case.

EXERCISE ONE

Complete these statements in the same way, using the verb in brackets.

1. We reduce the ore to pig-iron ...... it in a blast furnace. (*smelt*)
2. Production will be greatly increased ...... the new machinery. (*introduce*)
3. A hot steel bar can be hardened ...... it in water. (*quench*)
4. Bars of steel can be made ...... them through rollers. (*pass*)
5. The heat-resistant properties of steel are improved ...... more chromium and nickel. (*add*)
6. ...... roller bearings, the friction is reduced still further. (*use*)
7. ...... the bearing in an oil-bath, adequate lubrication is ensured. (*dip*)
8. ...... a flux to the metal, we can prevent oxidation. (*apply*)

9. ...... forced circulation in the boiler, better results are obtained. (*employ*)
10. ...... a gas rapidly in a cylinder, we raise its temperature. (*compress*)
11. ...... steam over the hot coke, producer gas is formed. (*blow*)
12. A casting is produced ...... molten metal into a mould. (*pour*)
13. Improved heat-transfer rates were achieved ...... fins to the outside of the cylinder. (*fit*)

EXERCISE TWO

Complete these statements with *by*, *by means of* or *with*, whichever you think most suitable.

1. Production can be greatly increased ...... the introduction of new machinery.
2. We can prevent oxidation of the metal ...... a flux.
3. Rapid heating in the boiler is achieved ...... forced circulation.
4. The work is firmly held in the lathe ...... the centres.
5. Better combustion is obtained ...... a hemispherical combustion chamber.
6. The heat-resistant properties of the steel can be improved ...... the addition of chromium and nickel.
7. Frequent measurements of the bar were made ...... a micrometer.
8. Lubricant is forced into the bearing ...... pressure of the grease gun against the nipple.
9. A soldered joint may be made ...... a soldering iron made of copper.
10. The temperature of the liquid is raised ...... the application of heat.
11. Greater speeds can now be attained by modern aircraft ...... the new metals which are now being developed.
12. More rapid burning is made possible ...... the use of pulverised fuels.

2. Purpose (Clauses)

See also Section 7.

Here is a further structure which is used to indicate purpose.

The steam is superheated	***so that*** ***in order that***	**it**	**is** **may be** **can be** **should be**	**fairly dry.**

EXERCISE

Complete these statements in the same way.

1. Phosphorus is added to the metal ...... better castings ...... produced.
2. ...... the iron ...... demagnetised, it is necessary to apply a negative magnetising force.
3. ...... the metal ...... properly soldered, the metal and the solder should both be made clean.
4. The steam velocity across the tubes is kept high, ... any stationary air ...... swept away.
5. The storage tank is elevated, ... its contents ...... withdrawn by gravity.
6. The condenser water is cooled ...... it ...... re-used in the condenser.
7. The coal gas is sometimes compressed ...... condensation in the gas mains ...... avoided.
8. A by-pass road is being constructed ...... the traffic ...... (not) need to go through the city centre.
9. ...... deposits ...... not form on the tubes, only pure feed water should be used.
10. Water is sprayed into the cylinder ...... immediate condensation of the steam ...... occur.
11. ...... the amount of expansion ...... calculated, the coefficient of expansion of the metal must be known.
12. The diameter of the bar should be measured frequently ...... too much metal ...... (not) taken off.

3. Noun + Noun

The normal way of describing an object in greater detail is by putting an adjective in front of it:

mild steel
hot water
wet steam.

But English allows us very often to put another noun in front of the noun, and sometimes two or three:

steam jacket
heat content
steel bar
carbon dioxide.

The relationship between the two nouns may vary quite a lot, as you can see from these examples:

Steam consumption	= the consumption *of* steam.
Metal tubes	= tubes *made of* metal.
Heat treatment	= treatment *with* or *by* heat.
Steam jackets	= jackets *containing* steam.
Cooling towers	= towers *for the purpose of* cooling.
Butt weld	= weld *of the type called* 'butt'.
Friction losses	= losses *caused by* friction.

N.B. The possessive form ('s) is very seldom used in technical writing.

EXERCISE

Expand these Noun + Noun phrases to show the full meaning:

1. air supply
2. water tube
3. heat transfer
4. mercury thermometer
5. concrete structure
6. cylinder walls
7. steel bar
8. stop valve
9. boiler feed water
10. steam chest
11. nickel alloy
12. roller mill
13. power cable
14. cylinder head design
15. blast furnace
16. workshop machinery
17. gear mechanism
18. grease gun
19. lock nut
20. temperature drop
21. petrol engine
22. heat content
23. turret lathe
24. machine testing conditions
25. power transmission problems
26. condenser extractor pump
27. generator power output
28. cylinder condensation losses
29. gravity feed lubrication system
30. fire tube boiler inspection door

Section 9

Reading: Centrifugal Governors

Most engines in industrial use are rated to run at a constant speed, irrespective of the load they carry. In order to keep the engine speed within the limits which it was designed for, a device which is known as a governor is incorporated in the engine. Its **function** is to control the running speed under all conditions of load.

The simplest form of governor consists of a pair of balls which are attached to a vertical shaft by means of arms. These balls **act as** weights. *While they are* stationary, they are acted on only by gravity. Now the vertical shaft is geared to the engine, and rotates with it. *When the engine starts*, it causes the shaft to rotate, and this forces the rotating balls outwards under the influence of centrifugal force. This movement of the balls at the end of their arms is transmitted to a sleeve which is free to slide up and down the shaft. *As the engine increases* speed, it rotates the shaft more quickly, and the weights rise further against the force of gravity. The sleeve also rises up the shaft, and *when it rises* beyond a certain point, it operates a throttle valve lever, and so reduces the flow of steam. The engine speed will then decrease, and *as the sleeve slides down*, it opens the throttle valve again. *When the engine is running* at constant speed, it produces a state of equilibrium in the governor, with the centrifugal force equal and opposite to the controlling force – that is, the weight of the governor and its gear. Governors which are required to work at very high engine speeds are normally weight-loaded. A weight is attached to the sleeve, and **serves to** prevent the sleeve from rising too far.

Both the simple and weight-loaded governors depend on gravity and must therefore be kept in a vertical position. This is often a disadvantage, and may be obviated by the use of a spring instead of a weight. The spring performs the same **function** as the weight, and keeps the sleeve depressed. It can be mounted in any position. By making simple adjustments to the loading on the spring, the governor speed can easily be altered. The governor is mounted in a dome-shaped housing which contains the spring and the bell-crank levers, on which the rotating balls are pivoted. Ball bearings at the pivots and at the top of the spindle **serve to** reduce wear and friction. *As the spindle rotates*, it causes the weights to fly outwards, and this movement about the pivot raises the sleeve against the pressure of the spring. Equilibrium is attained at a constant engine speed by the balancing of the centrifugal force and the compressive load on the spring.

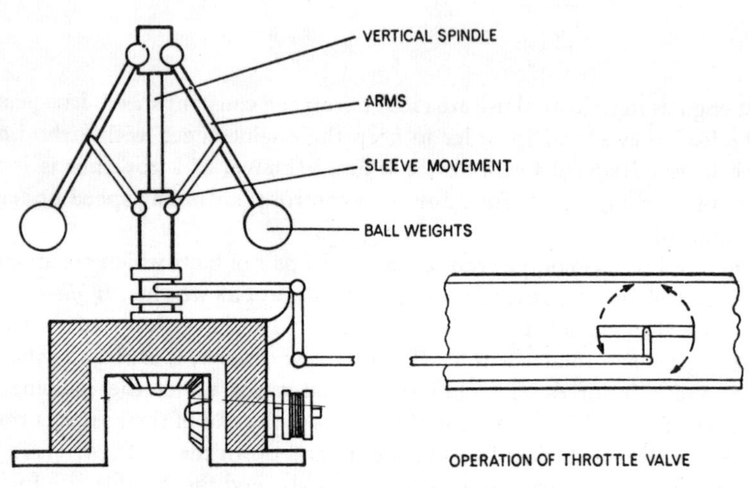

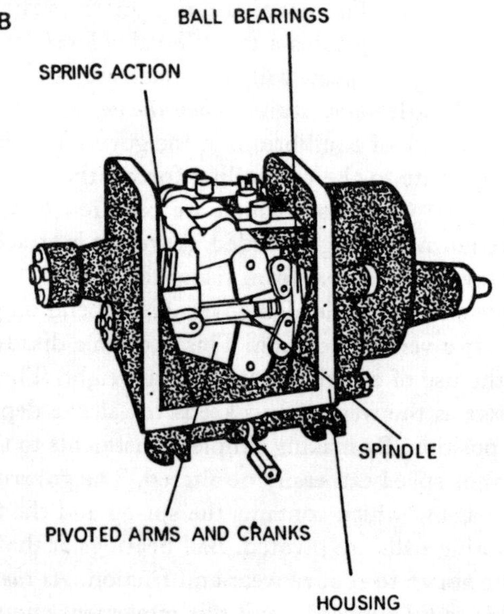

(A) Elementary governor principle
(B) Spring-loaded governor

WORD STUDY

Devise, Device, Instrument, Apparatus

1. We must *devise* some way of overcoming the difficulty. (= think out)
   A separation process was *devised* for the extraction of plutonium.

2. A *device* is (usually) a clever *mechanism* which is *devised* or *invented* to solve some particular mechanical problem.
   A thermostat is a *device* for regulating temperatures.
   A clutch is a *device* for engaging and disengaging gears.
   A burglar alarm is a *device* for giving warning that thieves are trying to enter a building.

3. An *instrument* is (usually) a small manufactured object which enables us to perform some precise action or measurement.
   A pyrometer is an *instrument* for measuring high temperatures.
   A seismograph is an *instrument* for recording earth tremors.
   A spectroscope is an *instrument* for measuring the spectra of rays.

4. An *apparatus* is (usually) a complicated mechanism or assembly of many different pieces used for some scientific experiment or test.
   An Orsat *apparatus* is used to analyse the products of combustion.
   A bomb calorimeter is an *apparatus* for finding out the calorific value of a solid or liquid fuel.

State, Condition, Conditions

1. *a.* The pig-iron comes out of the blast-furnace in a molten *state*.
   b. Metal which is hardened by cold-working may be brought back to its original {*state* / *condition*} by annealing.

<table>
<tr><td>2. a. The inspector found that working</td><td rowspan="4">conditions</td><td>in the factory were very bad.</td></tr>
<tr><td>b. Flying was impossible, for weather</td><td>became much worse.</td></tr>
<tr><td>c. The engine should be under normal working</td><td>during the test.</td></tr>
<tr><td>d. The initial steam</td><td>for this turbine are 500 lb/in² and 800° F.</td></tr>
</table>

Elevate, Depress (= lift up, push down)

1. The cooling tower is *elevated* above the level of the condenser.
2. The railway was *elevated* above street level.

<table>
<tr><td>3. The high-pressure air</td><td rowspan="3">depresses</td><td>a piston against a spring.</td></tr>
<tr><td>4. Evaporation of the fuel</td><td>the temperature to freezing point.</td></tr>
<tr><td>5. The engineer</td><td>a plunger to set off the explosive charge.</td></tr>
</table>

Assemble, Dismantle

1. The machine was *dismantled*, or *taken to pieces*, in order to transport it more easily.
2. When the machine arrived at its destination, it was quickly *re-assembled.*

3. This type of machine can be *assembled* in a few hours.
4. The components are shipped abroad, and *assembled* in local factories.

5. The *assembly-line* of the factory is where all the components are put together.

6. The delegates to the conference *assembled* in the *Assembly* Hall.

PATTERNS

1. Time Statements (1)

Look at these double statements:

1. John finished his work. John went home.
2. The steam leaves the boiler. The steam enters the turbine.

In both, the subject of the two parts is the same (*John* and *the steam*).
They both describe two events in a time-sequence.
So we can write them together in this way:

---

1. *After* John finished his work, he went home.
2. *After* the steam leaves the boiler, it enters the turbine.

The other common 'time-links' we can use are these:

---

1. *Before* the steam leaves the boiler, it is passed through a superheater.
2. *As* the products of combustion circulate, they heat the feed water.
3. *While* the metal is still molten, it is poured into moulds.
4. *As soon as* the steam passes over the metal tubes, it is condensed.
5. *When* the clutch is engaged, the car is in gear.
6. *Until* the machines are properly tested, they must not be used.
7. *Once* the machines are tested, they may be put into service.

EXERCISE

Join these double statements, using the most suitable 'time-link'.

1. The steam reaches a certain pressure. Immediately the steam lifts the valve.
2. The rivet cools. The rivet contracts and draws the plates together.
3. The air enters the furnace. The air is pre-heated by the turbine exhaust.
4. The first stage of the rocket burns out. Immediately the first stage is ejected.
5. The piston descends. The descending piston creates a partial vacuum above it.
6. Metal plates are prepared for a weld. But first the metal plates are clamped together.
7. The fuel travels along the conveyor chain. The fuel burns.
8. The ore cannot be used industrially. The ore is smelted and reduced to iron.

9. Gases pass through the turbine. They are still very hot afterwards.
10. The throttle valve closes. It reduces the supply of steam.
11. A bearing is properly lubricated. The bearing will last much longer.
12. The fuel enters the boiler. It is first pulverised.
13. New water pipes are installed. They should first be given cathodic protection against corrosion.
14. The velocity of the air is increased. Finally it reaches the speed of sound.
15. The pulverisers rotate. The pulverisers repeatedly strike the coal.
16. The piston moves along its stroke. The piston ejects the exhaust steam.

2. Function, Duty

The idea of *function* is very common in technology. It is rather similar to the idea of *purpose*, but it emphasises the *use* rather than the *purpose*.

The following are the common structures which express it:

1. *a.* The *function* *b.* The *duty*	*of*	the superheater the governor the spring	is to	raise the temperature of the steam. control the speed of the engine. keep the weights depressed.

2. *a.* The superheater *b.* The governor *c.* The spring	has performs	the *function* the *duty*	*of*	raising the steam temperature. controlling the engine speed. keeping the weights depressed.

3. *a.* The superheater *b.* The governor *c.* The spring	*serves to*	raise the temperature of the steam. control the speed of the engine. keep the weights depressed.

4. *a.* The superheater	*serves as*	a means of raising the steam temperature.
b. The governor	*acts as*	a method of controlling the engine speed.
c. The spring	*is used as*	a way of keeping the weights depressed.
d. The balls	*serve as*	weights.
e. The firebricks	*act as*	insulators to prevent heat radiation.
f. The slide-valves	*are used as*	a means of admitting steam to the cylinder.

EXERCISE ONE

Use each of these structures to complete the following statements:

1. A fan ...... (*induce*) a forced draught over the firegrate.
2. A thermometer ...... (*measure*) the temperature of a body.
3. A distributor ...... (*provide*) a spark in each of the cylinders.
4. A chuck ...... (*hold*) the work firmly on the lathe.
5. The safety valve ...... (*prevent*) excessive pressure in the boiler.
6. The vice ...... (*clamp*) the work on to the drilling machine.
7. The intermediate gears ...... (*connect*) the stud and lead-screw gears on the lathe.

8. Baffles ...... (*direct*) the flue gases round the boiler tubes.
9. Piston rings ...... (*prevent*) steam leakage past the piston.
10. The limestone ...... (*remove*) the non-metallic impurities in the iron ore.
11. A re-heater ...... (*re-heat*) the steam between one cylinder and the next.
12. The examination ...... (*test*) the students' knowledge.

EXERCISE TWO

State the function of:

1. The water-tubes in the boiler.
2. An anvil.
3. A liquid pump.
4. The lubricant in a bearing.
5. Steam jackets round a cylinder.
6. A die.
7. The tuyeres at the bottom of a blast furnace

3. Forces (Impel, Exert, Act, Balance, etc.)

---

1. *a.* The impeller blades *b.* The expanding gases	*force* *drive* *impel* *push*	the water forwards. the piston down the cylinder.

---

2. *a.* The weight *b.* The fluid *c.* The load which a spring	*exerts*	a turning force *on* the lever. a pressure *on* the walls of the container. may be varied by adjusting nuts.
d. The gases *e.* We have to	*exert*	a force *on* the piston. great force to prevent the expansion of the heated metal.

---

3. *a.* The force *acts* perpendicular to the axis of the spindle.

b. These two forces	*act*	in line with each other. in opposition to each other. against each other.
c. The force of gravity *d.* Friction *e.* A lift force	*acts on*	all objects vertically downwards. moving bodies and brings them to a stop. the undersurface of the aircraft wing.

---

4. *a.* One substance *reacts* with another in a chemical *reaction.*
   b. A force which *acts on* an object is opposed by an equal and opposite *reaction.*

---

5. *a.* Bodies with similar charges *repel* each other. They exert a *repulsive* force.
   b. Bodies with opposite charges *attract* each other. They exert an *attractive* force.

---

6. *a.* The weights at opposite ends of the lever } *balance* { each other.
   b. The two opposing forces } *counterbalance* { each other.

   c. When opposing forces balance each other, a state of *equilibrium* or *balance* is reached.

---

7. *a.* The power of the engine must be sufficient to } *overcome* { the resistance of friction.
   b. The aircraft must develop enough power to } *overcome* { the force of gravity.

Section 10

Reading: Impulse Turbines

In an impulse turbine steam is admitted through a nozzle and directed against one or more rows of blades. *Prior to passing* through this nozzle, the steam is at high pressure but low velocity. The nozzle normally consists of a convergent and divergent section. In the former, the steam suffers a drop in pressure, but its velocity is increased. The function of the divergent section is to reduce to a minimum the tendency of the fluid to turbulence, and thus to ensure that the fluid flow is as smooth as possible.

On emerging from the nozzle at its maximum velocity, the steam impinges on the row of moving blades which project radially from the turbine shaft. In this axial-flow type of turbine, the steam flow is along the axis of rotation of the shaft, and therefore the blades radiate outwards from the shaft. *On entering* the blades, which are set at a definite angle to the steam flow, the steam is deflected from its original path. *In being deflected*, it exerts an impulsive force on the blades, which causes them to rotate. *While passing* over the blades, the steam suffers a slight reduction in velocity through friction. In a simple turbine, it is then passed out into the atmosphere, or to a condenser, where it is condensed and led back to the boiler.

However, *after leaving* the blades of the turbine, the steam still possesses a considerable velocity, and this may be utilised in another type of turbine by passing it through a series of two or more turbine wheels. This is known as velocity-compounding. *On passing* through the first row of moving blades, the steam encounters a row of stationary blades which deflect the steam on to a second row of moving blades, and so on. Each time part of the kinetic energy of the steam is lost through friction, and therefore the velocity of the steam is progressively reduced. In order to compensate for this, the blades in each successive row are made progressively larger in cross-section, and their pitch is increased. In this way, a larger proportion of the kinetic energy of the steam can be utilised than in the simple turbine.

Another type of turbine in common use is known as the pressure-compounded turbine. It incorporates several rows of blades, but each one is enclosed between diaphragms to form a separate pressure stage. *After passing* through the first set of blades, the steam is directed through nozzles set in the succeeding diaphragm, and impinges on the following row of blades.

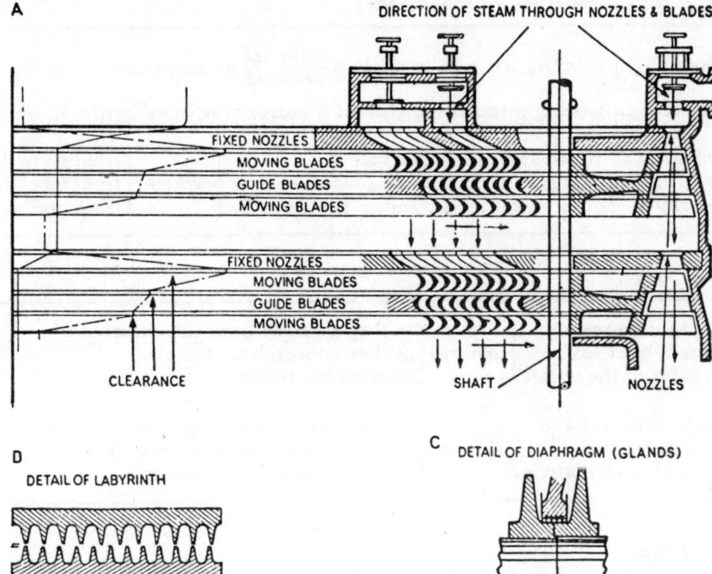

Cross-section of impulse turbine

WORD STUDY

Tend, Apt, Inclined

1. A person 2. Wet steam 3. Cast-iron 4. Turbulence	*tends to* *is apt to* *is inclined to*	put on weight when he eats too much. erode the blades of a turbine. fracture under excessive tension. dissipate the kinetic energy of the steam.
5. Leaks 6. Steam pockets	*tend to* *are apt to* *are inclined to*	develop around the tips of the turbine blades. form in the water tubes.

7. There is a *tendency for* { leaks to develop round the tips of the blades. / cast-iron to fracture under excessive tension. }

8. The present *tendency is* to use pulverised fuels in large boilers.

Impinge on, Encounter

1. The flames from the furnace should not *impinge on* the joints. (= strike)
2. On entering the turbine, the steam *impinges on* the rotating blades.
3. The beam of accelerated protons *impinges on* a beryllium target.
4. On entering the turbine, the steam *encounters* a row of fixed blades. (= meet)

Deflect, Refract (bend); *Reflect* (bend back)

---

1. A ray of light entering water at an angle is *refracted* / *deflected* at the surface.
2. A ray of light passing through the glass of a mirror is *reflected* by the silver.

3. A billiard ball which strikes another ball is	*deflected*	from its path.
4. Steam which impinges on the turbine blades is		from its course.
5. A nearby piece of iron causes a compass needle to be		from north.

Diverge, Converge

---

1. Railway lines seem to	*converge*	as they go away from the observer.
2. All roads tend to		as they approach a large city.
3. The sides of the nozzle		towards the throat.

4. Railway lines seem to	*diverge*	as they approach the observer.
5. All roads tend to		as they go away from a large city.
6. The sides of the nozzle		as they go away from the throat.

PATTERNS

1. Contracted Time Statements (1)

In the previous section, we practised time statements in which the subjects of both parts of the statement were the same.

e.g. Before *the steam* enters the nozzle, *it* is at very high pressure.
Before *it* enters the nozzle, *the steam* is at very high pressure.

These time statements are very often shortened or contracted to:

Before entering the nozzle, the steam is at very high pressure.

Here are the different possibilities of this structure:

Before *Prior to*	entering the nozzle, the steam is at high pressure.	= *before* it enters.
When *While* *In*	passing through the blades, the steam is deflected.	= *while* it is passing through.
After *On*	leaving the blades, the steam passes out to the atmosphere.	= *after* it leaves.

EXERCISE

Change these statements in the same way.

1. Before it mixes with the products of combustion, the air is pre-heated.
2. As the piston rises, it carries the exhaust gas upwards.
3. The aircraft exploded as it was landing.

4. After the gases pass through the boiler, they are still very hot.
5. As the shaft rotates, it splashes oil up into the bearings.
6. When the metal surfaces reach welding heat, they are pressed together.
7. As the rivet cools, it contracts.
8. When bearings rotate at high speeds, they generate frictional heat.
9. Before it enters the furnace, the fuel is pulverised.
10. When it leaves the furnace, the molten metal is channelled into moulds.
11. While the fuel is travelling along the conveyor chain, it burns.
12. Before it becomes molten, the metal is in a plastic state.
13. The structure of the metal begins to change as soon as it exceeds the critical temperature.
14. The hot gases pass up the flue to the chimney after they transmit their heat to the boiler water.
15. The gas may be compressed before it is circulated through the mains.
16. As they rotate, the pulverisers break up the coal into fragments.
17. As soon as the steam passes into the discharge pipe, it condenses.
18. After the liquid is heated for 10 minutes, it should be allowed to cool.
19. While it was entering the harbour, the vessel collided with the sea-wall.
20. Before it is passed back to the boiler, the condensate should be re-heated.

2. Contracted Time Statements (2)

These contracted forms *on*, *before*, *while*, etc. + *-ing* are normally used when the subject of both statements is the same, as you have just seen.
They are not normally used when the subjects are different. But one other type of statement can be expressed in the same way.

On removing the impurities, the water can be passed back to the boiler.
When installing a boiler, the floor space which is available is very important.

You will notice that this really means:

When we remove the impurities ......
and *When we are installing a boiler* ......

EXERCISE

Use the contracted structure to re-write the following statements:

1. Before we apply heat for a weld, the plates should be clamped together.
2. When we use superheated steam, compounding becomes less effective.
3. When we are drilling deep holes, the feed movement should be released from time to time.
4. While we are making an efficiency test on an engine, certain precautions should be observed.
5. When screws are being cut, the lead-screw on the lathe is engaged.
6. When railway tracks are being laid, allowance must be made for expansion.

7. In the construction of locomotives, the provision of a large heating surface is very important.
8. After the roughing cut is taken, the cutting tool should be sharpened.
9. Before the final cut is taken, the exact size of the bar should be measured.
10. Before the dam can be built, the course of the river will have to be diverted.
11. After you have read the book, a summary should be made of the important chapters.
12. Before starting production, extensive tests must be made.
13. In the course of construction of the motorway, vast quantities of earth have to be moved.
14. While the engine was being examined, a number of defects were found.
15. After £1,000,000 were spent on research and development, the whole project was suddenly abandoned.

3. Sequence

When steam enters the turbine, it has a very high *initial* velocity.
When it leaves the turbine, it has a much lower *final* velocity.
As it passes through the turbine, its velocity is *progressively* reduced.

The rows of blades in the turbine are made *progressively* larger.
Each row is a little larger than the *previous* or *preceding* row.
From January to August, the weather gets *progressively* warmer.
Each month is slightly warmer than the *previous* or *preceding* one.

The first steam engine was built during the nineteenth century.
During the *following* or *succeeding* hundred years, it became the main source of power.
The *initial* attempt to solve the problem ended in failure. So did the three *succeeding* attempts. The *final* attempt succeeded.

Subsequent or *later* attempts to repeat the experiment failed.
The condensate is stored in a cooling tower, for *subsequent* use in the condenser.

In a turbine, the steam passes through a *series* or *succession* of wheels holding blades. It passes through them one after the other. Each *successive* row reduces the kinetic energy of the steam. The energy of the steam is *progressively* reduced as it passes through the *successive* rows.

Not every row of blades rotates. There is a rotating ring, *followed by* a stationary ring, and this is *succeeded by* another rotating ring.
Every second ring is a rotating ring.
Every other ring is a rotating ring.
Each alternate ring rotates.
The rotating rings *alternate with* the stationary rings.
Each *alternate* stroke on a two-stroke engine is a working stroke.
Only *one* stroke *in four* of a four-stroke engine is a working stroke.
The strokes occur in a *sequence.*

EXERCISE

Complete these statements:

1. During the past century, there has been a ...... increase in the size of boilers.
2. The metal which was ...... heated is now quenched in a cold liquid.
3. A complicated ...... of operations is necessary to produce steel.
4. As the metal cools, its surface grows ...... harder and tougher.
5. The pneumatic riveter closes the rivet by a quick ...... of blows.
6. The ...... cost of the machines is high, but maintenance and operating costs are low.
7. Modern boilers are designed for higher pressures than those of the ...... century.
8. The exhaust steam is condensed, and can ...... be used again in the boiler.
9. The original design was not very satisfactory, and a ...... of modifications were made over several years.
10. The ...... pressure of the steam before expansion is 60 lb/in^2.
11. The neutrons lose their energy gradually by ...... collisions with other particles.
12. As work went on, the dam grew ...... higher.
13. The manager retired and was ...... by his assistant.
14. After a ...... of tests, the model was put into production.
15. He works ...... shifts: this week he is on the day-shift, and next week he will be on the night-shift.

Section 11

Reading: The Petrol Engine

In the internal combustion engine, heat is generated by the combustion of an inflammable charge inside a cylinder, and the heat energy is immediately converted into mechanical energy. Some heavy internal combustion engines use a gas fuel *or else* Diesel oil, and the fuel/air mixture may be ignited *either* by a spark *or* by compression of the mixture. However, for small i.c. engines, such as those which are used in motor-cars, the charge is a mixture of petrol and air, and is ignited by a spark from the distributor.

When the mixture is ignited, the products of combustion expand down the cylinder, which is fitted with a reciprocating piston. The downward movement of the piston is converted into a rotational movement of the crankshaft by means of a connecting rod. **As the crankshaft rotates,** the piston is driven upwards again, and the exhaust gases are expelled through the exhaust valve in the cylinder head. **When the piston nears** the top of this stroke, the inlet valve is opened and the exhaust valve closed. The piston then descends on the induction stroke, and draws a fresh charge into the cylinder. **As the piston rises** again on the compression stroke, the charge is compressed and ignited, and the cycle begins again. This is the four-stroke cycle which is in common use. An *alternative* cycle is the two-stroke cycle, which combines the exhaust and compression strokes into one.

The combustion of the mixture does not take place instantaneously. The spark is therefore timed to occur **before the piston reaches** top dead centre, *otherwise* maximum pressure would not be reached in time. **By the time the piston is** at top dead centre, combustion is well under way and the expansion of the gases is beginning. **Once combustion starts,** it should be carried through the mixture very rapidly, and this is assisted by making the clearance space above the piston as small as possible, and by careful design of the cylinder head. Rapid propagation of the flame through the compressed gas is also assisted by creating turbulence in the gas.

Most small i.c. engines in common use have four cylinders, which fire in a definite and regular sequence. This is necessary, *otherwise* the torque which the pistons impart to the crankshaft will be irregular and uneven. The torque is liable to be uneven in any case **when the engine is running** slowly, and a flywheel is fitted to the crankshaft to damp out these variations.

It is essential for the inlet and exhaust valves to open and close at exactly the appropriate moment in relation to the position of the piston. Therefore they are actuated by a cam-shaft running in phase with the crankshaft.

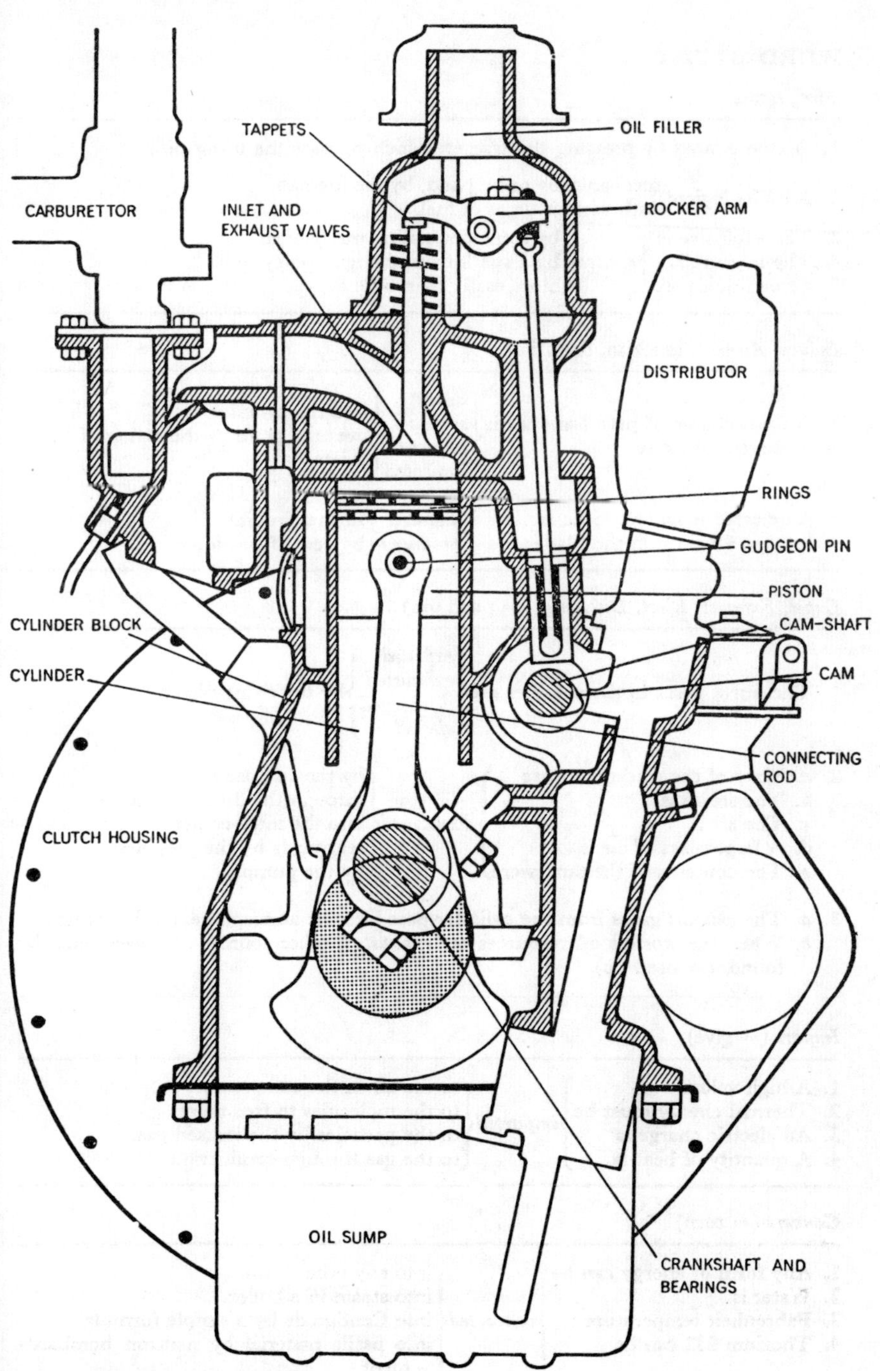

Cross-section of a petrol engine

WORD STUDY

Fire, Ignite

1. A rifle is *fired* by pressing the trigger, which releases the firing-pin.

2. A boiler is *fired*		mechanically or by hand, by the fireman.
		with various types of fuel.

3. The explosive is	*ignited*	by some detonating mechanism.
4. The mixture is		by a spark from the ignition system.
5. Some liquids are		more easily than others.

Induce, Aspirate (suck in, draw in)

1. A fresh charge of petrol and air is	*drawn*	into the cylinder.
2. A current of air is	*sucked*	over the grate by the action of steam jets.
	induced	
	aspirated	

3. An electro-magnetic force is	*induced*	in the circuit.
4. Intense stresses on the blades are	*produced*	by centrifugal force.

Expel, Exhaust, Eject, Discharge (= push out)

1. The burnt gases in the cylinder are	*expelled*	by the rising piston.
	exhausted	
	discharged	
	ejected	

2. *a.* Sixty of the workmen were	*discharged*	by the company.
b. The steam is		through the divergent nozzle.
c. The air is		into the inter-cooler.
d. A large mass of air is		rearwards by the propeller.
e. The contents of the tank were		by the pump.

3. *a.* The *exhaust* gases from the cylinder pass into the atmosphere. (= burnt up)
   b. When the world's oil resources are *exhausted*, other sources of power must be found. (= used up)

Impart (= give)

1. A high velocity is	*imparted*	to the air in the compressor.
2. Thermal energy must be		to the molecules to free them.
3. An electric charge is		to the particles by the ionised gas.
4. A quantity of heat is		to the gas through conduction.

Convert (= turn)

1. Any form of energy can be	*converted*	into any other form.
2. Water is		into steam in a boiler.
3. Fahrenheit temperature is		into Centigrade by a simple formula.
4. Thorium 232 can be		into fissile material by neutron bombardment.

5. The *conversion* of Fahrenheit into Centigrade temperatures is achieved by a simple formula.

Propagate, Distribute

---

1. The initial flame is	*propagated*	rapidly through the mixture. (= spread)
2. Heat is		by conduction through an iron bar.
3. A pressure wave is		through the gas near the speed of sound.
4. The new theory was		by lectures and articles.
5. The heat is	*distributed*	evenly throughout the material. (= shared)
6. The weight should be		evenly over the foundations.
7. The current is		to each of the plugs by the distributor.
8. The mixture is		to each of the cylinders in turn.

PATTERNS

1. Time Statements (2)

In the previous two sections, we have seen examples of Time Statements which had the *same subject* in both parts of the sentence.
Here are examples of Time Statements which have *different subjects* in the two parts of the sentence. Notice that they are not usually contracted.

Before the piston reaches the top of its stroke, the mixture is ignited. It continues to burn *until* combustion is complete. *By the time* the piston reaches top dead centre, combustion is well under way. *While* any unburnt gas remains in the cylinder, combustion will continue. *As* combustion proceeds, the gases expand and drive the piston down. *As soon as* the piston reaches bottom dead centre, the exhaust valve is opened. *When* the piston nears the top of its stroke again, the inlet valve is opened. *Once* all the exhaust gases are driven out, the exhaust valve is closed. *After* one cycle is completed, another cycle begins.

EXERCISE

Use the appropriate 'time-link' to join these statements.

1. Steam in the boiler reaches a certain pressure. The safety valve is lifted.
2. The fuel travels along the conveyor chain. The flame ignites it.
3. Combustion proceeds. The temperature of the mixture rises.
4. The steam engine was invented. Water could not be pumped out of coal-mines.
5. The critical temperature is exceeded. The steel undergoes structural changes.
6. Steam passes through the turbine nozzle. Its velocity increases.
7. The second world war was over. Jet engines were in common use.
8. The gas leaves the turbine blades. Expansion takes place in the jet-pipe.
9. The condensate is led back to the boiler. Oil and dirt from the engine are removed.

10. The steam is cooled below its condensation temperature. It turns to water.
11. The crank was invented. The steam engine could not be used to produce rotary motion.
12. Light falls on certain substances. Electrons are emitted.
13. The fluid passes through the blades. Frictional losses occur.
14. Heat transfer will continue. The system attains a uniform temperature throughout its mass.
15. The speed of sound is reached. Shock waves are formed.
16. The development programme is completed. It will have cost £10,000,000.
17. The fire engines reached the scene of the fire. The factory was already half-destroyed.
18. The material is available. Tests will start immediately.

2. Alternatives

Ignition can be produced *either* by a spark *or* by compression of the mixture.
Bearings are lubricated *either* by gravity feed *or* by forced feed. They can be lubricated *in either way.*
Bearings can be lubricated *either* by gravity feed *or alternatively* by forced feed.
The drive can be transmitted *either* by a flexible belt *or alternatively* by a chain.
The drive can be transmitted *either* by a flexible belt *or else* by a chain.
An *alternative* method of transmitting the drive is by an inelastic chain.
There are several *alternative* methods of lubricating bearings.

The temperature must not exceed 650° C	*or* *or else* *otherwise*	the metal will melt.

The toughness of the steel depends on *whether* it contains a smaller *or* a greater proportion of carbon.
The type of condenser we use will largely depend on *whether* (*or not*) there is a plentiful supply of pure water.

EXERCISE ONE

Complete these statements with *otherwise* and *or else.*

1. The governor should not be over-sensitive ...... it will cause the engine speed to oscillate continuously.
2. The furnace should not be overcharged with fuel ...... heavy smoke will be produced through poor combustion.
3. Some means of cooling the compressed air is necessary ...... the losses in the compressor will be large.
4. A high octane fuel has to be used ...... detonation is liable to occur.
5. Turbulent conditions are required in the combustion chamber ...... the flame will not propagate itself rapidly enough.

6. A compensator jet is necessary ...... the carburettor will not work properly at low speeds.
7. A flywheel is always fitted to the crankshaft ...... the vibration would be excessive at low engine speeds.
8. Piston rings must be replaced when they are worn ...... gas will leak past the pistons into the crankcase.
9. The project must be carefully prepared before work is actually started ...... a great deal of time will be wasted.
10. The aircraft will have to jettison some of its fuel ...... it will not be able to land safely.

EXERCISE TWO

Complete these sentences.

1. An ...... method of reducing the risks of detonation is by adding dopes to the fuel.
2. The use of ...... aluminium ...... magnesium alloys is now quite common.
3. The heat which is required for welding is produced by an oxy-acetylene torch or ...... by an electric arc.
4. ...... a centre ...... a chuck is fitted into the spindle depending on ...... turning ...... boring work is being done.
5. The fuel may be intimately mixed with the moderator or ...... spaced at intervals through it.

3. Transmission

a) *Mechanical*

1. The power from the engine is	*transmitted*	to the machine through a belt.
2. The piston movement is	*communicated*	to the wheels through a crankshaft.
3. The movement of the spindle is		to the lead-screw through gears.

b) *Radio*

The broadcasting station	*transmits* *broadcasts*	television and radio programmes.

c) *Transfer*

1. The molten metal is	*transferred*	from the ladle to the mould.
2. The heat from the reactor is		to the heat exchanger by a liquid coolant.
3. Heat is not easily		from a dry vapour to a metal surface.

d) *Convection*

1. The warm air is } *conveyed* { upwards and displaces the cold air.
2. The heat from the engine is } *carried* { away by the air-stream.

3. The heat from the engine is *transmitted* by *convection* into the air.
4. When the liquid is heated from the bottom, a *convection* current is set up.

e) *Conduction*

1. The heat from the furnace is } *conducted* { through the cylinder walls.
2. The heat of the soldering iron is } { to the metal of the joint.
3. Power from the generator is } *transmitted* { through cables to every house.

4. The heat from the steam is *transmitted* through the tubes by *conduction.*
5. Some substances are better *conductors* of electric current than others.
6. Copper is a better *conductor* of heat than iron.

f) *Radiation*

1. The heat of the sun is } *radiated* { to the earth by *radiation.*
2. Heat from the fire is } *transmitted* { to the walls of the furnace.

g) = *Carry* or *Take*

1. Boiler tubes } *convey* { the water from the upper drums to the lower drum.
2. Lorries } { the machinery to the docks ready for loading.

3. The exhaust steam is } *conducted* { through a blast pipe.
4. The steam is } *led* { through nozzles onto the blades.

Section 12

Reading: The Carburation System

Since it is essential to secure rapid and complete combustion in the cylinder of an internal combustion engine, the fuel and air mixture must be thoroughly mixed; and further, it must be in the correct proportions for all running conditions of the engine. This is accomplished by means of a device **called** a carburettor. In this carburettor, a stream of air **blown** over a jet mixes intimately with a spray of petrol **drawn** out of it. The jet is inserted into a choke or venturi in the intake manifold, and is supplied with petrol at atmospheric pressure.

During the suction stroke of the piston, the pressure in the intake manifold is below atmospheric, and air is induced through the intake and over the jet. *As there is a further drop* in pressure at the venturi, the pressure difference **produced** is large enough to draw petrol up out of the jet and atomise it. The level of the petrol in the jet is kept constant by the float and needle valve in the float chamber, which acts as a reservoir for the fuel. Above the venturi there is a throttle valve **operated** by the accelerator pedal, which controls the amount of mixture **admitted** to the cylinder.

However, this simple form of single-jet carburettor will not give correct mixture strength for all engine speeds. The chief difficulty **encountered** is that, at high running speeds, the amount of petrol **taken** up at the jet will increase faster than the increase in air-flow. Therefore a carburettor **set** to give correct mixtures at low speed will give a progressively richer mixture as the speed increases. To compensate for this, a second jet is provided, **fed** from a well open to the atmosphere and **supplied** with petrol from the float chamber. *Owing to the fact that this compensating jet is larger* than the main jet, it can supply petrol at a quicker rate than the main jet until the well is emptied. As the speed is increased, more and more of the petrol **required** is drawn from the main jet. The compensator jet can now supply only as much petrol as can pass through the small compensator orifice in the float chamber.

Another problem **to be solved** is that of starting. In order to obtain the rich mixture **required** for starting, the throttle must be almost closed. *As the air velocity is then very low* in the venturi, insufficient petrol is drawn out of the jet. This difficulty is overcome by the provision of an idler jet in the wall of the intake manifold near the throttle valve. This jet will only function when the throttle is nearly closed. When it is opened for faster running, the suction round the edge of the throttle decreases, and the idler automatically ceases to act.

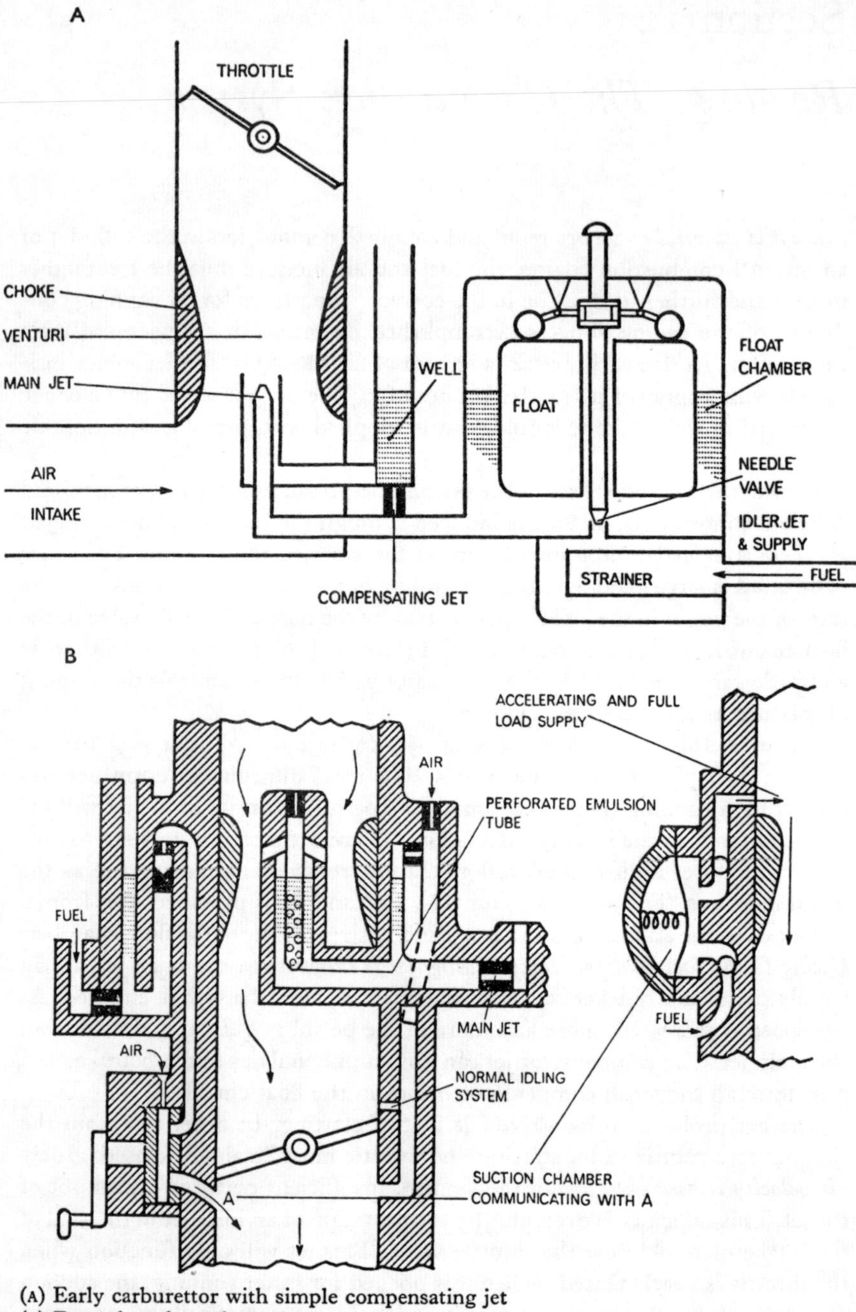

A

THROTTLE
CHOKE
VENTURI
MAIN JET
WELL
FLOAT
FLOAT CHAMBER
NEEDLE VALVE
AIR
INTAKE
IDLER JET & SUPPLY
STRAINER
FUEL
COMPENSATING JET

B

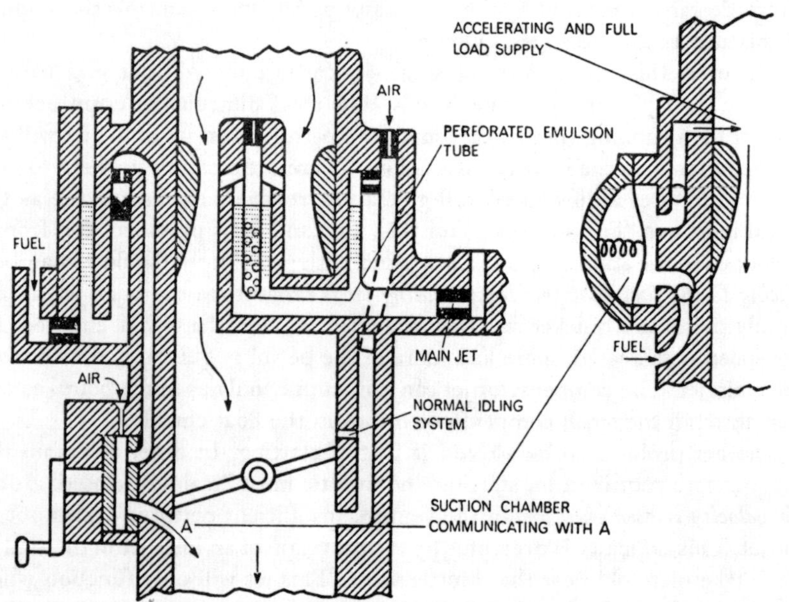

(A) Early carburettor with simple compensating jet
(B) Downdraught carburettor

WORD STUDY

Supply, Provide, Fit

1. A generating station	*supplies*	electricity *to* the city.
2. The compressor		compressed air *to* the engine.

3. A generating station	*supplies*	the city *with* electricity.
4. The compressor		the engine *with* compressed air.

5. Electricity	*is supplied*	*to* the city by the generating station.
6. Compressed air		*to* the engine by the compressor.
7. Cold water		*to* the condenser.
8. Air for combustion		*to* the furnace.

9. The city	*is supplied*	*with* electricity by the generating station.
10. The engine		*with* compressed air by the compressor.
11. The condenser		*with* cold water.
12. The furnace		*with* air.

13. Expansion joints of various kinds are	*fitted*	on steam pipes.
14. Drains are	*provided*	on the underside of the casing.

15. Steam pipes are	*fitted with*	expansion joints of various kinds.
16. Boilers are	*provided with*	safety valves.

17. The *provision* of a drain on the underside of the casing is necessary.
18. *Provision* must be made for draining the casing.
19. One way of *providing for* expansion is by a bend in the pipes.

Equip, Install

1. The new factory was	*equipped with*	the latest machinery.
2. The hospital is		X-ray facilities.
3. Divers have to be		oxygen apparatus.

4. The latest machinery was	*installed*	in the factory.
5. Several turbo-generators have been		at the dam.
6. A central-heating system was		in the house last year.

7. The *installation*	of these generators was a long and costly undertaking.	
	of atomic engines in ships and aircraft is not likely for a year or two.	

Insert (= put into)

1. A film of oil is	*inserted*	between the sliding surfaces of a bearing.
2. The workpiece is		between the lathe centres.
3. Diaphragms are		between the stages of the turbine.
4. The advertisement was		in the newspaper yesterday.

Allow for, Compensate for

1. The candidate left home ten minutes early to	*allow for*	delays on the journey.
2. The turbine is built in sections to		expansion.
3. The pattern maker has to		contraction of the casting as it cools.

4. *Allowance* must be made for expansion or contraction of the metal.
is always made for frictional losses and leakage losses in the turbine.

5. You must work twice as hard today to	*compensate*	*for* your absence yesterday.
6. The employers paid him £4000 to		*for* his injury.
7. An idler jet is provided to		*for* low air velocity in the venturi.

8. The loss of pressure through condensation is	*compensated for*	by the admission of more steam.
	offset	
9. The disadvantages of the jet engine are	*counteracted*	by its many virtues.

PATTERNS

1. Explanations of Cause (1)

Since the compensating jet is larger, it can supply more petrol.
The compensating jet can supply more petrol, *since it is larger.*

In these statements, the part which begins with *since* is a clause explaining *why* the main event took place.
The common 'cause-words' which are used in this structure are:

1. *Because*
Since
As } he was tired, he went to bed early.

2. *In view of the fact that*
On account of the fact that
Owing to the fact that
Seeing that } he was tired, he went to bed early.

Notice three more useful structures:

1. *The reason why* he went to bed early *was that* he was tired.
2. He was tired. This *explains why* he went to bed early.
3. He was tired. This *accounts for* { *the fact that* he went to bed early.
his going to bed early.

EXERCISE

Use each of the structures given above to link these statements:

1. The steam from the boiler is wet. It has to be passed through a superheater.

2. The temperatures reached are very high. Some method of cooling must be adopted.
3. This type of turbine is very widely used. It has a much greater efficiency.
4. Metal expands when it is heated. Expansion joints are fitted to steam pipes.
5. Exhaust gases still possess a great deal of heat. They can be used to heat the incoming air to the boiler.
6. Atomic power is not available in sufficient quantity. Coal is still a very valuable source of power.
7. The carburettor may become choked with dirt. An air filter is fitted.
8. Vertical boilers were installed in the factory. Only a limited floor-space was available.
9. The earliest steam engines could be used only for pumping. The crank had not been invented.
10. Gas turbines are not self-starting. A starting motor must be fitted, to drive the compressor.
11. The neutron is an uncharged particle. No repulsive forces are exerted on it by the nucleus.
12. The apprentices had very little training. Their work was very poor.

2. Contracted Relative: Passive

Look at these three sentences. Each one contains a *relative clause* with a *passive verb.*

The petrol mixes with a stream of air *which is blown* over it.
There is a throttle valve *which is operated* by the accelerator.
The locomotive *which was invented* by Trevithick revolutionised transport.

This type of statement is very common indeed in technical writing and speech, and it is usually shortened by leaving out the words *Which is* and *Which was*:

The petrol mixes with a stream of air *blown* over it.
There is a throttle valve *operated* by the accelerator.
The locomotive *invented* by Trevithick revolutionised transport.

EXERCISE

Change these statements in the same way:

1. The exhaust steam is passed over tubes which are filled with cold water.
2. The tube area which is exposed to the incoming steam is relatively large.
3. The efficiency of an engine is the ratio of the work which is done to the heat which is received.
4. The power which is demanded from modern turbines is continually increasing.
5. The research which is being carried out on this subject is extensive.

6. The steam which is extracted from the turbine is passed through a condenser.
7. The torque which is exerted on the crankshaft should be even.
8. The manufacturing process which was adopted was a revolutionary one.
9. Generators which are not required for service are stopped.
10. The steel which is obtained in this way is suitable for machine tools.

3. Problems, Difficulties and Solutions

Various	*problems* *difficulties*	*arose* *were encountered* *were met with*	in the development of a satisfactory carburettor.
These *problems* were		*approached* *tackled*	by a study of the air-flow in the choke.
		solved *dealt with*	by the provision of a compensating jet.
The *difficulty* was		*overcome* *avoided* *got round*	by providing a compensating jet.

Note: *Solution* has two meanings:

1. Knowing certain values enables us *to solve* the equation.

The diagram will help	*to solve* *in the solution of*	some of these problems.

The problem is quite	*incapable of solution.* *insoluble.*

2. *a.* Joints should be dipped in a *solution* of ammonium chloride to neutralise the acid.
   b. The gases are passed through *solutions* of various chemicals in water.

c. Various chemicals are *d.* A *soluble* substance is one which can be *e.* A *solute* (e.g. sugar) can be	*dissolved*	in water, and gases are passed through them. in a liquid. in a *solvent* (e.g. water).

Section 13

Reading: The Jet Engine

Jet engines *with which* most modern high-speed aircraft are equipped develop thrust on the same principle as the propellers of conventional aero-engines. In both, the propulsive force is derived from the reaction produced by a stream of air driven rearwards at high velocity. However, in jet-propulsion the air is directed rearwards in a jet from the engine itself. The earliest forms of jet-propulsion, such as the pulse jet utilised in the Flying Bomb, were incapable of functioning at rest, **in view of** the absence of any means of air-compression. But the introduction of the turbo-jet overcame this problem, since the turbine developed sufficient power to drive a compressor.

Air enters the engine through a divergent inlet duct, *in which* its pressure is raised to some extent. It then passes to a compressor, *where* it is compressed, and *from which* it is delivered to the combustion chambers. These are arranged radially round the axis of the turbine, *into which* the products of combustion pass on leaving the combustion chambers. A proportion of the power developed by these gases is utilised by the turbine to drive the air-compressor, and the residual energy provides the thrust *whereby* the aircraft is propelled. **Due to** the expansion of the exhaust gases in the jet-pipe behind the turbine, their exit velocity is very high.

In each of the combustion chambers, there is a perforated flame-tube, *into which* kerosene is sprayed and ignited. **Owing to** the need to limit temperatures in the combustion chambers, a large volume of excess air is required. The air/fuel ratio necessary to reduce combustion temperatures to an acceptable level is about 60 : 1. However with this ratio of fuel to air, the mixture would be difficult to ignite. Therefore only a small proportion of the compressed air is fed into the flame-tube, *where* it is ignited in a ratio of about 15 : 1. The remainder enters the flame-tube further down, or mixes with the products of combustion as they leave the tube. **By virtue of** this dilution of the hot gases with cooler air, the temperature *at which* they reach the turbine is reduced to about 850° C.

On entering the turbine, the gases pass through nozzles, *by means of which* they are directed through a ring of blades. These blades, the shape *of which* is determined by the need to reduce the torque to a minimum, rotate at high speed. **Because of** the tendency of fast-running blades to creep and change their shape, a special high-nickel alloy is used for them. After passing through the turbine, the gas expands down the jet-tube and is ejected into the

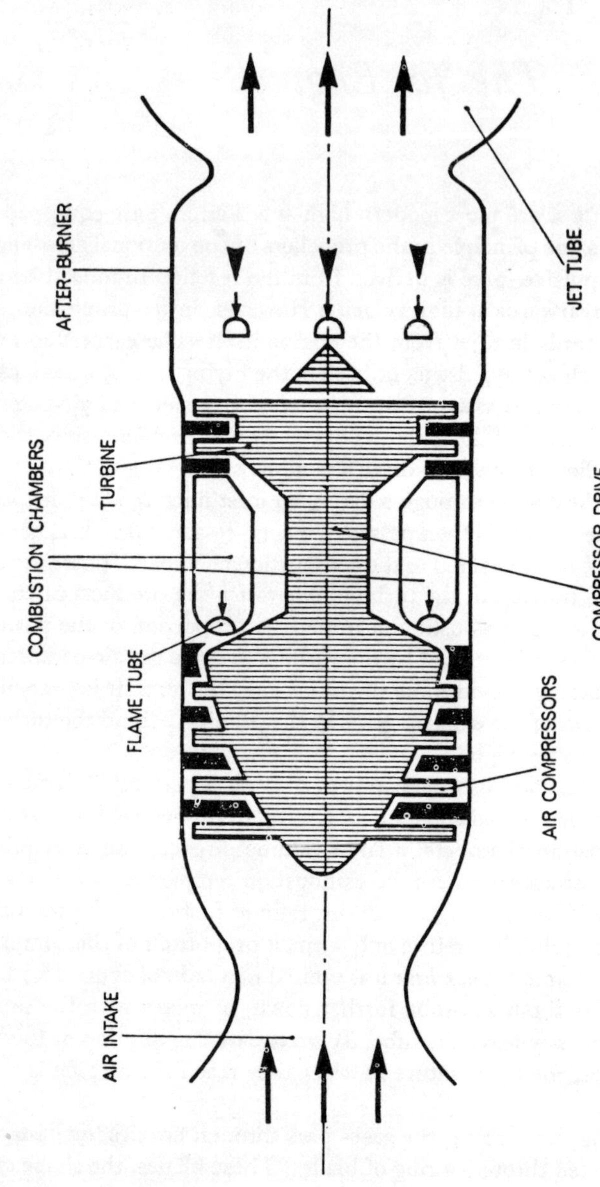

Cross-section of turbo-jet engine with after-burner

atmosphere. **Owing to** the high proportion of unburnt oxygen in this efflux, after-burners are often provided in the jet-pipe, *whereby* the hot gases are again ignited. This increases their velocity, and provides extra thrust for take-off.

WORD STUDY

Work, Function, Operate, Run

<table>
<tr><td>1. This compressor is designed to</td><td rowspan="3">run
work
operate
function</td><td>at relatively low speeds.</td></tr>
<tr><td>2. This type of engine will</td><td>for long periods without repair.</td></tr>
<tr><td>3. Jet engines are able to</td><td>over a wide range of mixture strengths.</td></tr>
</table>

<table>
<tr><td>4. The machines should be tested under normal</td><td>running
working
operating</td><td>conditions.</td></tr>
</table>

<table>
<tr><td>5. When the engine speed increases, the governor</td><td>is brought into operation.
comes into operation.</td></tr>
</table>

Control, Regulate

<table>
<tr><td>1. The steam supply to the engine is</td><td rowspan="4">regulated
controlled</td><td>by the governor.</td></tr>
<tr><td>2. The movement of the valve is</td><td>by a servo-motor.</td></tr>
<tr><td>3. Working conditions nowadays are</td><td>by government acts.</td></tr>
<tr><td>4. The temperature in the vessel can be</td><td>to within strict limits.</td></tr>
</table>

Govern, Determine, Fix

<table>
<tr><td>1. The type of engine adopted is</td><td rowspan="3">determined
decided
governed
fixed</td><td>by the use to which it is put.</td></tr>
<tr><td>2. The amount of excess air provided is</td><td>by the combustion temperatures required.</td></tr>
<tr><td>3. The angle at which the deflection plates are set is</td><td>by the need to achieve maximum turbulence.</td></tr>
</table>

Residue, Remainder

<table>
<tr><td>1. What remains
2. The remainder
3. The residue</td><td>of the heat from the exhaust gases is used to heat the incoming air.
of the energy of the steam is not recoverable.</td></tr>
</table>

<table>
<tr><td>4. The residual
5. The remaining</td><td>heat of the gases is used to heat up the incoming air.
energy of the gases is ejected from the jet-pipe.</td></tr>
</table>

Dilute, Diffuse, Disperse

1. Liquid is added to the acid in order to *dilute* it. (= weaken)
2. Zinc and copper electrodes are put into *dilute* sulphuric acid.
3. The hot gases have to be *diluted* by the addition of cool air.

4. The acid *diffuses* into the rest of the solution in the cell. (= spreads out)
5. The dust particles in the air *diffuse* the light.
6. The air in the pump is *diffused* in a divergent cone.

7. The light passing through a prism is *dispersed* into a band of colours. (= scatter)
8. The factory buildings are *dispersed* over a wide area.

PATTERNS

1. Explanations of Cause (2)

In the previous section, we saw some examples of 'cause-words' which are used when a verb follows: that is, they introduce a *clause.*
Now we shall look at 'cause-words' which are used when a noun only follows. That is, they introduce a *phrase.*

The steam pressure falls	*because of* *on account of* *owing to* *due to*	condensation in the cylinder.

Because of *On account of* *Owing to* *Due to*	the high temperatures, special alloys are used.

The two following expressions are used less commonly, as their meaning is rather restricted:

In view of	the importance of this problem . . . the difficulties involved . . .
By virtue of	its simplicity of construction . . . its heat resistance properties . . .

EXERCISE

Practise this pattern with the following statements:

Because of On account of Due to Owing to etc.	the high cost of labour, a mechanical stoker was installed. the velocity of the steam, the blades are caused to rotate. expansion of the shaft, misalignment occurs at the bearings. the provision of heat exchangers, the efficiency was increased. the increase in temperature, there is an increase in pressure. their enormous lifting capacity, electro-magnets are used. the high air/fuel ratio, a lot of oxygen is present in the products of combustion. the wetness of the steam, it must be superheated. the intense stresses involved, a high-carbon steel must be used.

dust particles in the atmosphere, accurate observation is very difficult.
the need to dispose of waste products, the installations must be sited near the sea.
the size and complexity of the plants required, only a few countries possess them.
expansion or contraction of the shaft, axial movement of the bearing takes place.
their greater viscosity, liquids are less likely to leak than gases.
the expense of the project, government assistance is necessary.

2. Prepositions with 'which'

In technical writing, the preposition is usually placed before **which** (or **whom**) and not at the end of the sentence, as it normally is in speaking.

Jet engines, **with which** most modern aircraft are equipped, . . .

Notice:

1. The air passes to a compressor **where** it is compressed. (= *in which*)
2. After-burners are provided **whereby** the hot gases are again ignited. (= *by means of which*)

EXERCISE ONE

Insert the correct word or words in these sentences.

1. The exhaust steam is passed to a condenser . . . . . . it is condensed.
2. 10 degrees is the limit . . . . . . the nozzle can control the steam flow.
3. There are a number of tubes . . . . . . the water circulates.
4. Radial flow turbines differ in the manner . . . . . . the steam flow is arranged.
5. This depends on the purpose . . . . . . the exhaust steam is used.
6. Cold water . . . . . . the condenser is supplied circulates in these tubes.
7. The rate of wear of the bearing depends on the efficiency . . . . . . it is lubricated.
8. There is an expansion period . . . . . . after-burning of the fuel may take place.
9. Openings in the crankcase . . . . . . the crankshaft passes are well sealed.
10. The material . . . . . . the apparatus is made is a good non-conductor of heat.

11. The shape of the electrodes ...... the breakdown strength depends can be altered.
12. This fuel is a mixture of gases, the chemical combination ...... is known.
13. There is a combustion chamber, in the top ...... is fitted an inlet valve.
14. Other materials are used in the workshop also, ... some details should be given.
15. The expansion will be greatest at those parts ...... the metal is hottest.
16. The heat is absorbed by a fixed weight of water, the temperature rise ...... can be measured.
17. The micrometer is an instrument by means ...... very accurate measurements can be made.
18. The hot water is taken to a heat exchanger ...... steam is generated.
19. The dew point is the temperature ...... a gas is saturated with vapour.
20. Resistors are devices ...... a resistance is interposed in a circuit.

EXERCISE TWO

Join these sentences using a preposition + relative.

1. The earliest turbine consisted of a sphere. Steam was passed into the sphere.
2. The air is passed to a compressor. Here it is compressed.
3. The brush is depressed by a spring. The tension of the spring is adjustable.
4. The lathe can also cut screws. For this, the lead-screw is engaged.
5. There is a perforated flame-tube. Kerosene is sprayed into it.
6. Iron is converted into steel by various processes. All of these processes involve heating it to very high temperatures.
7. The soil was sandy. The road surface was laid over the soil.
8. The light passes through a prism. The prism disperses the light.
9. The fuel is contained in a metal can. The purpose of this can is to prevent reactions between the fuel and the coolant.
10. The power station is in the north of the country. Plutonium is produced in this power station.

3. Ratio and Proportion

---

1. *a.* There is one professor to every ten students. They are *in a ratio of* 1 *to* 10.
   b. There are 15 parts of air to every part of fuel. They are *in a ratio of* 15 *to* 1.
   c. The professor/student *ratio* is 1:10.
   d. The air/fuel *ratio* is 15:1.
   e. The *ratio of* the clearance volume *to* the swept volume in a cylinder differs in different types of engine.
   f. A compression *ratio* of about 4:1 can be obtained with a turbo-compressor.
   g. The efficiency of a cyclic process is the *ratio of* the work done *to* the heat received.

---

2. *a.* The *proportion* of students to professors is 10 to 1.
   b. The proportion of air to fuel in the combustion chamber is 15 to 1.
   c. The air and fuel are mixed *in a proportion of* 15 to 1.
   d. Manganese and magnesium are present *in equal proportions* in duralumin.

e. The linear speed of rotation of a pulley is *f.* The electromotive force induced in the circuit is	*proportional to*	its diameter. the rate of change of flux.

g. The volume of a mass of gas at constant pressure is *directly* *h.* The power of an engine is *directly*	*proportional to*	its absolute temperature. the area of cross-section of the cylinder.

   i. The insulation resistance of a cable is *inversely proportional to* its length.

   j. As the demand for power increases, the supply *is proportionately* increased.

k. The machine is simple but much too heavy. It is *l.* The new machine is slightly better but twice as expensive. It is	*disproportionately*	heavy. expensive.

---

3. *a.* This bridge will be very costly *b.* The evaporative capacity is large *c.* The machine is very heavy	*in relation to* *for*	its limited usefulness. the size of the boiler. its small size.

Section 14

Reading: The Turbo-prop Engine

The efficiency of a turbo-jet engine varies with the speed and altitude at which it operates. *Whilst* it is very efficient at supersonic speeds and high altitudes, it is not suited to the low speeds involved in taking-off and landing. Under these conditions, thrust augmentors or after-burners are often required to boost the power, and this entails heavy fuel consumption and restricts the range of the aircraft. *On the other hand*, propeller-driven aircraft cannot attain speeds much in excess of 500 m.p.h., *whereas* at low speeds they have a much better performance. Since subsonic speeds are still acceptable for most civilian airliners, a type of engine known as the turbo-prop was developed, which combined some of the advantages of both jet and piston-driven engines.

In the turbo-jet, the turbine is required to develop enough power to drive the compressor only, *whereas* in the turbo-prop engine, it must supply power also for the propeller, to which it is coupled by means of reduction gearing. As the propeller rotates, it drives rearwards a much larger column of air than that which is expelled from the jet-tube of the turbo-jet, but at a much lower

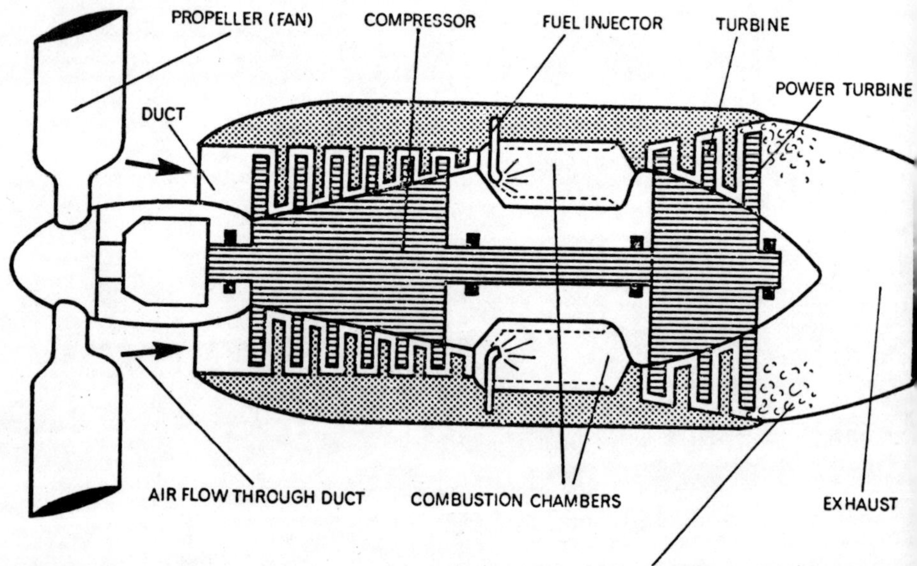

Cross-section of ducted fan engine

velocity. **Consequently** it is quieter than the turbo-jet, since the volume of noise produced by an aircraft engine increases with the velocity of the air column. Most airports are situated in or near large centres of population, **with the result that** any reduction in the noise level is a decided advantage. Furthermore, a large proportion of the energy of the products of combustion is needed to drive the compressor and the airscrew. As this proportion increases, so the amount of thrust developed in the jet-pipe diminishes. **In consequence,** the destructive blasts of hot gas which emanate from the jet-pipe of the turbo-jet while taxiing on runways or taking-off are greatly reduced.

The main disadvantage of the turbo-prop engine is of course the limitation imposed on speed by the airscrew, **as a result** of which it is likely to become obsolete on all except short-haul aircraft.

A more recent development in jet propulsion is the ducted-fan jet, in which the turbine drives a multi-bladed fan enclosed in a duct. A certain proportion of the air which enters the engine by-passes the compressor and combustion chambers, and is impelled by the fan down the outside of the duct, **so that** it is expelled at considerable velocity from the rear of the engine. It amplifies the mass of hot exhaust gases, and thus serves to augment the thrust derived from them. **Consequent on** the more moderate speed of this ducted air, the noise level is kept reasonably low. In addition, this type of engine performs well both below and above the speed of sound, *whereas* the other types of engine are efficient only at certain speeds.

WORD STUDY

Involve, Entail (= implies, makes necessary)

1. *a.* The fitting of a superheater		a considerable extra cost.
b. Rapid compression of a gas		a rise in temperature.
c. The Diesel cycle	*involves* / *entails*	compressing the air to a very high pressure.
d. A re-entry turbine		large frictional losses.
e. The planning of road gradients		moving large quantities of earth.

2. *a.* Less manual labour is		the handling of oil than coal. (= engaged)
b. All the engineers are	*involved in*	the dispute over wages.
c. A number of factors are		measurements of radiation dose.

Augment, Boost, Amplify, Diminish

1. The velocity of the molecule is		by the addition of heat. (= increased)
2. The jet thrust may be	*augmented*	by after-burning in the jet-pipe.
3. Cylinder condensation is		by the presence of water on the clearance space walls.

4. The jet thrust needs to be 5. Pressure in the induction passages is 6. The aircraft's speed can be	*augmented* *boosted*	during take-off and landing. by the use of a supercharger. by the use of rockets.

7. The efflux from the jet-pipe is 8. The sound in the radio is	*amplified*	by the ducted air. (= made bigger) by a valve called an amplifier.

9. The arrangement of levers *amplifies* the movement of the bar.

10. During winter, stocks of coal *diminish* owing to heavier consumption. (= lessen)
11. The steam enters each successive row of blades at a *diminishing* velocity.

Couple

---

1. The turbine wheel is *coupled to* the driving shaft through helical gearing.
2. The metal strips are *coupled together* to form a thermo-couple.
3. The wagons are *coupled together* by couplings to form a train.

4. The low initial cost of the engine, *coupled with* its ease of maintenance, make it very suitable for this purpose.

Perform

---

1. Work is *performed* by the steam during expansion. (= carry out)
2. Compression can be *performed* in two or more stages.
3. Tests must be *performed* on the material to establish that it can be safely used.

4. The *performance* of the aircraft is very satisfactory. (= what it can do)
5. Modifications to the engine improved its *performance* considerably.

Limit, Restrict, Impair, Impose

---

1. The length of the runway 2. The low melting point of the metal 3. The limited floor-space available	*restricts* *limits*	the landing speed of aircraft. its usefulness to industry. the size of the engine.

4. The metal is 5. The aircraft is	*limited in* *restricted in*	its usefulness by its low melting point. speed to about 500 m.p.h.

6. The usefulness of this machine is 7. The insulating properties of rubber are	*impaired*	by its low efficiency. (= *spoiled*) by long exposure to sunlight.

8. The length of the runway 9. The low melting point of this metal 10. The available floor-space	*imposes limits on* *imposes limitations on* *imposes restrictions on*	the landing speed of the aircraft. its usefulness. the size of the engine which can be installed.

PATTERNS

1. Results (1)

a)

1. The temperature of the gas rises.	*Consequently*	it expands in the cylinder.
2. After-burners have to be used.	*Therefore*	fuel consumption is heavier.
3. The aircraft speed is limited.	*As a result*	it will soon become obsolete.
	Hence	

4. The temperature of the gas rises,	*so that*	it expands in the cylinder.
5. After-burners have to be used,	*with the result that*	more fuel is consumed.
6. The aircraft is limited in speed,		it will soon become obsolete.

b)

1. *As a result of*	its rise in temperature the gas expands.
2. *In consequence of*	having to use after-burners more fuel is consumed.
3. *Consequent upon*	its limited speed the aircraft is now obsolete.

4. A rise in the temperature of the gas	*results in*	its expansion.
5. The use of after-burners	*leads to*	increased fuel consumption.
6. Superheating the steam		greatly increased efficiency.
7. Standardising the size of the blades		production costs being lowered.

EXERCISE ONE

Use the patterns given in a) to link these statements:

1. Heat flows in from the surrounding air. The ammonia evaporates.
2. The circulation in the unit is effected by gravity. No working parts are involved.
3. The friction losses are greatly reduced. They may be neglected.
4. The crystal boundaries of the metals are broken down. The metals disintegrate.
5. Water was sprayed into the steam causing condensation. A partial vacuum was produced.
6. There is a pressure and heat drop through the blades. The velocity of the steam increases.
7. The valve closes some of the low-pressure nozzles. The speed drops.
8. 30% of the working steam is used for feed heating. There is an improvement in thermal efficiency.
9. A corrosive acid is liable to be produced. Special precautions have to be taken.
10. Superheating dries the steam. Blade erosion is considerably reduced.
11. The cooling water and condensate are kept separate. The condensate is not contaminated.

12. The draught is thus increased. More air is available for combustion.
13. The fissile material is rapidly used up. The elements have to be frequently replaced.
14. The weather was very bad for some weeks. Progress with the building of the bridge was not so good as was expected.
15. Labour-management relations are very good. There are seldom any serious disputes.

EXERCISE TWO

Use the patterns given in b) to link these expressions in order to form a statement in each case:

1. heating the metal in air. it oxidises.
2. mass production. the goods become cheaper.
3. lubrication of the bearings. the friction is reduced.
4. working the metal cold. internal stresses are set up in it.
5. a drop in pressure. partial evaporation of the liquid.
6. increased demand for power. large capacity turbines were produced.
7. condensation. a partial vacuum was produced.
8. the development of the jet engine. much greater speeds can be attained.
9. the inefficiency of this type of engine. it was abandoned.
10. a pressure drop through the blades. an increase in the steam velocity.
11. increase in traffic density. underpasses and fly-overs were built.
12. overheating in the cylinder head. the mixture was detonated.
13. a rise in temperature. an increase in the pressure energy of the fluid.
14. the bad weather. progress on the bridge was held up.
15. the intensive research which was carried out. development of the engine proceeded very rapidly.

2. Contrast

Here is the structure commonly used to show the contrast or opposition between two facts:

---

a) At high speeds the turbo-jet is more efficient, *while* / *whilst* / *whereas* at low speeds the propeller is more efficient.

b) *While* / *Whilst* / *Whereas* at high speeds the turbo-jet is more efficient, at low speeds the propeller is more efficient.

---

c) The contrast can be emphasised by adding *on the one hand, on the other hand.*

A hot engine will run on a weak mixture, *while on the other hand* a cold engine requires a richer mixture.
Whereas on the one hand a hot engine can run on a weak mixture, a cold engine requires a richer mixture.

On the other hand is often used alone, after a full-stop.

A hot engine will run on a weak mixture. *On the other hand* a cold engine requires a richer mixture.

d) Notice the expression *in contrast to* + Noun.

In contrast to the rich mixture needed to start a cold engine, a weak mixture is sufficient to keep a warm engine running.

EXERCISE

Use these contrast words to link these statements:

1. The live centre on the lathe rotates with the spindle. The dead centre is stationary.
2. A belt drive provides a flexible link between shafts. A chain drive provides a positive link.
3. Unlubricated bearings develop a great deal of friction. Bearings which are properly lubricated develop much less.
4. Mercury has a very regular coefficient of expansion. Water has a variable coefficient of expansion.
5. Fuels rich in paraffin are liable to detonation. Aromatics are anti-detonators.
6. Insufficient air will prevent complete combustion. Too much air will reduce the temperature of combustion.
7. The traffic density on the road is very high during the peak hours. It is very low at midday and during the night.
8. A skilled craftsman can earn high wages. An unskilled worker earns very little.
9. Uranium 235 requires slow neutrons for its fission. The neutrons emitted during fission are fast neutrons.
10. The steam in contact with the steam chest is comparatively dry. The steam in contact with the piston is much wetter.

3. Variables

1. *a.* *The higher* the velocity of steam, *the greater* (is) the turbine speed.
   b. *The further* the flame-front travels, *the greater* (is) the detonation risk.
   c. *The thinner* the layer of solder, *the higher* (must be) the soldering temperature.

---

2. *a.* *As* { the velocity of the steam increases, } (so) { the turbine speed increases.
   b. *As* { the flame-front advances, } (so) { the risk of detonation increases.
   c. *As* { the temperature of a solid rises, } (so) { the molecular agitation increases.

---

3. *a.* The specific heat of ice *decreases* } *with* { a reduction in temperature. / the temperature.
   b. The magnetic field *increases* } *with* { an increase in current. / the current.

   c. The saturation pressure of a vapour *varies*
   d. The number of blades in each wheel *varies*
   e. The melting point of brass *varies*
   } *with* / *according to* { the temperature. / the size of the turbine. / its composition.

   f. Friction losses in the pipe *vary as* the square of the velocity of flow.
   g. During expansion the pressure *varies inversely as* the volume.

---

4. The temperature of the water film in the condenser *remains constant* at 50° C.
   So long as vapour is being produced, the temperature *remains constant.*
   Air passes through the pre-heater at a *constant* pressure.
   R is a *constant*, and has a *constant* value for any particular gas.

   Water has a *variable* coefficient of expansion. It varies with the temperature.
   The flow of heat through a condenser tube involves many *variables.*
   The ratio k/x is replaced by h, a *variable* known as the film coefficient.

EXERCISE ONE

Use the patterns of (1) and (2) to link these statements.

1. The population of the world goes up. The demand for food goes up.
2. The cost of living rises. Wages must rise.
3. Industrial towns attract more people. Few people are available for farming.
4. The steel is hard. It is difficult to work.
5. The rivet gets cool. The plates are drawn tighter together.
6. The shaft rotates faster. More friction is developed.
7. Expansion proceeds. The intrinsic energy of the steam decreases.
8. The steam pressure falls in the nozzles. Its velocity increases.
9. The fuel/air mixture is richer. The temperature in the engine is higher.
10. The turbine blades rotate faster. The stresses imposed on them increase.
11. The rate of evaporation is high. More steam will be generated.
12. The mass flow of air decreases. The compressor delivery pressure falls.

EXERCISE TWO

Complete these statements as in (3) above, using *vary*, *increase* or *decrease* as appropriate.

1. The efficiency of the turbo-jet ...... a decrease in speed and height.
2. The efficiency of the turbo-jet ...... an increase in speed and height.
3. The efficiency of the turbo-jet ...... speed and height.
4. The wages of the workmen will ...... their skill and experience.
5. The strength of the steel ...... the amount of carbon it contains.
6. The air temperature ...... an increase in altitude.
7. The speed of rotation of a pulley ...... its diameter.
8. The risk of detonation ...... a higher fuel octane number.
9. The wind velocity ...... increased height above the ground.
10. The molecular agitation in a solid ...... an increase in its temperature.
11. The proportion of CO_2 in the flue gas ...... the amount of excess air supplied.
12. The noise level produced by a stream of gas ...... decrease in speed.
13. The ratio of heating surface to grate area ...... the size of boiler.
14. The coefficient of expansion of water ...... its temperature.
15. The internal energy of a gas ...... a rise in temperature.

REVISION (SECTIONS 8–14)

Read these statements, choosing the correct word from the alternatives in brackets.

1. The factory is now (*furnished*, *equipped*, *installed*) with automatic lathes, and this has (*involved*, *implied*, *insisted*) a heavy capital (*output*, *outlay*). On the other (*hand*, *side*) part of the labour force has been (*eliminated*, *dispensed*, *dispensed with*) as a result, since (*less*, *fewer*) men are required to (*drive*, *function*, *operate*) this type of (*machine*, *machines*).
2. The (*rate*, *speed*) of heat (*transfer*, *transference*, *transmission*) from the cylinder may be increased by (*supplying*, *providing*) cooling fins on the outside of the cylinder. (*Hence*, *Thereby*) the total (*volume*, *area*) (*susceptible*, *instrumental*, *available*) for cooling is (*largely*, *greatly*, *highly*) increased, and the heat is (*diffused*, *disseminated*, *dissipated*) more rapidly.
3. There (*is*, *was*, *has been*) a (*progressive*, *successive*, *subsequent*) increase in production over the (*last*, *latest*, *recent*) ten years owing to the (*equipment*, *installation*, *instalment*) of these new (*machines*, *machinery*) in the factory. A (*success*, *succession*, *progression*) of changes has been (*done*, *made*) in the management of the company, and a number of new techniques have been (*produced*, *introduced*, *achieved*).
4. (*While*, *During*, *As*) passing through the turbine blades, the steam is

(*refracted*, *reflected*, *deflected*) from its (*initial*, *original*) course, and (*in*, *on*, *when*) being (*refracted*, *reflected*, *deflected*) it (*exerts*, *imparts*, *entails*) an impulsive (*force*, *power*, *weight*) on the blades, which (*makes*, *causes*) them to (*rotate*, *circulate*, *encircle*).

5. The cylinders (*fire*, *ignite*, *burn*) in a regular (*cycle*, *sequence*, *series*), so that the (*downward*, *downwards*) movement of the pistons is (*transmitted*, *conducted*, *conveyed*) to the crankshaft as an even turning (*movement*, *motion*, *moment*). In this (*method*, *way*, *means*) the stresses on the crankshaft are reduced as (*much*, *little*) as possible.
6. Turbulent (*states*, *conditions*) in the (*cylinder*, *cylinder's*) head are (*conductive*, *conducive*, *appropriate*) to (*effective*, *efficient*, *affective*) combustion of the mixture, and this is (*greatly*, *largely*) (*performed*, *achieved*, *done*) by careful design of the cylinder head.
7. (*Since*, *For*) hundreds of years, men (*are trying*, *have tried*, *tried*) to (*develop*, *evolve*, *discover*) some means (*for*, *of*) overcoming the (*power*, *force*) of gravity.
8. The water (*under*, *into*, *in*) which the hot metal rod is immersed (*obtains*, *acquires*, *attains*) heat by (*conduction*, *convection*, *radiation*). Heat continues to flow from the metal (*unless*, *until*, *while*) the water temperature is equal (*with*, *to*, *as*) that of the metal.
9. A mixture of fuel and air is (*induced*, *inserted*, *input*) into the cylinder, where it is (*ignited*, *burned*, *exploded*) by a spark passing across the (*gap*, *slit*, *slot*) between the electrodes of a spark plug. Combustion takes place as the flame (*diffuses*, *spreads*, *dissipates*) rapidly through the (*all*, *total*, *whole*) mixture.
10. (*On*, *When*, *In*) increasing the (*engine's*, *engine*) speed, the shaft rotates (*faster*, *quicker*), and (*subsequently*, *consecutively*, *consequently*) the weights on the governor are (*raised*, *risen*) by centrifugal (*force*, *power*), (*thereby*, *whereby*) raising the sleeve. This has the (*affect*, *effect*) of (*functioning*, *operating*, *regulating*) a throttle valve lever and reducing the flow of steam.
11. (*In*, *On*, *During*) planning the new motorway, it was necessary to (*allow*. *compensate*) for the (*big*, *great*) increase in traffic which is expected (*over*, *through*, *in*) the next few years. (*Provided*, *Unless*, *In case*) this was done, the road (*would*, *will*) quickly become (*incapable*, *inadequate*, *insufficient*) for its purpose.
12. The Diesel (*cycle*, *circle*, *series*) involves (*to compress*, *compressing*) the air in the cylinder head to an (*extremely*, *intensely*) high pressure, with a (*consequent*, *consecutive*) rise in temperature, until the temperature is (*sufficiently*, *enough*) high to cause the (*injected*, *introduced*, *induced*) fuel (*to ignite*, *ignite*) (*instantaneously*, *spontaneously*, *simultaneously*).
13. The (*expenditure*, *value*, *cost*) of (*equipping*, *installing*, *inserting*) the factory with the new machinery has to be balanced (*with*, *against*, *on*) the savings

which are (*liable, likely, possible*) to be (*affected, effected, performed*) as a result of increased production and a more (*efficient, effective*) use of man-power.

14. The (*purpose, function*) of the flux which is (*supplied, fitted, applied*) to the (*work, works*) to be welded is the removal of any existing oxides, and the (*protection, prevention, disposal*) of further oxidation (*during, while*) heating.
15. The amount of steam which is (*evolved, developed, generated*) by a boiler increases (*as, with*) the (*rate, ratio, speed*) of combustion increases, and this can be (*achieved, acquired*) by providing a forced (*draught, current*) of air across the fire-grate.

Section 15

Reading: Aerofoils

Apart from the fuselage and the engines, the most important parts of an aircraft are the surfaces known as aerofoils. These include the rudder, elevators and ailerons, whose function is to control the aircraft in flight; and the wings which provide the lift necessary to overcome the weight of the aircraft and lift it through the air. A substantial horizontal thrust, provided by the jet or the propeller, drives the aircraft through the surrounding air, while the wing deflects downwards the mass of air *flowing* on to it. This produces a reactive force *acting* in the opposite direction, which lifts the wing upwards. Without some means of horizontal propulsion, no lift can be produced by the wing. Modern aircraft are **so heavy that** the wings must develop a very large lift force in order to sustain the aircraft.

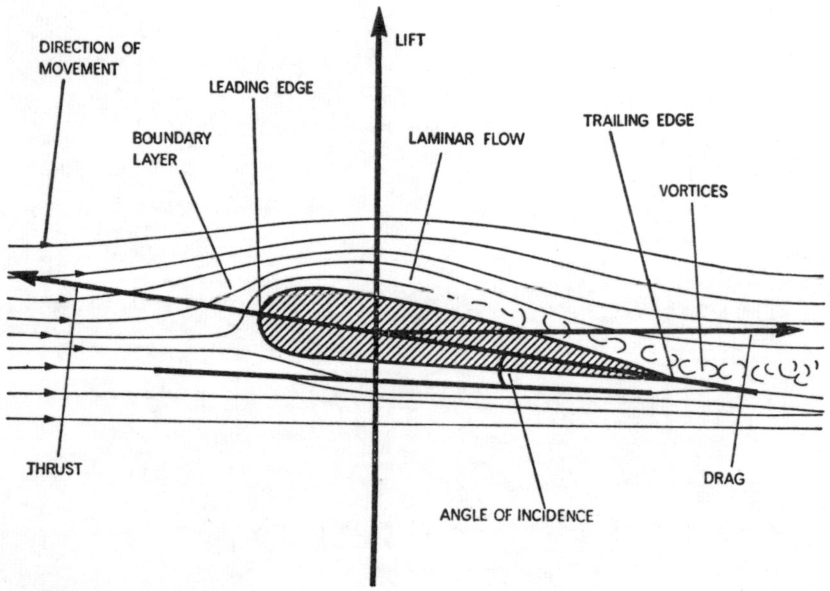

Cross-section of aircraft wing

The design of the wings is therefore very important, and various factors have to be considered. Wind-tunnels *reproducing* flight conditions are used to examine the behaviour of air *flowing* over different types of wings at different speeds. The lift produced by a wing will depend on, among other factors, the wing area, its profile, and the angle of incidence – that is, the angle at which the wing is inclined to the direction of motion. Air *flowing* over the top of the aerofoil should flow smoothly and without turbulence. This laminar flow is achieved by streamlining the profile and by making the skin of the aerofoil smooth. As a result, the air-flow will follow the contour of the wing, except for a narrow boundary layer of stationary air on its surface. However, above a certain angle of incidence, which varies with the type of wing, the air-flow is liable to break up and become **so turbulent as to** destroy the low-pressure region above the wing. This causes **such a rapid loss of lift that** the aircraft may stall. To counteract this, slots are sometimes fitted to the leading edge of the wing, *guiding* the air-flow more steadily over the aerofoil. Since low speeds are essential for landing, extendable flaps are also fitted to the trailing edge. These extend the effective area of the wing, and thus prevent the aircraft from stalling.

The force exerted by the deflected column of air beneath the wing has a vertical component called lift, and a horizontal component called drag. Drag in its various forms represents a loss of the energy available to provide lift, but it always accompanies lift. It can never be entirely eliminated, since the wing itself offers resistance to the air through which it moves. A laminar flow over the wing, *reducing* drag to a minimum, is the optimum condition. But around the wing-tips and on the trailing edge, some turbulence is inevitable. The air, *flowing* through a region of higher pressure under the wing, swirls up at these edges into a region of low pressure above the wing and produces a vortex, which may be **so violent as to** produce vapour trails at the wing-tips.

WORD STUDY

Effective

a) = having the desired effect

1. Heavy water is more	*effective*	in slowing down neutrons than graphite.
2. Compounding is more		when high compression ratios are involved.
3. Ring hydrocarbons are		in reducing the tendency of a fuel to detonation.

b) = real or actual

The *effective*	working time is only six hours, because work stops for an hour at lunch.
	power of an engine can be measured by a dynamometer.
	pressure is reduced by the back pressure in the cylinder.

Factor

1. In choosing an engine, one *factor* to be considered is ease of transportation.
2. In the development of high speed engines, a limiting *factor* is the rate at which fuel can be burnt.
3. Thermal efficiency depends on a number of *factors*, including nozzle efficiency.
4. In converting lb/in^2 to lb/ft^2, the *factor* 144 must be introduced into the calculations.

Thrust

1. A thrust bearing takes the longitudinal	*thrust*	down the axis of a shaft.
2. The pillars of a building take the		from the arches.
3. The engines provide the forward		that drives the aircraft through the air.
4. This engine develops 100,000 lb of		

Laminar, Laminated, Agitated, Turbulent

1. The air-flow over the aerofoil becomes	*agitated*	at low speeds.
2. The designer aims to prevent	*turbulent*	steam flow through the turbine nozzle.

3. Combustion in a cylinder is assisted by *turbulence* in the mixture.

4. The design of the aerofoil encourages a	*laminar*	airflow over it.
5. Below a certain velocity, the liquid will have	*smooth*	flow through the pipe.

6. Thin layers of wood are stuck together to form *laminated* wood.
7. The plastic material is made of thin layers bonded together to form *laminated* plastic.
8. The direct current armature core is *laminated*.

PATTERNS

1. Result (2)

Here is another common structure for expressing Result.

1. The increase in population is *so rapid that* there is a food shortage.
2. The population is increasing *so rapidly that* there is a food shortage.
3. The country has *so many* natural resources *that* it can support itself easily.
4. The country has *so much* coal *that* it can export large quantities.
5. The problem is *so complex that* it can only be solved by computers.

6. The increase in population is *so rapid*	*as to* cause a food shortage.
7. The population is increasing *so rapidly*	
8. There is *such a* rapid increase in population	
9. There are *such* rapid increases in population	

10. The country has *so little* coal *as to* make it necessary to import large quantities.

EXERCISE

Complete these statements with the appropriate words:

1. The fuel is ...... volatile ...... it cannot be weighed in an open crucible without loss.
2. The load on the turbine may be ...... great ...... stop the blades from turning.
3. The temperature of the gas may rise to ...... extent ...... the hydrocarbons decompose.
4. The molecular agitation becomes ...... violent ...... the molecules break away from each other.
5. The friction losses are ...... much reduced ...... become negligible.
6. The temperatures in the turbine are ...... high ...... special nickel alloys must be used.
7. Steam is now required in ...... large quantities ...... very large capacity boilers have to be built.
8. There are ...... few moving parts ...... maintenance is reduced to a minimum.
9. The temperature may become ...... high ...... ignite the charge before the passage of the spark.
10. ...... interest has been shown in the new model ...... large scale production is to start at once.
11. The development costs are ...... great ...... government assistance is essential.
12. The steel is in ...... brittle condition ...... it can only be scrapped.
13. Tungsten carbide is ...... hard material ...... it can cut metal at very high speed.
14. The problem presents ...... many difficulties ...... no satisfactory solution has yet been found.
15. The engine proved ...... more reliable than the earlier ones ...... it has gradually replaced them.
16. The mixture would have ...... large air/fuel ratio ...... make it difficult to ignite.

2. The Active Relative (-ing)

Look at these sentences:

The man *who operates the lathe* is a skilled worker.
The spark *which passes between the electrodes* ignites the fuel.
Wind-tunnels *which reproduce flight-conditions* are used.

Each of these statements contains a relative clause which is *active* in form. When it is in the Present tense (and rarely in the Past tense) a shortened form is used:

The man *operating the lathe* is a skilled worker.
The spark *passing between the electrodes* ignites the fuel.
Wind-tunnels *reproducing flight-conditions* are used.

EXERCISE

Change these statements in the same way:

1. The engineers who designed the motorway had many problems to overcome.
2. Bearings which rotate at high speeds must be well lubricated.
3. The gases which expand down the cylinder drive the piston downwards.
4. Steel which contains very little carbon is known as mild steel.
5. Rapid cooling produces irregular contractions which weaken the metal.
6. The shafting which transmits power to the machines is supported on bearings.
7. The molten iron which comes from the furnace is cast into pigs or ingots.
8. There are enormous oil deposits which lie under the surface of the earth.
9. Some of the heat of combustion is absorbed by water-tubes which line the walls.
10. The steam impinges on moving blades which lie along the periphery of the wheel.
11. Turbine efficiency is reduced by steam which leaks past the packing.
12. Sand which has a high porosity is suitable for moulding operations.
13. Pure iron is a soft metal which has a crystalline structure.
14. The oil-hole which leads to each bearing is fitted with a nipple.
15. A wooden pattern which has a similar shape to the part required is made.
16. The steam encounters droplets of water which fall through it.
17. All aeroplanes are fitted with navigational aids which enable them to fly blind.
18. The hot gases which emanate from the jet-pipe produce a large volume of noise.
19. The contractors who installed the machinery are responsible for the damage.
20. The aircraft which is standing on the runway is bound for Istanbul.
21. Part of the light which strikes the surface will be reflected from it.
22. Current which enters the ground from an electrode will spread out in all directions.
23. The quantity of fluid which passes a given section of the pipe can be measured.
24. Liquids which contain suspended solids can easily be handled by these pumps.
25. The bridge which now spans the river was built nearly a century ago.

3. Exceptions

It is important not to confuse the following three items:

---

1. *a.* Everyone in the room comes from Egypt,	*except* (for)	the teacher. (= he does not)
b. None of the planets is inhabited,		the earth.
c. All solids expand when they liquefy,		ice and a few others.

Except for / *With the exception of*	the teacher, everyone in the room comes from Egypt.
	the earth, none of the planets is inhabited.
	ice and a few others, all solids expand when they liquefy.

---

2. *a.* An engine cannot run	*without*	fuel. (= in the absence of fuel)
b. Toughened steel machines easily		tearing.
c. The engine would quickly overheat		an efficient cooling system.
d. Gases cannot be quickly compressed		generating heat.

---

3. *Apart from* / *Besides* / *In addition to*	the lecturer, there are twenty people here. (= not counting him)
	coal, the most important natural fuels are gas and oil.
	its lightness, aluminium has several other advantages.
	the earth, how many planets revolve round the sun?

EXERCISE

Complete these statements with the appropriate word:

1. The lathe can perform a variety of other operations ...... turning.
2. A carburettor will not give correct mixture strength at high speeds ...... a compensating jet.
3. Several other losses must be taken into account ...... friction-loss at the blades.
4. The whole of the energy of the exhaust gases, ... a small amount required to drive the compressor, is used to provide thrust.
5. ...... its high cost, this type of machine would be very suitable.
6. ...... iron and steel, aluminium is the commonest metal used in the workshop.
7. The bearings would rapidly become worn ...... proper lubrication.
8. Nowadays all ...... the smallest aircraft have power-assisted controls.
9. An ordinary spring governor could not control a large flow of steam ...... the help of an oil-relay.
10. ...... its use in accumulators, lead is also used as the base for lead paint.
11. There was no means of approaching the mountain ...... from the north.
12. The construction of the dam cannot be started ...... a thorough investigation of the problems involved.

13. ...... mercury, the coefficient of expansion of liquids varies with the temperature.
14. The furnace is in continuous operation, ... when it is shut down for repair.
15. ...... one small deposit in the south, there is no oil at all in this country.

Section 16

Reading: Radioactivity

Atomic nuclei consist of combinations of protons, or positively-charged particles, and neutrons, or uncharged particles. The number of protons and neutrons in each element can vary, but only certain combinations are stable. For example, calcium-48, having 20 protons and 28 neutrons, is a stable isotope of calcium. But *if there is* an excess or deficiency of neutrons in any combination, the isotope will be unstable. A nucleus is more likely to be unstable *if it is* a heavy one – that is, *if it contains* a large number of protons and neutrons. Unstable nuclei attempt to achieve stability by emitting some form of radiation, until they transform themselves into stable isotopes.

There are radioactive isotopes of every element, either those existing in nature or else those activated artificially by bombardment of stable nuclei with nuclear particles such as protons, alpha-particles or neutrons. However, a particle will not be absorbed by the target nucleus *unless its velocity corresponds* with one of the energy levels of the nucleus. Heavy nuclei, having more energy levels than light nuclei, are more likely to effect capture of a particle –

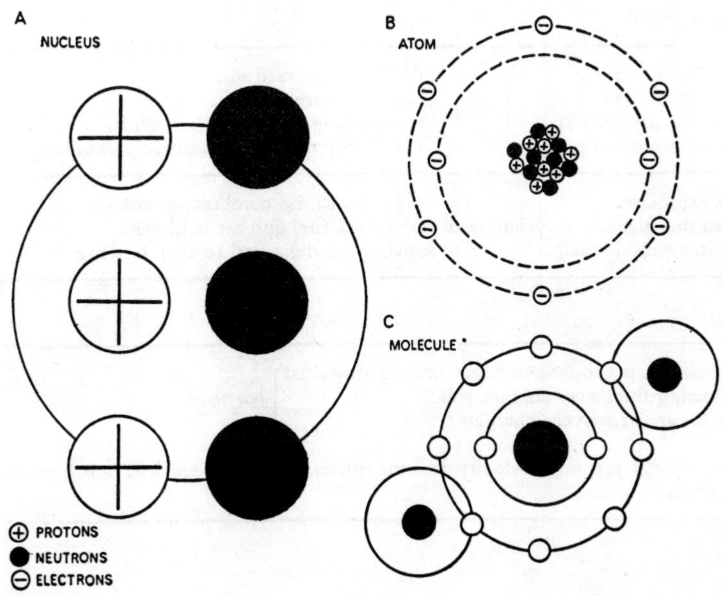

a fact which helps to explain the importance of uranium, thorium and other very heavy atoms in nuclear research.

Since the neutron is uncharged, it is not affected by the charged electrons and protons of the target atom, and is therefore more likely to be captured than any other particle, ***provided that it is*** in resonance with an energy level of the nucleus. **In the event of** neutron capture, the mass number of the nucleus will be raised, and it will thus become unstable and radioactive. As radiation continues, the level of radioactivity falls exponentially, and the time taken for it to reach half its original value is known as the half-life of the isotope, which may vary from a fraction of a second to millions of years. Isotopes with long half-lives have many uses in medicine and industry, but they must be handled and disposed of with great care, **in case** they cause radiation damage.

Neutron bombardment of the very heavy uranium atoms may have a quite different result. It may cause the nucleus of the fissile U-235 atom to split into two parts. This nuclear fission releases large quantities of energy which finally takes the form of heat energy, and at the same time other neutrons are ejected from the nucleus. The fission fragments are highly radioactive, and will contaminate the fissile uranium ***if they are not removed*** periodically. A number of these fission products, such as Caesium-137, are very useful as irradiation sources, and it is now possible to separate out the desired isotope from the spent fuel.

WORD STUDY

Charge

1. The cylinders are	*charged*	*with* compressed air.
2. The furnace is		*with* pulverised fuel and air.
3. The accumulator is		by passing a current through it.
4. Electrons are negatively		while the nucleus is positively charged.

5. An explosive	*charge*	is induced into the combustion chamber.
6. Into the furnace, a		of pulverised fuel and air is blown.
7. At intervals a small		of lubricant is delivered to each bearing.

Particle

Condensation is thought to begin around tiny dust	*particles.*
The flowing fluid may contain solid	
Electrons are negatively-charged	

Alpha-*particles* are high-velocity helium nuclei, and beta-*particles* are high-velocity electrons.

Element, Filament

1. He learned the *elements* of geology at school. (= basic facts)
2. Oxygen, hydrogen, carbon and potassium are all *elements.*
3. The problem involves a number of different *elements.* (= parts)
4. The red-hot wires of an electric fire are *elements.*
5. Uranium rods inserted into a moderator are fuel *elements.*

6. The white-hot tungsten wire of an electric bulb is a *filament.*
7. A thin *filament* of coloured fluid is injected into the main stream.

Nucleus, Nuclear

<table>
<tr><td>1. The organisation was built up round a small</td><td rowspan="3">nucleus</td><td>of scientists.</td></tr>
<tr><td>2. The flame spreads from the initial</td><td>to the main body of the mixture.</td></tr>
<tr><td>3. By bombarding it with thermal neutrons, the</td><td>of the uranium atom can be fissioned.</td></tr>
</table>

4. *Nuclear* energy is liberated as a result of *nuclear* fission.

Active, Activate, Excite

<table>
<tr><td>1. a. Zinc chloride forms the</td><td rowspan="3">active</td><td>base for many proprietary fluxes.</td></tr>
<tr><td>b. The drug's</td><td>constituent is only a small fraction of the total.</td></tr>
<tr><td>c. The volcano has not been</td><td>for thousands of years. It is inactive.</td></tr>
</table>

2. A nucleus can be artifically *activated* / *excited* by neutron bombardment.

3. Unstable nuclei are *radioactive,* and emit *radioactivity.*

Stable, Stabilise (= not easily changed)

Boron is a *stable* substance, which does not burn below 700° C.
Mineral oils are fairly *stable,* and do not decompose when heated.
Ships are designed to be *stable,* and should return to an upright position after heeling over.
Only certain combinations of neutrons and protons are *stable.*
Unstable nuclei emit electrons until they reach a *stable* configuration.
Embankments and dams must be *stable* enough to resist all forces on them.

Sandy soils can be *stabilised* by adding cement to them.
The heavy keel acts as a *stabiliser* on a ship.

PATTERNS

1. Conditions (if)

Here is the commonest way of showing that one event is dependent in some way on another event taking place.
In this section we shall deal only with the 'open' condition, and leave the other forms until we consider the *hypothesis* in Section 21 (1).

If the weather is good, I shall go for a walk.
Unless the weather is good, I shall stay at home.

Notice that *unless* is equivalent to *if . . . not.*

If the water is pure, it will not need further treatment.
Unless the water is pure, it will need further treatment.

Tenses: If + Present, Subject + Future (or Present)

EXERCISE ONE

Complete these statements with the correct form of the verb.

1. If the turbine speed (*increase*), the governor automatically (*come*) into operation.
2. If the supply of coolant (*fail*), emergency controls (*operate*) immediately.
3. If the nucleus (*contain*) an excess of neutrons, one or more of them (*be converted*) into protons.
4. Neutrons (*be admitted*) if the uranium (*be fissioned*).
5. The cylinder temperature (*rise*) if the quantity of steam flowing through the cylinders (*be increased*).
6. Unless the steam (*be superheated*), higher pressures (*be*) necessary.
7. If an indicator (*be fitted*), the pressure at any part of the stroke may be measured.
8. If current (*be passed*) through a solenoid, a magnetic field (*be set up*).
9. If no external forces (*act*) on a system, the momentum of the system (*remain*) constant.
10. Harmful radiations (*result*) unless the isotopes (*be shielded*) properly.
11. A sudden loss of lift (*be experienced*) if the aircraft speed (*fall*) below a certain level.
12. The conveyor belt (*be*) liable to slip off the drive if it (*stretch*).
13. If the fuel (*reach*) this critical temperature, it (*ignite*) spontaneously.
14. If the combustion gases (*not be diluted*), the temperatures at the turbine (*be*) too high.
15. The mixture may ignite spontaneously unless the combustion chamber (*be designed*) properly.

EXERCISE TWO

An alternative form of this condition is sometimes used:

Should the temperature fall, condensation of the steam *will result.* (= if the temperature falls, ...)

Now turn these statements into 'if'-statements:

1. Should the neutron flux increase, the flow of coolant must also increase.
2. Should the work not be completed by March, the contract will be cancelled.
3. Should the supply of lubricant fail, the bearings will become overheated.
4. Should the airspeed fall below a certain value, the airflow over the wings will be broken up.
5. Should the oil deposits prove extensive, the national revenue will be greatly increased.
6. Should the gases be allowed to escape unburnt, there will be appreciable heat losses.
7. Should the neutron flux rise any further, more control rods should be inserted into the core.
8. Should the boiler scale not be removed regularly, heat transfer will be impaired.

2. Conditions (Restrictive)

In addition to the ordinary 'if'-clause, we can express conditions in a more restrictive way:

---

a) I will come home *providing* / *provided* / *on condition* (that) you come with me. (= otherwise I won't)

b) I will come home *only if* you come with me.
I will *only* come home *if* you come with me. (= not come unless)

---

c) *Given* + *Noun*

Given plenty of labour, the job will be completed on schedule.
Given sufficient turbulence in the combustion chamber, detonation is unlikely to occur.

EXERCISE ONE

Use the patterns of a) and b) where appropriate to complete these statements:

1. This design is likely to be accepted ...... the cost is reasonable.
2. Steam flow through the nozzle will be smooth ...... the nozzle is properly designed.
3. A reactor can be used to produce power ...... an efficient heat-transfer system is employed.
4. Temperatures of up to 700° C are acceptable ...... special heat-resisting alloys are used.

5. The engine can be run at very high speeds ...... the vibrations can be damped out.
6. A chain reaction can be sustained ...... there is a critical mass of fissile material available.
7. Concrete can be used for shielding ...... it contains a high proportion of neutron absorbent material.
8. Fuels of high ash content may be burnt in the furnace ...... the fusing point of the ash is high enough.
9. Steam leakage can be reduced by fitting separate steam and exhaust valves, ... they are compensated for expansion.
10. These oil deposits will be worth exploiting ...... they are extensive enough.
11. The operation can proceed indefinitely ...... the controls are pre-set correctly.
12. The changes in dimension during heating are not serious ...... allowance is made for them.

EXERCISE TWO

Practise the c) pattern by adding *Given* to these statements, and compare them with the relevant sentences from Exercise One.

1. ...... a properly designed nozzle, the steam flow will be smooth.
2. ...... an efficient heat transfer system, a reactor can be used to produce power.
3. ...... effective means of damping out the vibrations, the engine can be run at very high speeds.
4. ...... a critical mass of fissile material, the chain reaction can be sustained.
5. ...... correct pre-setting of the controls, the operation can proceed indefinitely.

3. Eventuality

Eventuality refers to the *unlikely* (and usually *unwelcome*) chance that something (usually *unfortunate*) may happen.

We can of course express this idea simply by saying:

It is (just) possible that . . .
or There is a remote chance that . . .

But there are three other patterns which are useful here:

a) *A normal if-clause + should*

If a fire *should* break out, }
If there *should* be a fire, } all workers will leave the building.

---

b) *In the event of*, or occasionally *in case of* + *Noun*

In the event of fire, *In case of fire,* *In the event of a fire breaking out,*	all workers will leave the building.

c) The phrase *in case*, which means 'because of the risk that . . . (something may happen)'.

All workers will leave the building, *in case* the fire spreads to the chemicals.

EXERCISE ONE

Practice with a).

1. If there (*be*) a power breakdown, the emergency generator is switched on.
2. If the boiler pressure (*rise*) too high, the safety valve will blow off.
3. If any flaw (*be*) detected in the finished product, it must be rejected.
4. If high level radiation (*escape*), it can be very dangerous.
5. If there (*be*) a large leakage of steam, the engine efficiency will fall.
6. If the pipes (*become*) too heavily corroded, they must be replaced.
7. If the oil-pump (*fail*), the moving parts will become overheated.
8. If one control system (*break down*), the aircraft can be controlled by a duplicate system.

EXERCISE TWO

Practice with b).

1. ...... a power-breakdown, the emergency generator can be switched on.
2. ...... the boiler pressure rising too high, the safety valve will blow off.
3. ...... flaws being found in the finished product, it must be rejected.
4. ...... an explosion, the blast will be contained by the pressure vessel.
5. ...... a large leakage of steam, the engine efficiency will fall.
6. ...... the pipes becoming too heavily corroded, they must be replaced.
7. ...... an oil-pump failure, the moving parts will become overheated.
8. ...... fog, aircraft can be guided down to the runway from the control tower.

EXERCISE THREE

Practice with c).

1. An emergency generator is provided ...... there is a power breakdown.
2. A safety valve is fitted ...... the pressure in the boiler rises too high.
3. The finished products must be carefully examined ...... they are flawed.

4. Miners carry special detecting devices ...... any poisonous gases should be encountered underground.
5. Fission products must be carefully stored ...... they emit dangerous radiations.

Section 17

Reading: Chain Reaction

When fission occurs, an average of 2·5 neutrons are emitted from the nucleus. If the fission process can be *so arranged that* one of these liberated neutrons is captured by another U-235 nucleus to produce another fission, then the reaction will become self-sustaining.

When emitted, neutrons travel at a high velocity, and it is known that such fast neutrons have little chance of being captured by the fissile uranium. However, **if slowed down** to thermal speeds, their probability of capture is greatly increased. In the normal thermal reactor, the uranium is surrounded by a large mass of moderating material. The liberated neutrons *collide* repeatedly with the light atoms of the moderator *in such a way that* they lose much of their energy and eventually become thermalised. The moderator may be either a liquid such as heavy water, or a solid such as graphite. Both these substances are of low atomic weight and have low neutron absorption cross-sections. With the graphite moderator, the uranium which is generally in the form of rods is inserted into channels cut out of the graphite. These channels are *so arranged as to* form a lattice structure, the object of which is to reduce neutron escape to a minimum. Provided that a sufficient mass of uranium is disposed in a number of rods through the moderator, a high enough proportion of the emitted neutrons will find their way to fissile nuclei to produce a chain reaction. The minimum quantity of uranium required to initiate the chain reaction is called the critical mass.

Once irradiated, the uranium fuel elements tend to lose strength and become wrinkled. It is therefore necessary to encase them in a can or cladding of some material such as aluminium or magnesium. These cans are *designed so that* they not only support the uranium inside, but also contain the highly radioactive fission products, and prevent reaction taking place between the fuel and the coolant.

A chain reaction can be initiated by inserting more and more fuel elements into the reactor core until the critical mass is attained. It can be terminated by withdrawing the rods. **Once started,** the chain reaction must be *controlled in such a way that* a steady neutron flux rate, and thus a steady production of heat energy, is maintained. The simplest method of control is by inserting control rods of cadmium, or some similar material with a very high neutron absorption cross-section, into the moderator. The purpose of the control rods is to absorb the neutrons emanating from a fissioned nucleus. If therefore

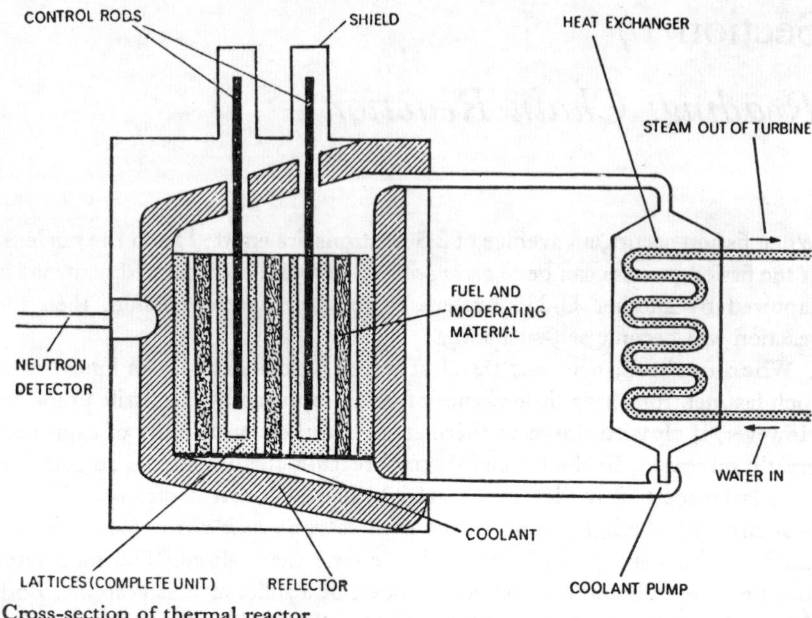

Cross-section of thermal reactor

there is an increase in the neutron flux rate in the reactor, more control rods can be inserted until the reaction rate is stabilised again: that is, until the multiplication factor is exactly 1.

WORD STUDY

Maintain

The aircraft *maintained* the same speed for several hours. (= keep up)
Steam tightness is *maintained* by means of asbestos packing.
The back pressure is *maintained* at a constant value by the condenser.
The flow of steam must be sufficient to *maintain* the pressure.
These nickel alloys *maintain* their strength at very high temperatures.

The machinery is very simple to *maintain*. (= keep in good condition)
Maintenance should be carried out regularly. (= inspection and repair)

Sustain

The car driver *sustained* serious injuries in the crash. (= suffered)
The factory *sustained* heavy damage in the fire.

The shield must be capable of *sustaining* very high temperatures. (= withstand)
The metal *sustained* a lot of hammering, and needed normalising.

The lift from the wings must *sustain* the whole weight of the aircraft. (= support)

In order to *sustain* the chain reaction, the multiplication factor must be unity. (= keep going)

Contain

The tank *contained* ten gallons of petrol. (= hold)

The pressure vessel is designed to *contain* the effects of an explosion in the core. (= keep in)
All radioactivity must be *contained* within the biological shield.
The *containment* of radioactive particles is one of the chief concerns of the designer of a nuclear reactor.

Retain

Permanent magnets are capable of *retaining* their magnetism indefinitely. (= keep)
The exhaust steam *retains* a considerable amount of heat.
The nut is *retained* by a cotter pin. (= hold in position)

Flux

A *flux* is a substance added to a metal to assist its melting.
A welding *flux*, such as sand or borax, is applied to a weld to prevent oxidation of the metal.
The neutron *flux* in a reactor is the neutron density × the neutron velocity.
The luminous *flux* is the rate of flow of light from any source.
The magnetic *flux* is the number of lines of force passing through a medium.

Dispose of (= throw away, get rid of)

The government has a lot of surplus equipment it wants to *dispose of*.
Radioactive waste must be carefully stored until it can safely be *disposed of*.
These machines are obsolete, and will be *disposed of* as soon as possible.

Emit, Emanate

---

1. *a.* A radar transmitter	*emits*	radio pulses, which are reflected back.	(= throws out)
b. A heated body		radiations to its surroundings.	
c. An electron gun		electrons.	
d. A nucleus		neutrons when fission takes place.	

e. The biological shield reduces radioactive *emissions* from the reactor core to almost nothing.

---

2. *a.* The heat rays which	*emanate*	from a body can be measured by a pyrometer.	(= come from)
b. The hot gases which		from a jet-pipe travel at very high velocity.	
c. The neutrons which		from a fissioned nucleus are fast.	

d. The biological shield reduces radioactive *emanations* from the reactor core to almost nothing.

PATTERNS

1. Manner (1)

Compare these two statements:

a) The bridge was *so well built that* it lasted for a hundred years.
b) The bridge was *so designed that* it would last for a hundred years.

Or this variation of the statements:

a) The bridge was strongly built, *so that* it lasted for a century.
b) The bridge was *designed so that* it would last for a century.

The patterns used are almost identical, but the emphasis is different.
The a) statements emphasise the *result*, which is often *unintentional.*
The b) statements emphasise the *deliberate way* or *manner* in which the results are brought about.

Here are the patterns for this type of statement:

(i) (ii)	The air drier can be	modified *in such a way* modified *so* *so* modified	*that* it fits inside the boiler. *as to* allow it to fit inside the boiler.

EXERCISE ONE

Complete these statements following the (i) pattern.

1. The pressure vessel is (*designed*) it will withstand the blast of an explosion.
2. The waste products are (*stored*) they cannot contaminate their surroundings.
3. The chain reaction must be (*controlled*) it produces a steady flow of energy.
4. The reactor core must be (*shielded*) no dangerous radiations can escape.
5. The fuel rods are (*inserted*) they form a lattice structure in the moderator.
6. The neutron flux is (*controlled*) it neither increases nor decreases.
7. The coolant circuit is (*arranged*) no radioactivity will pass into the generators.
8. The steam pipes must be (*fitted*) longitudinal expansion or contraction can take place easily.
9. The coils are (*wound*) like poles come together.
10. The factory was (*designed*) there would be no waste of space.

EXERCISE TWO

Complete the same sentences from Exercise One, with the pattern from (ii). They will be slightly changed, and in some you will have to invent a suitable verb (*enable* and *prevent* are useful verbs for this). Example:

1. The pressure vessel is designed so as to withstand the blast of an explosion.

2. When, Once, If, etc. + *Past Participle*

We can shorten a *time clause* or *if-clause* in two ways:

a)	*After* *On* *Before* *During*	separat*ion* . . .	=	*After* *When* *Before* *While*	it	is was has been	separated.
b)	*When* *While* *Once* *If*	separat*ed* . . .	=	*When* *While* *Once* *If*	it	is was has been	separated.

When, while, once and *if* must be followed by an *-ed form of the verb* in this construction, not by a noun.

c) Notice that these four words can also be used with an *adjective*.

when necessary
if possible
once full
while still hot

EXERCISE

Complete these statements with the appropriate word.

1. ...... superheated, the steam is less likely to cause cylinder condensation.
2. ...... installation, the plant was slightly damaged.
3. ...... cleaned of all impurities, the engine condensate is ready to be passed back to the boiler.
4. ...... installed in a boiler designed for it, forced draught gives good results.
5. ...... construction, several modifications were incorporated.
6. ...... alloyed with tin, copper forms a series of alloys known as bronze.
7. ...... worked, the metal should be annealed.
8. ...... rolled into sheets, zinc can be used for roof-coverings, etc.
9. ...... delivery, the turbine was tested in the factory.
10. ...... freshly cut, thorium is very soft, but ...... exposed to the air it oxidises.
11. ...... expansion in the nozzles, the steam increases in specific volume.

12. ...... tested, the engine failed to reach its rated output.
13. ...... heated, the metal expands, and ...... allowed to cool it will contract.
14. ...... examined, the part was found to be faulty.
15. ...... examined, the part will probably be found to be faulty.
16. ...... stored carefully, the fission products can be used as a gamma source.
17. ...... bombarded by thermal neutrons, the U-235 is capable of fission.
18. ...... fission, neutrons are ejected from the nucleus.
19. ...... heavy irradiation, the fuel element becomes damaged.
20. ...... run at very high speeds, the engine is liable to vibrate.
21. ...... located, the wreckage of the aircraft was carefully examined by experts.
22. ...... testing, the engine was put into immediate service.
23. ...... necessary, the fuel rods can be removed and replaced.
24. ...... ignited, the combustible mixture expands rapidly.
25. ...... desired, any modifications can be made in the design.

3. Arrangements

a) = *Plans*

1. The government will *arrange to* employ the redundant workers elsewhere. / *arrange for* redundant workers to be employed elsewhere.

2. The employers must *arrange to* install safety devices on all machines. / *arrange for* safety devices to be installed on all machines.

3. *a. Arrangements* have been *made* to employ the redundant workers elsewhere. / to install safety devices on all machines.
   b. Arrangements are *made* to pass the flue gases up both sides of the boiler.

b) = *Positioning*

1. The boiler steam drums can be } *arranged* / *disposed* { in a variety of ways.
2. The fuel elements are } *arranged* / *disposed* { in a lattice in the moderator.
3. The orbiting electrons are } *arranged* / *disposed* { in shells at varying distances from the nucleus.
4. The engines can be } *arranged* / *disposed* { radially round the crankshaft.

5. The *arrangement* } of the heating surface varies with the type of boiler.
6. The *disposition* } of the tubes at an angle over the furnace ensures good water circulation.

c) = *System*

<table>
<tr><td>A system
An arrangement</td><td>of gears connects the turbine shaft to the air-compressor.</td></tr>
</table>

<table>
<tr><td>The heating</td><td>system
arrangements</td><td>in the factory</td><td>is
are</td><td>quite inadequate.</td></tr>
</table>

d) The idea of *arrangement* is closely connected with *Manner*

<table>
<tr><td>The cooling system of the reactor must be so</td><td>disposed
ordered
planned
arranged
organised
designed
set out</td><td>that the steam generators are not exposed to radiation.</td></tr>
</table>

Section 18

Reading: Reactor Cooling System

Various types of reactor *have been designed* and constructed for a number of different purposes, such as the production of fissile material, the production of radio-isotopes, and the generation of electrical power. In the case of reactors designed to produce power, it is essential to devise some method of transferring the heat generated in the reactor core to a heat engine, where it can be converted into electrical power. It is in any case necessary to provide some efficient cooling system, so that the temperatures in the core should not exceed the safe limit of about 600° C.

The cooling system adopted in a reactor depends on whether the moderator is liquid or solid. In the case of a liquid-moderated reactor, the moderator itself acts as a coolant, and can be circulated out of the core and through a heat exchanger. But in cases where the moderator is a solid (normally graphite), a

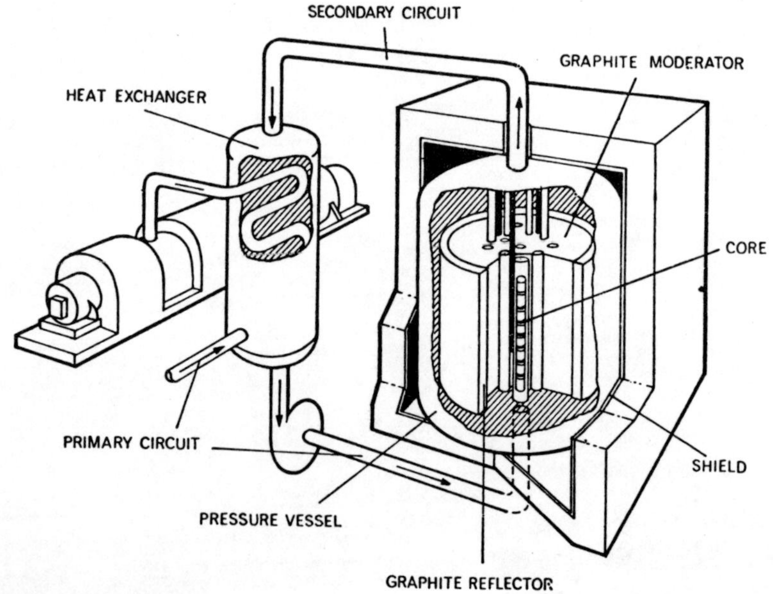

Reactor cooling system

separate cooling system must be provided. The coolant is circulated through the annular spaces between the fuel elements and the moderator, absorbing heat as it passes, and the heat **so absorbed** is conveyed out of the core to the heat exchanger. Very large quantities of heat are generated by fission, and in order that these may be rapidly dissipated, a large volume of coolant is required. It is therefore frequently pressurised, especially where a gaseous coolant is used, to increase its density. A number of different coolants *have been employed*, including water, carbon dioxide and liquid metals. It is essential that the fluid **so used** should have good heat-removal properties, and also a low neutron absorption. To pump such a large quantity of coolant through the core, large pumps are needed, and the power supply for these pumps is taken from the power output of the reactor. Since the power **thus consumed** diminishes the total useful output of the reactor, it should be kept as low as possible.

Coolant which *has been passed* through the reactor will be in some degree contaminated by radiation, and cannot therefore be allowed to come into contact with the turbo-generators. The coolant is circulated in a closed primary circuit, and its heat content is transferred to a secondary circuit through a heat exchanger. In some reactors a liquid-metal coolant is used, and it is likely to become heavily irradiated. In such cases, both the primary circuit and the heat exchanger are therefore included within the biological shield. The working fluid in the secondary circuit is fed into turbo-generators, where its energy is converted into electrical power. Reactors *have recently been built* which are capable of generating up to several hundred megawatts.

WORD STUDY

Core (= heart, or centre)

The *core* of an apple. The *core* of a problem.
When a steel bar is cooled, the case will cool before the *core* does.
The iron bar at the centre of a solenoid is called the *core*.
Cables can be made of aluminium with a thin *core* of steel wire.
When complicated castings are made, a *core* moulded from dried sand is used to form the hollow centre of the casting.
The coolant removes heat from the reactor *core*.

Contaminate, Pollute (= make impure)

1. Exhaust gases from boilers, vehicles, etc., cause air *pollution* in cities.
2. Rivers are *polluted* by the effluent from sewers and drains.

3. High-pressure steam may be	*contaminated*	by the material of the vessel which contains it.
4. Air in a cylinder may be	*contaminated*	by leaking lubricant.
5. Condensate will be	*contaminated*	if it mixes with impure cooling water.
6. Spots will appear on zinc crystals when they are	*contaminated*	by iron.
7. Objects and people may be	*contaminated*	by an escape of radiation.

In-, Out-, Through-

The air *intake* or *intake* manifold of an engine is the passage through which air is taken into the cylinders.
The *inlet* and *outlet* valves let the air in and out of the cylinder.
The power *input* is the power which must be fed into a machine to make it work.
The power *output* is the power delivered or sent out by an engine.
The heat *output* is the amount of heat which can be delivered.
The factory *output* is the number of items produced by a factory.
The *throughput* is the amount of oil, water, gas, etc. which is pumped through a pipeline.

PATTERNS

1. Uses of the Perfect Tense

The perfect tense is not nearly so common as the Present and the Past Tenses, but its main uses should be noted carefully.
The *passive* form is, as usual, more common than the *active* form.

i.e. *work has been started* rather than:
they have started work.

a) In structures which describe an event *before the present* but at *no* specific or definite time.

Work *has been started* on the new system of motorways.
Research *has shown* a probable connection between smoking and lung cancer.

b) In structures which describe an event or series of events happening *continuously* or *repeatedly up to the present.*

Various types of reactor *have been designed* for different purposes.
Engineers *have encountered* many problems with this material.

c) In structures associated with words like *already, not yet, for, since.*

Work on the motorway *has not been started yet.*
Work on the motorway *has already been completed.*
Work on the motorway *has been going on since* 1958.
Test borings *so far have indicated* the presence of large oil deposits.

d) In structures associated with the words *just, recently* and *lately.*

The company *has just developed* a new type of aircraft.
Recent research has shown a connection between smoking and cancer.
Work on the motorway *has recently been held up* owing to bad weather.

EXERCISE

Practise this pattern with the following statements:

1. The presence of large coal deposits ...... (*prove*) by preliminary surveys.
2. The whole area ...... (already; *photograph*) from the air.
3. Difficulties with the fuel injection system ...... largely (*overcome*).
4. These experiments ...... (*have*) very interesting results.
5. Work ...... (just; *begin*) on two 500 Mw nuclear power stations.
6. Several of the workers who were exposed to radiation ...... since (*die*).
7. The steam which ...... (*exhaust*) from the turbine is then condensed.
8. Studies ...... (*make*) over a long period to determine the best type of engine lubricating oil.
9. The government ...... (recently; *invite*) tenders for the construction of the coffer dam.
10. The engine, which ...... (*design*) primarily for aircraft, may also prove suitable for other purposes.
11. After these coal seams ...... (*exhaust*), the coal mine will be closed down.
12. Flying tests ...... (not yet; *complete*) on the prototype machine.
13. Considerable care ...... (*take*) to ensure the greatest reliability in performance.
14. The company ...... (*spend*) a great deal of money on research in recent years.
15. The plastics industry ...... (*expand*) enormously since the end of the war.
16. After the fuel elements ...... (*use*) in the reactor, they are removed and cooled.
17. This type of valve ...... (*prove*) very satisfactory over a great many years.
18. All the designs submitted ...... carefully (*consider*), but none of them ...... (*find*) adequate, and no contract ...... (*award*).
19. Once the metal ...... (*heat*) beyond the critical temperature, it is allowed to cool slowly.
20. The department, which ...... (*found*) in 1945, ... (*expand*) every year since then, and ...... (*do*) some very useful work.
21. If no allowance ...... (*make*) for expansion of the metal, severe stresses will be set up in it.
22. The company ...... (*suffer*) a severe financial loss over the past year.
23. Plans ...... (*make*) to increase production immediately, and this ...... (*necessitate*) taking on a number of extra craftsmen.
24. Steam which ...... (*condense*) in the condenser can be passed back to the boiler for re-use as feed water.
25. The first steam engine ...... (*build*) about two hundred years ago, and since that time steam ...... (*become*) the most important single source of power that man ...... (ever; *know*).

2. Manner (2)

In Section 12, we noticed the contraction of the passive relative:

The petrol mixes with a stream of *air blown* over it.
There is a throttle *valve operated* by the accelerator.

Now we often find the same structure enlarged by *so* or *thus*.

The houses are made of wood. Houses *so constructed* are much cheaper to build. (= houses which are constructed *in this way*)
Shareholders' dividends will be cut, and the money *thus saved* will be used for plant modernisation. (= the money which is saved *in this manner*)

So constructed and *thus saved* obviously refer back to the information given just before. *So* and *thus* are placed before the participle. *In this way* and *in this manner* are placed after it.

EXERCISE

Complete these statements using this contraction-pattern.

1. Dopes such as lead tetra-ethyl are sometimes added to the petrol. Petrol ...... (*treat*) is less liable to detonation.
2. Secondary air is mixed with the products of combustion, and the gases ...... (*cool*) then enter the turbine.
3. Fully automated machinery has been introduced, and the increase in production ...... (*achieve*) has been very satisfactory.
4. High-pressure air under the wings escapes round the wing-tips to the low-pressure region above, and the vortex ...... (*form*) is a source of drag.
5. The heat energy from the reactor is used to drive a turbine, and the power ...... (*generate*) is fed into the national grid.
6. The plates to be welded are placed between the electrodes, across which a current is passed. The heat ...... (*produce*) is sufficient to weld the plates together.
7. Alloy steels are quenched from a temperature of about 800° C, and then tempered. Steels ...... (*treat*) are very hard, and are used for making dies.
8. As the rotational speed increases, the governor arms are raised, and the slight movement ...... (*produce*) is communicated to the steam throttle through a relay.
9. The exhaust gases are ejected from the jet-pipe, and the thrust ...... (*develop*) drives the aircraft through the air.
10. Unless care is taken, steam will escape round the tips of the blades, and the losses ...... (*cause*) will reduce the turbine efficiency.

3. Cases

The word *case* and the phrases associated with it are very important.
In Section 16, we noticed two *case*-phrases connected with *eventuality*:

in case of fire . . .
in case it rains, I shall take my umbrella.

The word *case* has the general meaning of *a particular example or instance* as you can see from the following passages:

---

a) The doctor found one or two interesting *cases* of heart disease among the patients he examined. *In the case of* one patient, several heart attacks had already occurred, but *the other cases* were not so serious. This disease is *in any case* common among elderly people, but *in certain cases* quite young people may also suffer from it. *In such cases* there is often a history of heart disease in the family, and *in a few cases* a childhood illness may have been responsible.

b) The samples were all examined when they were unloaded. *In some cases* the packaging was inadequate, while *in several cases* the samples were not packed at all. *In every case where* the packaging was faulty, the samples were spoiled, and *in no case* were they properly labelled. This is probably *a case of* inefficiency on the part of the manufacturers, *in which case* the matter should be brought to their attention.

Note: 1. *in any case* has the idiomatic meaning of *anyway*.
2. *in no case* requires inversion of the subject and verb.
3. the use of *where* after *case*, or even instead of *case*:
(In *cases*) *where* the goods were found to be faulty, they were returned to the manufacturers.
4. *case* constructions such as the above should be used sparingly; not so frequently as in the examples or in the exercise which follows.

EXERCISE

Complete this passage with a suitable 'case' phrase.

The radioactive half-life of different isotopes varies enormously. ...... polonium 216, it is only a fraction of a second, while ...... such materials as uranium 238 or 235, it is several thousand million years. The penetrative power of the radiation from these unstable isotopes depends on the type of radiation. ...... gamma rays, the penetrative power is very great, and a heavy protective shield is required. There have been ...... workers have been exposed to dangerous radiation doses, and ...... severe illness or even death has resulted. Since these radioactive isotopes present such severe health hazards, they must be treated with great care. ...... may they be handled directly. Mechanical manipulators and conveyors must be used ...... It is obviously necessary ...... to view the irradiation process while it is going on, and ...... heavy shielding windows can be used, ... as much as three feet thick. ...... a maze and mirror system may be used, enabling the operators to view the process in safety. Great care must also be taken with the disposal of radioactive waste, especially ...... the level of radioactivity is high. ...... a nuclear reactor, the disposal of waste becomes extremely important.

Section 19

Reading: Conductors and Conductivity

It is usual to **consider** electric current **as** a flow of electrons from one point to another through a medium, or even through a vacuum. If the electron flow takes place in a vacuum, as in the case of electronic valves, the electrons will travel at considerable speeds, since little resistance is offered by the medium, and fewer impacts will occur between the electrons. If the medium is a solid – in which case the electrons are more tightly packed – the electron flow will be slower.

All substances may be **classified** electrically **as** conductors or insulators, according to the degree of resistance which the medium offers to the flow of current. Most liquids, particularly solutions in liquids, are good conductors. Most gases at normal temperature and pressure are good insulators, but gases maintained at low pressure in a sealed tube allow a flow of current to take place as a result of ionisation of the gas molecules. Solids vary greatly in resistance, some being very good conductors, while others are so resistant that they are **referred to as** insulators. Electric current is normally transmitted along annealed copper wire.

The resistance of any material to the flow of current is affected by a number of factors, such as the length and cross-section of the conductor, and by its resistivity, which is a specific property of the material at a specific temperature. The temperature therefore also has some effect on the resistance of a material: in most cases, an increase in temperature causes an increase in resistance. With certain metals, such as copper or iron, the change in resistance which attends on changes in temperature is relatively large – a fact which is utilised in the resistance thermometer, in which *it is possible to* measure temperature changes, as in the windings of an electric motor, for instance, by the change in resistance.

Some materials have a very high resistance, and **as such** they can be **used as** insulators to prevent the leakage of current. Among these materials are asbestos, celluloid, porcelain, cotton and rubber, and recently a number of new materials have been developed, including synthetic textiles such as nylon, and synthetic resins such as vinyl resins. The resistivity of most insulators decreases with an increase in temperature, for which reason the temperatures in insulated conductors must be kept reasonably low. A breakdown of insulation may occur under the application of very high voltages, and *it is necessary to* know the dielectric strength of any insulating material. Some materials, such

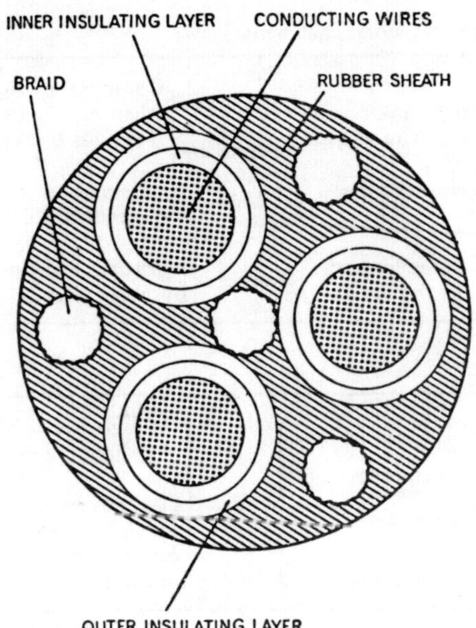

Cross-section of electric cable

as cotton, which is often **used as** insulation, are liable to absorb moisture, and this will adversely affect their insulating properties. Rubber, which is a standard insulating material, is liable to deteriorate under sunlight, and *it is therefore advisable* to protect it with some weatherproof material.

WORD STUDY

Affect (v); *Effect* (n)

1. The temperature of the conductor	*affects*	its resistance to current.
2. The presence of carbon in the iron	*influences*	its behaviour.
3. Machine vibration	*has an effect on*	the surface finish of the work.

4. The poor quality of the goods	*adversely affected* *had an adverse effect on*	the sales.
5. The high quality of the goods	*favourably affected* *had a beneficial effect on*	the sales.

6. The *effect of* the carbon in the iron *is to* change its behaviour.
7. The *effect of* vibration in the machine *is to* produce a poorer surface finish.
8. The *effect of* increased temperature in a conductor *is to* increase its resistance.

Deteriorate – Improve (get worse, get better)

1. Coal is likely to 2. Rubber will slowly 3. The performance of the engine will 4. The economic position of the country will	*deteriorate*	if stored for long periods in the open. when exposed to the sunlight. if serious leakages of steam occur. unless there is a rapid increase in production.
5. The efficiency of the engine was 6. The performance of the jet is	*improved*	by fitting a turbo-compressor. by using after-burners.

Medium

1. The temperature of the 2. Induction motors operate through the 3. Coal gas was the chief 4. Any working 5. Steam is used as the working	*medium*	through which heat is transmitted by radiation is not raised. of a moving magnetic field. for lighting in large towns. can be used with this cycle. in these turbines.

Specific – Specify

a) The *specific*	weight of an aero-engine is the weight in pounds for every pound of thrust. gravity of a substance is the ratio between the weight of 1 c.c. of the substance and the weight of 1 c.c. of water. heat of a substance is the number of calories needed to raise 1 gram of the substance by 1° C. heats of most substances vary with their temperature.

b) = definite and detailed

The engineer was given *specific* instructions on what to do.
The terms of employment must be clearly *specified* in the contract.
The exact dimensions and tolerances should be *specified* by the customer.
The *specification* should include all the information required by the contractors to carry out the work properly.

PATTERNS

1. It is + *Adjective* + to

This pattern, and similar ones which we shall look at in the following Sections, are an essential feature of the scientific style. By using this type of introduction to a sentence, we avoid using the personal form. Instead of saying:

We can measure temperature changes

the scientist can say:

It is possible to measure temperature changes

We have therefore an alternative to the normal passive statement:

Temperature changes can be measured.

The important words which can be used in this pattern are:

It	is was seems appears proves becomes	easy possible necessary essential advisable preferable useful instructive desirable advantageous practicable common usual	(difficult) (impossible) (unnecessary) (inadvisable) (useless) (undesirable) (disadvantageous) (impracticable) (uncommon) (unusual)	to	do something.

EXERCISE

Change these statements into the pattern shown above:

1. We do not want to allow cold water to enter the boiler.
2. There is no difficulty in pumping out the water from the condenser.
3. We must eliminate as far as possible eddy currents in the magnet core.
4. We normally connect the generator to a pair of feeding points.
5. The whole of the compression cannot practicably be carried out in one cylinder.
6. We prefer to obtain higher pressures by having more compression stages.
7. There is some advantage in working at lower temperatures.
8. Where there is a limited supply of water, one should not use a jet condenser.
9. We are now in a position to produce fissile material artificially.
10. We often use two separate condensers to do this.
11. You would be well advised to measure the dimensions of your work after each cut.
12. A film of lubricant must be maintained over the wire during manufacture.
13. The metal should be tempered after it has been quenched.
14. We can reduce the amount of friction by using rolling bearings.
15. We shall learn a lot by looking at the accompanying diagram.

2. As

In Sections 9 and 11, we noticed the use of *as* in time-statements, and in Section 12, we noticed its use in cause-statements.
Now in this section and the following ones, we shall look at some of the other uses of this important and difficult word.

a) *Known as*, etc.

1. This type of motor is	*known* *referred to*	*as*	an induction motor.

2. The efficiency of the engine is *expressed as* a percentage of the ideal efficiency.

3. Cylinder clearance is *defined as* the ratio of clearance volume to swept volume.

4. Electric current may be	*considered* *regarded* *looked on* *seen*	*as*	(being) a flow of electrons through a medium.

5. These materials may be *classified as* conductors.

6. The conductivity of copper wire is	*taken* *accepted*	*as*	(being) the standard for all measurements of conductivity.
7. The limestone in the furnace	*serves* *acts*	*as*	a flux to assist the melting.
8. A hollow tube is often	*used* *employed*	*as*	a conductor of current.

b) = *In the form of*

1. The condensate is returned to the boiler	*as*	feed-water.
2. The steam is cooled and condenses		a film of water.
3. The carbon in cast iron is present partly		free graphite.

c) *As + Past Participle* (with roughly the same meaning)

Natural uranium, *as* obtained from the refining plants, is a solid.
The uranium, *as* used in the reactor, is in the form of a thin rod.
The bridge, *as* originally planned, would have been too expensive.

d) *As such*

1. The earth is a conductor of electricity and	*as such*	may form part of an electrical circuit.
2. A simple governor is dependent on gravity;		it must be kept vertical.
3. This fuel has a high octane number and		it is less likely to detonate.

EXERCISE

Complete these statements, as shown above.

1. This is the main London–Manchester road, and ...... it carries a great deal of traffic.
2. The specific weight of a gas turbine ...... pounds weight per pound of thrust.

3. When the reactor is moderated by water, this water ...... the coolant also.
4. The petrol is mixed with air and injected into the cylinder ...... a spray.
5. The slip of the rotor usually ...... (express) ...... a percentage of the speed of rotation of the magnetic field.
6. The tailstock or dead centre on the lathe is stationary, and ...... it is liable to become heated.
7. Metals composed mainly of tin ...... tin-base metals.
8. A particle of gamma radiation ...... (sometimes) ...... a photon.
9. The work ...... projected will take ten years to complete.
10. The energy from nuclear fission is taken out of the reactor ...... heat.
11. The drag force acting on the fluid can be ...... being limited to the boundary layer close to the walls.
12. Increasing the moisture content ...... (usually) ...... humidification.
13. The vehicle, ... shown in the illustration, costs £2000.
14. The simple diode ...... (use) ...... a low-power rectifier.
15. This man is a skilled lathe-operator; ...... he is entitled to higher rates of pay.

3. Examples

It is sometimes possible to use *as* and *like* when we are giving examples. But the commonest and best expression is *such as*, used as in these examples.

1. Some substances, 2. Projects,	*such as*	tungsten, emit electrons when heated in a vacuum. this one, require a great deal of planning.

3. 4. *Such*	substances projects	*as*	tungsten emit electrons when heated in a vacuum. this one require a great deal of planning.

5. The metal must be able to withstand very high temperatures 6. Soldering is one way of making joints in wire	*such as* (= of the kind which)	are encountered in the high pressure compressor. occur in electrical work.

7. The temperatures at the turbine blades are as high as 600° C. 8. Some materials offer a very great resistance to the flow of current. 9. The rotor may have a voltage induced in it by the moving magnetic field.	*Such*	temperatures (*as* these) need special materials. materials are called insulators. a motor is known as an induction motor.

Section 20

Reading: Induction Motors

In almost every respect an a.c. motor is *similar* in construction *to* a d.c. motor. The essential difference lies in the fact that a d.c. motor requires a commutator to maintain moving contact between the rotating armature and the source of power. **It will be appreciated that** the necessity of providing a commutator with its carbon brushes complicates the construction of the motor, and limits its capacity. Furthermore, with an a.c. motor it is possible to have the windings on the stator and to rotate the magnetic field, rather than have a stationary magnetic field and place the windings on the rotating armature, *as is the case* with a d.c. motor. **It is obvious that** this simplifies the problem of insulating the windings.

The commonest form of a.c. motor is the polyphase induction motor. *As its name suggests*, the current in the rotor is derived not from an external power supply, *as in the d.c. motor*, but is induced by a moving magnetic field in the air-gap between the rotor and the stator. Excitation of the stator winding by a three phase current causes a rotating magnetic field, as each of the electromagnets in turn reaches its maximum strength. And this rotating magnetic field between the stator and the rotor induces a voltage in the rotor conductors.

It has been proved that induced voltage causes a current to flow in opposition to the force producing it. **It follows** therefore **that** the rotor will revolve in the same direction as the rotation of the magnetic field, so that the relative motion between the two is lessened. Now the rotating field will rotate at the synchronous speed of the supply – that is, the frequency multiplied by 60 and divided by the number of electromagnets in the winding. Since the speed of the rotor will always be less than the speed of the rotating magnetic field, a torque will be exerted on it. **It should be noted that** the slip, which is the difference in speeds of the two expressed as a percentage, will never be zero, or no current would be induced in the rotor. When the motor is put on load, the rotor speed will decrease temporarily, thus increasing the percentage slip. The result of this, however, is to increase the induced current and therefore the torque. **It will be seen** therefore that, as the load increases, the speed is only reduced by a fairly small amount.

For small motors, a squirrel-cage rotor is used, *as shown* in the diagram. It consists of a number of *identical* bars of copper or aluminium sunk into slots in a laminated steel core. It is cheap to produce, but has the disadvantage of a low starting torque and a lack of control of speed. In the case of large motors,

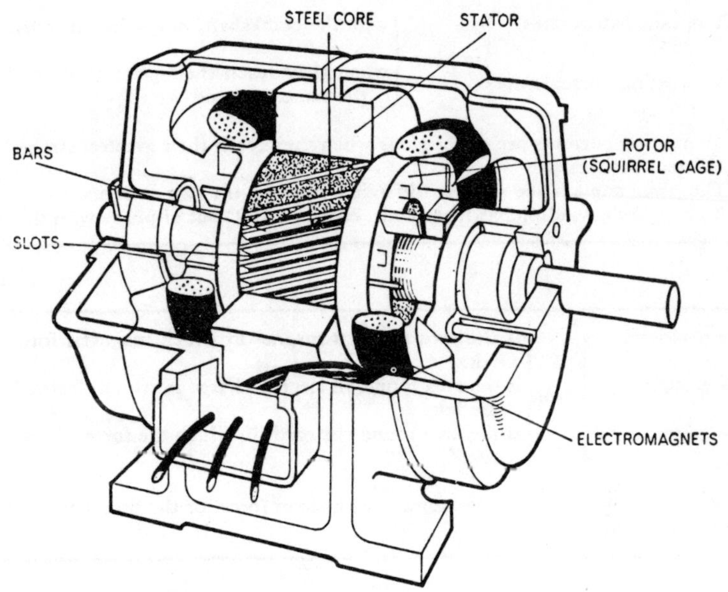

Squirrel-cage induction motor

it is desirable that there should be an adequate starting torque and some control over speed. For large motors therefore, a phase-wound rotor is used, with the windings connected at one end to each other and at the other end to slip-rings, thus enabling the resistance of the rotor to be varied at will, providing a greater starting torque, and some speed control.

WORD STUDY

Stage, Section, Phase

---

1. The first *stage* / *section* / *phase* / *part* of the building operation was completed in eight months.

2. *a.* Turbo-compressors have several *stages* of compression.
   b. The turbine has several pressure *stages*, each one being enclosed between diaphragms.
   c. The pressure is raised in *stages*.
   d. A system of *multi-stage* compression, with inter-coolers, is often used.

3. *a.* The machine was built in *sections* for ease of transport.
   b. The first 12-mile *section* of the road has already been completed.
   c. A *section* of the retaining wall gave way under the pressure.

4. *a.* The camshaft rotates	*in phase*	with the crankshaft, but at half its speed.
b. Alternating currents are	*in phase*	when they reach their greatest strengths at the same moment.

c. Alternating currents are *out of phase* when they reach their greatest strengths at different moments.
d. The *phase* angle is the angular difference between the two currents.
e. A *three-phase* winding has three coils, each one 120° out of phase with the next.

Field

---

1. The magnetic	*field*	is the area round a magnet in which magnetic forces are felt.
2. The electric	*field*	is the area round an electric charge in which electric forces are felt.
3. The gravitational	*field*	is the area round the earth in which the force of gravity is felt.

4. *Field* strength is defined as the number of lines of force, or the flux density at any point in the field.

Derive, Obtain, Source

---

1. The propulsive force of the aircraft is	*derived* / *obtained*	from the reaction of a jet.
2. Power for the machines is	*derived* / *obtained*	from an electric motor.
3. Pure aluminium is	*derived* / *obtained*	from aluminium ores by electrolysis.
4. A wide range of commercial fuels are	*derived* / *obtained*	from petroleum.

The *source* of the river is in the mountains a thousand miles away.
Radiation *sources* must be handled with great care and by remote control.
In an adiabatic heat change, no heat is received from any external *source.*
The sun is the primary *source* of the earth's light.
Oil is a *source* of great wealth for a number of countries.
Information and data were collected from all available *sources* throughout the world.

PATTERNS

1. It (is) + $\frac{\textit{Adjective}}{\textit{Verb}}$ + that . . .

This is another common impersonal start to a statement. Here are some of the typical forms of it.

It is	*likely* *possible*	that	eddy currents will be produced in the core of the magnet.
It is	*evident* *obvious* *clear*	that	these currents will generate heat in the core.
It is	*desirable* *essential*	that	these currents should be eliminated as far as possible.
It should be	*noted* *realised*	that	this energy cannot be destroyed, only changed into other forms.
It will be	*noticed* *seen* *appreciated*		
It can be	*shown* *proved* *demonstrated*		
It is	*known*		
It is	*assumed*	that	the gas temperature in the cylinder is constant.
It has been	*decided* *arranged* *planned*	that	production should begin in a few months.

EXERCISE

Add an impersonal introduction to these statements.

1. ...... convection currents can only take place in an upward direction. (*show*)
2. ...... current can be induced in a conductor by a moving magnetic field. (*prove*)
3. ...... with a squirrel-cage rotor, there can be little control of speed. (*appreciate*)
4. ...... for the purposes of the calculation, there are no frictional losses in the turbine. (*assume*)

5. ...... a large volume of coolant is required to keep the temperature down to a reasonable level. (*obvious*)
6. ...... the introduction of a variable resistance requires a more expensive wound rotor. (*clear*)
7. ...... the Carnot cycle has the highest thermal efficiency of all cycles. (*demonstrate*)
8. ...... the mass of the nucleus represents almost the whole mass of the atom. (*see*)
9. ...... the cost of nuclear power will soon be no higher than the cost of any other form of power. (*hope*)
10. ...... particles in solution carry the current through the liquid. (*know*)
11. ...... some of the electric energy is expended in producing light. (*note*)
12. ...... the temperature remains constant throughout the experiment. (*assume*)
13. ...... none of the tenders for the contract will prove acceptable. (*possible*)
14. ...... the distribution of current through the conductor is not uniform. (*know*)
15. ...... the machine should be tested under conditions which approximate as closely as possible to normal. (*desirable*)

2. Similarity

<table>
<tr><td rowspan="4">This machine is</td><td>exactly the same as
identical with</td><td rowspan="2">the other one</td><td rowspan="2">in design.</td></tr>
<tr><td>roughly the same as
similar to
like</td></tr>
<tr><td>exactly the same</td><td rowspan="2">in design</td><td rowspan="2">as the other one.</td></tr>
<tr><td>roughly the same</td></tr>
<tr><td>The two machines are</td><td colspan="2">alike
identical
similar
the same</td><td>in every respect.
in most respects.</td></tr>
<tr><td colspan="4">Sweden, like Finland, has very large resources of timber.
Argon, like neon, is an inert gas.</td></tr>
<tr><td colspan="4">An a.c. motor does not need a commutator, as the d.c. motor does.
Regenerative feed-water heating is used, as (it is) in ordinary steam power plants.</td></tr>
</table>

EXERCISE

Complete these statements with the correct words.

1. The cylinders must be machined with great care so that they are all ......
2. D.c. machines, ... a.c. machines, have an a.c. voltage generated in the armature.
3. Cobalt ...... steel, is classed as a ferro-magnetic material.
4. Cobalt is a ferro-magnetic material just ...... steel is.
5. The two engines are identical ...... size, but the new one develops greater power.
6. This new engine is identical ...... the earlier one, but develops greater power.
7. A blast furnace is ...... a cupola, except that it is bigger.
8. The new factory will be designed by Smith and Jones, ... the previous one ......
9. A spring-loaded governor is not dependent on gravity ...... is the weight-loaded governor.
10. The training here lasts for four years, ... in your country.
11. The lathe, ... the other machines in the shop, is driven from an electric motor.
12. The lathe is driven from an electric motor, ... the other machines ......
13. The compression ratio in a jet is not constant, ... in the reciprocating engine.
14. Light, ... heat, is a form of radiation.
15. In the induction motor the rotor is not connected to the power supply ...... in the ordinary d.c. motor.

3. As (cont.)

Notice these common expressions using *as* (meaning roughly *similar to what*):

a) Active form

As the illustration on page 246 shows . . .
As we have stated in the previous chapter . . .
As we have just proved . . .

b) Passive form (*notice that there is no 'it' subject*)

As is shown in the illustration . . .
As has been stated in the previous chapter . . .
As has just been proved . . .
As is well known . . .
As was mentioned a short time ago . . .

c) Contracted Passive form

As shown in the illustration . . .
As stated in the previous chapter . . .
As just proved . . .
As mentioned a short time ago . . .
As pointed out by Professor Smith . . .

d) Other contractions

As above . . .
As before . . .
As follows . . .

Section 21

Reading: Electrolysis

Many substances, when dissolved in water, undergo dissociation – that is, some of the molecules are broken down into charged particles or ions. For example, common salt dissolved in water partially dissociates into positively-charged sodium ions, and negatively-charged chlorine ions. The degree of dissociation which takes place varies with different substances, and also with the degree of dilution.

When an electric current is passed between two electrodes immersed in such a solution, the −charged ions move towards the anode, while the +charged ions are drawn to the cathode. **Assuming** that the electrolyte is a copper sulphate solution and the electrodes are of copper, then the sulphate ions will be attracted to the anode, where they unite with the copper of the plate to form new copper sulphate, while the metallic copper ions are deposited on the cathode as pure copper. **Assuming** that the process goes on long enough, the anode will gradually be taken into solution, and the cathode will increase in size through continuing deposition of copper. *If there were* no

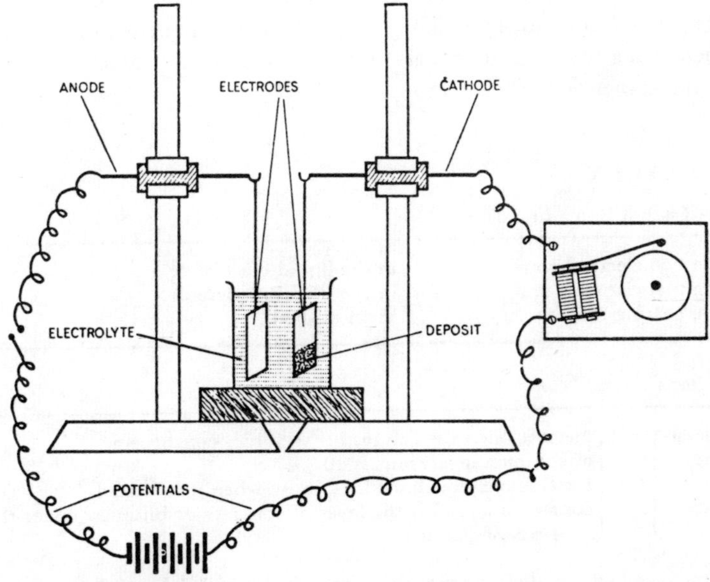

Illustration of electro-plating

losses in this process, the whole of the energy supplied *would be* used in forming pure metal on the cathode. But in practice deposits of gas round the electrodes reduce the electrolytic activity slightly, and *would interfere* more seriously with it *if some chemical agent were not introduced* to combat it.

Where both electrodes are of the same material, the potentials developed will be equal and opposite. But if dissimilar metals are used, the potentials will differ, and an electromotive force is set up. The cell may then be used as a source of electric energy. In primary cells, energy is produced only until the anode is consumed. Secondary cells, or accumulators, however, unlike the primary cells, can be recharged by passing a reversed current through them.

The principle of cathodic deposition, as it is called, has many industrial applications. It is employed, for instance, in the production of pure metals, such as aluminium or sodium, by using a fused ore of the metal as the electrolyte. Another application is in the process known as electro-plating, in which a thin surface of some metal such as chromium or tin is deposited on a metallic base so that it adheres firmly to the base. Electro-forming, as distinct from electro-plating, involves growing metal on to a base in such a way that the base can subsequently be melted out or removed, leaving only the electroformed deposit. **Assuming** that all the factors involved, such as temperature and current density, can be closely controlled, a surface of the exact shape and thickness required can be produced. **Supposing** it was desired to produce certain components of very complicated shape. *If this were done* by normal machining processes, it *would be* very costly and difficult to make within the required tolerances. But by making a cast of the component to be produced, and metallising it so that it acts as a cathode, a deposit of exactly the correct shape and dimensions can be grown on to it.

WORD STUDY

Immerse (= put into a liquid)

<table>
<tr><td>1. The two electrodes are</td><td rowspan="3">immersed</td><td>in the liquid electrolyte.</td></tr>
<tr><td>2. The fuel elements are</td><td>in the liquid moderator.</td></tr>
<tr><td>3. The bearing may be</td><td>in an oil-bath.</td></tr>
</table>

Base – Basis

<table>
<tr><td>1. A lead-</td><td rowspan="4">base</td><td>metal is one in which lead is the chief constituent.</td></tr>
<tr><td>2. The</td><td>of common logarithms is 10.</td></tr>
<tr><td>3. A</td><td>metal is one which oxidises easily when it is heated.</td></tr>
<tr><td>4. The</td><td>course on a road is the layer of concrete or bitumen under the top or wearing course.</td></tr>
</table>

5. Nimonic alloys are alloys with a nickel *base.* It is a nickel-*based* alloy.
6. The machine must rest on a firm *base.* It must be firmly *based.*

7. There is no factual *basis* for this theory.
8. He reached this conclusion on the *basis* of experimental data.

9. The synchroscope is } *based on* { the principle of the rotating field.
10. The thermostat is } *based on* { the fact that different metals have different co-efficients of expansion.

11. The *basic* / *fundamental* law in electric circuit theory is Ohm's law.

Accumulate, Collect

---

1. The fission products } *accumulate* / *collect* { in the fuel element and contaminate it.
2. The molecules } *accumulate* / *collect* { as a vapour above the heated liquid.
3. Gases are liable to } *accumulate* / *collect* { round the electrodes, interfering with the electrolytic action.
4. Soot or scale should not be allowed to } *accumulate* / *collect* { in the boiler tubes.

Accumulations { of gas round the electrodes interfere with the electrolytic action.
Accumulations { of scale on the boiler tubes will reduce the rate of heat transfer.

An *accumulator* { is a single electrolytic *cell*, or a series of *cells* in which electric current can be stored.
An *accumulator* { is used to store steam until it is needed by the engine.
An *accumulator* { is used to store liquid or air until it is needed by pumps.

Dissociate – Associate

---

1. Some molecules *dissociate* (break up) { into simpler molecules when they are heated. / when they are immersed in water.

2. *a.* Detonation in a cylinder is } *associated with* / *connected with* { accelerated flame speeds.
   b. The high temperatures } *associated with* / *connected with* { nuclear fission affect the structure of the fuel.
   c. Most of the mass of an atom is } *associated with* / *connected with* { the nucleus.
   d. There are many difficulties } *associated with* / *connected with* { the construction of fast reactors.

Potential

a) = possible in the future

The } *potential* { resources of this country are enormous.
The } *potential* { market for this new product is very wide.
The } *potential* { value of this new material in industry is doubtful.

The use of plastics for pipes is a development of great *potential* value.

The industrial *potential* of this country is enormous.

---

b) (energy)

Water stored on a hill-top has *potential* energy.
Energy can be stored in the form of *potential* energy.
There is a *potential* difference between the two electrodes.
All points on this conducting surface are at the same *potential.*

PATTERNS

1. Suppose (1)

In Section 16, we saw examples of the conditional statement, which says that something will happen *if* or *provided that* something else happens first.
The same structure, but with different tense-forms, is used when we *suppose* or *imagine* something happening which is, in fact, unlikely to happen or didn't really happen at all.
In ordinary life we like to play the game of imagining something that is unlikely to happen:

If I *were* rich, I *would buy* a large house.

or even something which definitely did not happen:

If I *had married* her, I *would have been* unhappy.

Scientists and engineers do not often play this game of make-believe in their work, but sometimes you will meet these forms of *supposition.*
Notice the tense-forms used:

a) *If* + Past, Subject + would + Infinitive. (unreal)
b) *If* + Past Perfect, Subject + would have + Past Participle. (impossible)

In this construction, *were* is often used instead of *was*
be is sometimes used for *is.*

EXERCISE

These sentences will show you the sort of occasions on which this suppose-form may be used. Complete them with the correct tense forms.

1. If the engine could be made to work in this way, it (*have*) an efficiency of 100%.
2. If the bearings (*not lubricate*), they would rapidly overheat.
3. If there was an explosion in the reactor, the pressure vessel (*be able*) to contain it.
4. Unless the work had been finished on schedule, the contract (*cancel*).
5. If the compressor blades were made of ordinary steel, they (*be unable*) to withstand the very high temperatures.
6. If the world's population (*rise*) more slowly, there would not have been such a grave shortage of food.
7. If there (*be*) no thrust to provide the forward movement of the aircraft, there (*be*) no lift force either.

8. If the radioactive material were not carefully stored, it (*contaminate*) its surroundings.
9. If the concrete (*not seal*) against the air, it would have dried out too quickly.
10. If the whole operation (*not plan*) carefully beforehand, a great deal of time and money would have been lost.

2. Suppose (2)

Here we are concerned with the idea of *assuming* or *assumption.*
We do not know whether something is true or not, but we are going to *assume* or *suppose* that it is true for a certain limited purpose.

a) A *hypothesis* is a kind of assumption which we make as a starting-point for a line of reasoning.

Ancient geographers *assumed* that the world was flat.
It is *assumed* that petroleum originates in marine deposits.

---

b) For the purposes of some *calculation* or *experiment,* we assume certain facts: they may not be true, but it *simplifies* the calculation to assume that they are true.

The medium is *assumed to be* atmospheric air only.
The cylinder is *assumed to be* a perfect non-conductor of heat.
The heat loss is *taken to be* negligible, and is disregarded.

The *assumption* is made that
- the cylinder is a perfect non-conductor.
- there is no heat loss from the cylinder.

Assuming (that)
- there is no loss of speed over the blades, calculate the outlet velocity of the steam.
- the deflection of the galvanometer is 45 degrees, find the weight of copper deposited.

Assume (that) / *Suppose* (that) / *If*
- '*v*' is the velocity of the steam, then *R* is its relative velocity.
- the rise in the temperature of the water is 15 degrees. – How much water must be delivered to the condenser?

---

3. Difference

Be careful with the prepositions which are used in these statements of difference or distinction.
You will find some similar forms, expressing contrast, illustrated in Section 14.

This machine	*differs* *is different*	*from*	the other one	*in*	its shape. several respects. the fact that it is more powerful. that it is more powerful.
	can be distinguished			*by*	its shape.

It is useful to	*differentiate* *distinguish* *make a distinction*	*between*	a blower and a liquid pump.

This engine,	*unlike* *as distinct from* *as opposed to*	the earlier one, has six cylinders.

This engine has six cylinders	*as against* *as compared with* *as opposed to*	the four cylinders of the earlier one.

EXERCISE

Complete these statements.

1. Heat waves ...... light waves only ...... their different wavelengths.
2. Conduction ...... convection ...... the way in which the transfer of heat is effected.
3. Iron ...... rubber is a good conductor of electric current.
4. We normally ...... those substances which are good conductors of current and those which are not.
5. The low-pressure compressor has four stages of compression, ... the high-pressure compressor, which has eight stages.
6. The low-pressure compressor has four stages of compression ...... the eight stages of the high-pressure compressor.
7. The petrol engine ...... the Diesel engine ...... the mixture is ignited in the cylinder by a spark.
8. ...... the Diesel engine, the petrol engine is spark-ignited.
9. Jet aircraft can fly at supersonic or hypersonic speeds ...... the 600 m.p.h. maximum speed of a propeller driven aircraft.

REVISION (SECTIONS 15–21)

Read these statements, choosing the correct word from the alternatives in brackets.

1. The radioactivity which is (*accompanied, associated, involved*) with the majority of fission products (*dissipates, diminishes, augments*) (*fairly, rather*) rapidly, but a certain (*amount, number*) of these take a very long time to (*decline, decay, decrease*). These must be stored until the (*level, degree, dose*) of radioactivity is low enough for them to be safely (*disposed, dispensed*) of.
2. Workers in atomic power (*factories, plants, works*) are (*liable, apt, tended*) to be (*exposed, disposed, revealed*) to dangerous (*degrees, doses, supplies*) of radiation, and in order to (*counteract, overcome, dispense with*) this danger, certain precautions always have to be (*made, done, taken*), such as the wearing of (*preventive, protective, irradiated*) clothing.
3. The air (*across, through, into*) which the wing of the aircraft is moving (*affords, imposes, offers*) considerable (*resistance, restriction, reaction*) to it. (*Varied, Various*) means have been (*designed, devised, adapted*) to minimise (*this, that*), including streamlining the wings and fuselage, but it can never be (*thoroughly, entirely*) (*obviated, eliminated, disposed*).
4. The moderator (*contains, comprises*) a number of (*canals, channels*) into which are (*inserted, introduced, injected*) the fuel (*elements, filaments*) and also the control rods, (*which, whose*) (*function, object*) is to (*determine, regulate, govern*) the neutron flux (*ratio, rate, proportion*).
5. The principle of the hovercraft (*involves, necessitates, implies*) the (*supply, provision*) of some means of (*maintaining, sustaining, retaining*) a cushion of air underneath the craft. For this purpose, air from a fan is (*emanated, emitted, discharged*) through ducts on the undersurface, forming an air curtain which (*contains, retains*) the region of high-pressure air on which the craft is (*suspended, sustained, maintained*).
6. The metallic (*filament, element*) is placed inside a (*vacuous, vacated, evacuated*) tube, and a voltage is (*applied, supplied, provided*) to it. The heat (*generated, evolved, delivered*) in this way is sufficient for electrons to be (*emanated, expelled, emitted*), and these (*impress, impinge, induce*) upon an anode to which an (*alternate, alternating*) potential is (*applied, supplied, provided*).
7. The airport runways are being (*expanded, extended, increased*), with the result that it will be able to (*accommodate, accumulate*) all (*apart from, except for*) the largest aircraft. A ground control system is also being (*installed, inserted, fitted*) to assist aircraft (*in case, in the case*) of bad weather.
8. The engine is identical (*to, as, with*) the (*late, last, latest*) model, (*apart*

from, except for) the introduction of an eight (*section, stage, phase*) compressor, which is (*able, capable*) of (*delivering, developing, generating*) air at higher pressures (*as, than*) before.

9. (*Since, During, For*) the past ten years, a number of bridges (*has been, have been, were*) constructed. As (*the, a*) result, communications with the interior of the country have been (*greatly, largely*) (*accelerated, increased, facilitated*) and (*work, works*) (*has, have*) been found for many (*unemployed, unemployeds*).
10. In (*case, the case, the event*) of the compression ignition (*engine, motor, machine*), the spark plug can be (*dispensed with, eliminated, disposed of*) since ignition is (*acquired, developed, effected*) by (*rising, raising*) the (*temperature, heat*) of the air through compression to the point (*when, where, whereby*) it produces ignition of the oil (*induced, injected*) into it.
11. An accumulator (*provides, produces, supplies*) low tension (*current, voltages*) to the primary coil. This primary (*circle, circuit*) is repeatedly broken by an interruptor (*actuated, activated, actioned*) by a cam rotating (*at, on, in*) synchronism (*with, to, as*) the engine, (*this, thus*) causing a high tension (*current, voltage*) to (*run, circulate, flow*) through the (*second, secondary*) winding of the coil.
12. The fission (*products, productions*) formed in the reactor (*constitute, include, comprise*) a large number of chemical elements, (*including, containing*) rare gases (*as, like, such as*) krypton and xenon.
13. The design of an aircraft which is able to (*acquire, attain, accomplish*) a speed of 2000 miles per hour (*entails, entrains, implies*) a great deal of preliminary (*research, researches*). (*Without, Except, Unless*) certain difficulties can be overcome, (*little, few*) progress can be (*done, made*).
14. Modern plastics possess (*qualities, properties, accomplishments*) which make them satisfactory (*substitutes, exchanges, displacements*) for the traditional materials in a wide (*number, range, scope*) of products. They are not (*effected, affected*) by corrosion (*as, like*) iron and steel are, and (*while, as*) they do not (*convey, transmit, conduct*) electricity, they are widely used (*for, as*) insulators.
15. The main (*cause, source, origin*) of the country's wealth lies in the rich (*metal, mineral, material*) deposits in the north. Mining (*works, operations*) have been going on (*for, since*) many years on an increasing (*amount, scale, extent*), and would have (*extended, expanded, augmented*) even more rapidly if an adequate transport system (*was, is, had been*) available.

Section 22

Reading: Liquid Flow and Metering

The behaviour of a fluid flowing through a pipe is affected by a number of factors, including the viscosity of the fluid and the speed at which it is pumped. Below a certain critical velocity, the flow is streamline, but when the velocity is increased beyond this value, the fluid becomes unstable and the smooth flow will eventually break up, *eddies being formed* which give rise to turbulence and loss of kinetic energy. The velocity at which this occurs varies both with the internal diameter of the pipe and with its surface characteristics. Small roughnesses on the pipe walls do not materially affect the flow, since they do not protrude beyond the laminar sub-layer at the pipe wall. But if the roughness is **such that** it projects into the main stream, then the turbulence in this region will be increased, *more of the kinetic energy of the fluid being dissipated* as heat.

Liquids flowing through pipes are subject to loss of head due to frictional

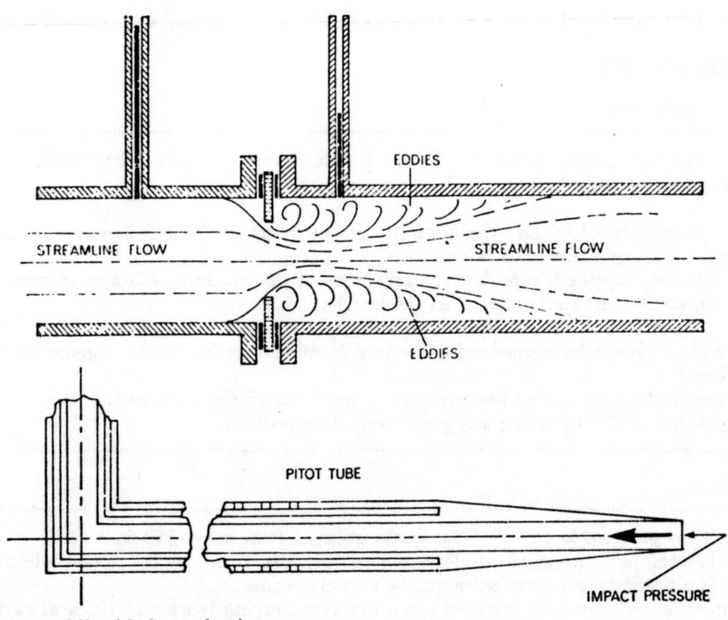

The flow of liquid through pipes

forces at the surface of the pipe. The fluid flow close to the pipe walls is retarded by contact with them, *this drag being transmitted* through the viscous fluid, so that a velocity gradient exists at right angles to the flow. Thus it is not possible to measure the rate of flow by a single velocity measurement, and a number of readings should be taken at radial intervals through the flow.

An accurate estimation of the probable loss of head in a pipe is important, since it will determine the horse-power required to ensure discharge at the required rate and pressure. It is theoretically possible to calculate the frictional pressure drop in a given length of pipe of a given diameter and roughness from the following data: the rate of flow of the fluid, its viscosity and its density. Additional allowances, however, have to be made for losses due to the presence of sharp bends or elbows in the pipe, provided they are **such as to** impede the normal flow to any appreciable extent.

The rate of flow at any section of a pipe can be measured by a variety of metering devices, *the commonest being* those in which the fluid is either retarded or accelerated at the measuring point, *the pressure difference being then measured.* In a pitot-tube, a small filament of the fluid is brought to rest in a small-bore tube, *the impact pressure being measured* against the static pressure of the fluid in an outer tube. In other instruments, the stream is accelerated through a Venturi or nozzle. Its kinetic energy is thereby increased, and the rate of flow can again be determined from the pressure difference involved. Flow meters, like valves, are liable to be a source of friction, and their design should be **such that** they obstruct the fluid flow as little as possible.

WORD STUDY

Datum, Data, Given

Mean Sea Level is the *datum* from which measurements of altitude are made.
The Equator is the *datum* from which latitudes are calculated.

The melting point of ice and the boiling point of water are the fixed points or *data* on which the Centigrade scale is based.
From the *data* supplied, calculate the efficiency of the machine. (data = information)
A certain amount of *data* is given in the article.

The rise in pressure for a *given* reduction in volume of a gas is constant. (given = stated or fixed)
The size of engine required for any *given* purpose can be determined.
The quantity of fluid passing any *given* point is measured.

Gradient

The railway *gradient* is 1 : 350. The tracks go up 1 ft in every 350 ft.
There is a temperature *gradient* along the cooling fins, from the tip to the cylinder.
There is a potential *gradient* between the two electrodes.
To construct an easy road *gradient* often involves moving large quantities of earth.

Liquid – Fluid

When ice is melted, it changes from the solid to the *liquid* state.
Benzol, petrol and kerosene are *liquid* fuels.
Liquid metal is sometimes used as a reactor coolant.
Gases, when cooled sufficiently, *liquefy*. The liquefaction temperature of hydrogen is – 252·8° C.
A *liquid* pump is one which pumps *liquids*, such as water, oil, etc.

A *fluid* is any substance which *flows*.
The working *fluid* used in this reciprocating engine is steam.
A gas turbine uses hot gases as the working *fluid*.
In a hydraulic system, oil is normally used as the working *fluid*.
The rate of flow of a *fluid* through the pipe is measured.

Pipe, Tube, Rod

A *pipe* is normally made of metal; fluid flows through a pipe.
A steam *pipe*; a drain-pipe; an oil-pipe; an oil-pipeline; a jet-pipe.
The oil is *piped* from the oil-well to the refinery.

A *tube* may be made of metal, glass, rubber, plastic, etc.
A *tube* often is smaller in diameter than a pipe.
A thermometer is a graduated *tube* containing mercury or alcohol.
A condenser contains rows or banks of *tubes* in which water circulates.
Tubular steel is used sometimes in bridge-building.
The apparatus consists of a flask and a length of *tubing*.

A *rod* is a thin stick of metal; it is not hollow like the pipe or tube.

PATTERNS

1. The Final -ing Clause

We have already examined a large number of ways in which statements can be joined together to form complex sentences. There are still a few others to be noticed, including this *final clause* which technical writers are very fond of using.
This type of clause has at least three different uses:

a) *In place of 'And'*. It is a simple addition to the preceding statement. The subject of the second part is normally different from the subject of the first part, and must be stated.

The starter motor is switched off, *the engine accelerating* under its own power.
The normal type of crankshaft is used, *the upper pistons being operated* by cross-heads.

b) *In place of 'Since'*. It is an explanation of what has just been said. The subject of the second part is very often the same as the subject of the first part, and is omitted.

The proton is the opposite of the electron, *being a particle* of positive electricity.
Mercury is most commonly used in thermometers, *having a constant coefficient* of expansion.

c) To show the result or consequence of the first statement. Examples will be given in Section 23 (1).

EXERCISE

Join these statements in the same way, and notice whether they are simple *additions* to what has been said, or *explanations* of it.

1. The machines may be arranged in groups. Each machine is driven from a countershaft.
2. An oil-pump delivers oil to the bearings. The oil then drains into a sump.
3. A number of fast reactors are now being constructed. The production of fissile material is one of their main purposes.
4. A number of fast reactors are now being constructed. The production of fissile material is essential.
5. Compression takes place in the inlet duct. Some of the kinetic energy of the air which enters is converted into heat.
6. Small roughnesses on the surface of the pipe have no effect on the fluid flow. They are restricted to the sub-layer close to the wall.
7. Cooling of the piston is necessary. The coolant is conveyed to it through a hollow piston rod.
8. 0·7% of U-235 is present in natural uranium. The remaining 99·3% is the fertile isotope U-238.
9. Three fixed coils are arranged radially. Each coil is connected to one line conductor.
10. This metal shows good resistance to corrosion. It forms a film of oxide which prevents corrosion.
11. The air/fuel ratio in the flame tube was about 15 : 1. The remaining air passes over the outside of the tube.
12. The air/fuel ratio in the flame tube is reduced to about 15 : 1. A large part of the air from the compressor is passed round the outside of the tube.
13. The sulphate ions are attracted towards the anode. They are negatively charged.
14. The copper ions are attracted towards the cathode. They are deposited on it as pure copper.
15. The probable resistances are calculated; a temperature rise of 40° C is assumed.
16. There are several ways of finding the moment of inertia. The two most convenient ones are as follows.
17. The metal is heated to about 800° C. It is then allowed to cool slowly.
18. The steam reaches the cylinder in a fairly dry state. It has passed through the superheater first.

2. Such that, Such as to

Look at these statements:

The size of the flow-meter The job	is *such that*	the flow is unaffected by it. it demands the greatest skill.
The size of the flow-meter The job	is *such as to*	have no effect on the flow. demand the greatest skill.

In this type of statement, the phrases *such that* and *such as to* are contractions of:

of such a kind of such a size of such a value etc.	that. as to.

EXERCISE

Practise this structure by completing the following statements.

1. The diameter of the pipe must be ...... permit the liquid to flow at a moderate speed.
2. The diameter of the pipe must be ...... the liquid flows at a moderate speed.
3. The design of the nozzle is ...... an almost frictionless flow takes place.
4. The characteristics of this alloy are ...... make it very suitable for this purpose.
5. The expense of colour television is likely to be ...... not enough people will be able to afford it.
6. Working conditions in the factory are ...... few workers stay for longer than three months.
7. The aircraft will remain airborne until its speed is ...... the lift force on the wings no longer exceeds the weight of the aircraft.
8. The level of radioactivity is ...... the waste material can be safely disposed of.
9. The depth of the coal seam is ...... make working uneconomical.
10. The depth of the coal seam is ...... working it would be uneconomical.
11. The temperatures in the turbine are ...... special materials have to be used.
12. The velocity of the liquid must be ...... a streamline flow is maintained.
13. The difficulties encountered have been ...... little progress has yet been made.
14. The effect of the fission products on the fuel element is ...... make it necessary to remove them periodically.
15. The construction of the impeller vanes is ...... suspensions can readily be pumped through.

3. Measurements and Calculations

a) *Metre, Meter, Measure*

A kilo*metre* is a thousand *metres*, or five-eighths of a mile.

A pyro*meter* is an instrument for measuring high temperatures.
An am*meter* is an instrument for measuring the amperage of a current.
A volt-*meter* is an instrument for measuring voltage.
A flow-*meter* is an instrument for measuring the rate of fluid flow.

The rate of flow can be *metered* / *measured* by a variety of *metering* / *measuring* devices.

1. The luminous flux from a light source is
2. The current flowing in a conductor is
3. The pressure of the steam is

} *measured in* { lumens. / amperes. / lb/in^2.

Readings of the thermometer / *Measurements* of temperature } should be *taken* every ten minutes.

b) *Calculations* (work out mathematically)

Calculate / *Work out* / (*Determine*) {
the brake horse power developed by the engine at 2000 rev./min.
the amount of air required for complete combustion of the fuel.
the mass of copper deposited in 40 minutes.

c) *Determine* (= find out)

The constituents of the fuel can be *determined* by chemical analysis.
The purpose of the test is to *determine* the calorific value of the fuel.
It is necessary to *determine* the effect of the particles on the flow.
Other types of thermometer must be used for accurate *determination* of very high temperatures.

d) *Estimate, Gauge, Judge* (= roughly)

1. The temperature of the metal may be { *estimated* / *judged* / *gauged* } from the colour of the oxide film.
2. The age of a rock may be { *estimated* / *judged* / *gauged* } from the fossils embedded in it.

A pressure *gauge* gives an indication of the pressure in the boiler.
A plug *gauge* is a tool used to measure dimensions accurately.
A micrometer is a *gauge* which gives a very exact measurement of size.

The surveyor *estimates* the quantity and cost of the materials.
In the *estimate* produced by the surveyor, the cost of each item is noted down.
The *estimated* time of arrival of the aircraft is 11.00 today.
It is *estimated* that the world's oil resources will last for 100 years.

e) *Deduce* (= one thing from another)

From the information given, we can / From the fossils embedded in it, we } *deduce* { the specific heat of the oil. / the age of a rock.

Section 23

Reading: Liquid Pumps

A wide variety of liquids are now being used in chemical plants, and these usually have to be pumped through pipelines. In choosing the type of pump most suitable for any specific operation, a number of problems have to be taken into account. In the first place the quantity of liquid, and the pressure at which it is required to be pumped, must be considered. Neglecting all other considerations, the reciprocating pump is ideal for pumping small quantities of liquid at high pressure, the amount of fluid delivered depending on the volumetric displacement of the pistons. The delivery however is rather uneven – a defect which can only be remedied by compounding a number of cylinders, **thus making** the machine rather large and expensive.

The viscosity of the liquid is another factor which must be taken into account, *in that* it largely determines the frictional losses which will occur. Rotary-type pumps are widely used in the handling of highly viscous liquids. They differ from reciprocating pumps *in that* they deliver an even flow of liquid, but they are unsuitable for pumping liquids of low viscosity, which tend to leak past the tips of the gear teeth. They are mainly used for the pumping of oils and similar liquids of high viscosity, which are less liable to leakage and which moreover provide the necessary lubrication for the moving parts of the pump, **thus obviating** the need for a separate lubricant. A further consideration involved in the choice of pump is whether or not the liquid is corrosive or contains solid particles in suspension. In such cases, precautions have to be taken to avoid damage to the mechanism. *With regard to* suspensions, the clearances in the pump must be large enough to permit the particles to pass, and *from this point of view*, the rotary pump is not suitable, clearances necessarily being small to reduce leakage. The centrifugal type of pump is more commonly used when suspensions are present, since various types of impeller can be fitted, **thus enabling** the pump to handle a wide variety of liquids, including those with suspensions.

The centrifugal pump is compact and requires little maintenance. But it suffers from a certain disadvantage, *in that* there are considerable friction losses in the entry and discharge passages of the impeller, and further losses due to turbulence in the impeller itself. The pump consists essentially of one or more impellers rotating in the centre of a casing. This impeller contains a number of vanes so designed that the fluid entering the pump is carried round by the vanes at a speed depending on their speed of rotation. It is then dis-

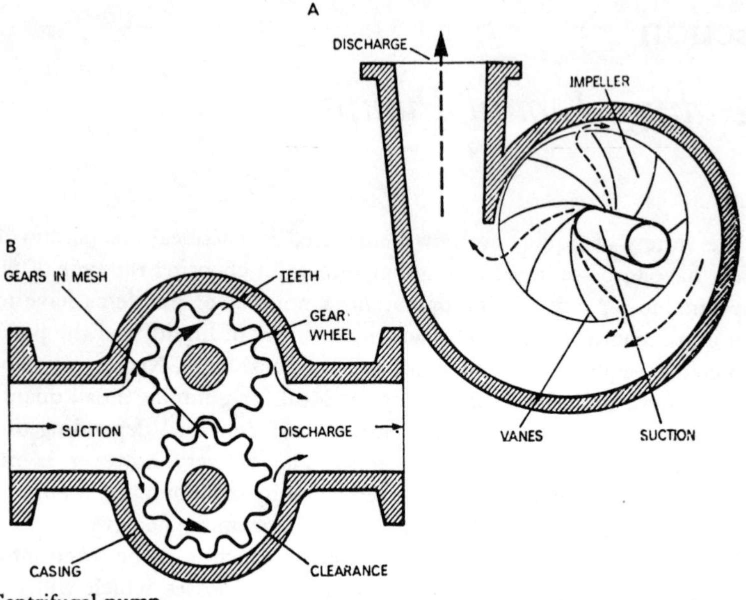

(A) Centrifugal pump
(B) Gear pump

charged into a delivery chamber with a high kinetic energy imparted by the action of the vanes. This energy is then converted into pressure energy, **thus adding** to the large pressure difference between the suction and delivery sides of the pump. Excessive speed of rotation of the impeller is liable to cause the pressure on the suction side to fall so low that the liquid will vaporise, **thus causing** damage to the impeller.

WORD STUDY

Plant, Unit, Machinery

---

1. The power *plant* / *unit* driving the machines is a 200-hp induction motor.

2. New *plant* / *machinery* has recently been installed in the factory.

3. The concrete-mixing *plant* / *equipment* was set up on the building site.

Suspend

Lengths of shaft can be	*suspended*	from beams by means of hangers.
The cradle was		from the roof by ropes.
The roadway is often		by suspenders from steel cables spanning the river.
Dust particles are		in the air.
Solid particles are		in a liquid.

The river Forth will soon be spanned by a	*suspension*	bridge.
Dust particles are held in		in the air.
Solid particles are held in		in the liquid.

Every modern car has independent front *suspension.*

Erode (wear away); *Corrode* (eat away)

The top soil has been	*eroded*	by the rain and carried away by the river.
The coastal rocks are		by the sea.
The turbine-blades are		by wet steam.
The blades are liable to be		by high-velocity steam or gas.

Acids will gradually	*corrode*	metals by electrolytic action.
The carbon dioxide of the air will		metals.

Pipes can be protected against *corrosion* by galvanising them.
Some metals are more resistant to *corrosion* than others.

The pump may be damaged by contact with the *corrosive* liquid.

Defect, Fault, Remedy

The car tested has a number of *defects,* / *faults,* including a *defective* / *faulty* heater.

The engine is so constructed that any *defective* component can be easily removed and replaced.

A geological *fault* is a break in a bedding of rock, so that the strata appear discontinuous.

Any *defects* which appear during testing are to be *remedied* / *put right* by the makers.

PATTERNS

1. The Final -ing Clause (Result)

As we noticed in the previous Section, this pattern is also used to express the consequence or effect of what has been stated before. The subject of the second part is normally the same as the subject of the first part, so that it is not stated.

The rivet contracts as it cools, drawing the plates together.

Frequently the words *thus* or *thereby* are added to emphasise the meaning.

The rivet contracts as it cools, thereby drawing the plates together.

EXERCISE

Join these statements together in the same way, using *thus* or *thereby* and the *-ing* form of the verb.

1. The compressor may not be able to maintain the delivery pressure. This causes a reversal of flow.
2. A substance may capture a neutron. This raises its mass number by one.
3. The unburnt air can be burnt in the jet-pipe. This increases the thrust from the jet.
4. The excess air mixes with the products of combustion. This lowers their overall temperature.
5. A number of new machines were installed in the factory. This resulted in an increase in production.
6. Polythene sheets are laid over the wet concrete. This prevents the concrete from drying out too quickly.
7. A thin stream of the fluid is forced through a Venturi. This has the effect of accelerating it.
8. A variable resistance is led into the rotor. This gives the motor a better starting torque.
9. The surface area of pulverised fuel is greatly increased. The combustion process is hastened by this.
10. The steam is discharged into the water through nozzles. This brings about condensation.

2. In that . . . (points of view, etc.)

Notice these useful idiomatic expressions.

The reciprocating pump is superior to the rotary pump The reciprocating pump differs from the rotary pump	*from certain*	*points of view.*
	in certain	*respects.* *features.* *ways.*
	from the point of view of *with regard to* *in*	efficiency.
	in	being more efficient. giving greater efficiency.
	in that *in so far as* *inasmuch as*	it is more efficient.

N.B. Notice particularly the expression *in that.*

EXERCISE

Practise by completing the following statements.

1. This is an ideal site for the factory ...... it is close to the sources of supply of the raw materials.
2. The new bridge is likely to prove very useful ...... it will provide a direct route to the north.
3. The new bridge is likely to prove very useful ...... providing a direct route to the north.
4. The transformer differs from the ideal ...... there are losses in the core and windings.
5. The Trident is similar to the Caravelle ...... both aircraft have engines mounted at the rear of the fuselage.
6. The Trident is similar to the Caravelle ...... having its engines mounted at the rear of the fuselage.
7. The gear pump has one advantage over the reciprocating pump ...... it gives an even delivery of fluid.
8. This method of analysis is open to criticism ...... not being sufficiently rigorous.
9. Rubber differs from synthetic plastics only ...... it is produced naturally and not in the laboratory.

10. This is a difficult course ...... it involves a general knowledge of all branches of engineering.
11. High steam velocities are not desirable ...... they often introduce serious tube erosion.
12. The motorway is much safer than the old road ...... dispensing with dangerous intersections and junctions.
13. The motorway is much safer than the old road ...... it dispenses with dangerous intersections and junctions.
14. This engine differs from the earlier one ...... the bearings are made of white metal.

3. Consider, Neglect

a)

1. A number of factors must be 2. Certain losses should be	*considered* *taken into consideration* *taken into account*	when designing a road. in estimating the efficiency of an engine.

3. The losses due to leakage past the pistons can be 4. The resistance of the bearings to the rotation of the shaft can be	*ignored* *neglected* *disregarded*	since they are negligible. as it is relatively small.

b) Notice that this type of word is frequently used to introduce working procedures or instructions.

Taking into account all losses, the efficiency of the engine is still fairly high.
Neglecting all radiation losses, calculate the amount of steam required . . .
Assuming radiation losses to be 5%, calculate the amount of steam required . . .
Disregarding variations in specific heat, the air temperature will be raised from T_2 to T_6.
Multiplying the results by 9/5, we obtain the Fahrenheit temperature.
Using these values of temperature, the value of x can be found.

Section 24

Reading: Petroleum

Petroleum is the largest source of liquid fuel, and, *in spite of* attempts to develop synthetic fuels, and the continued use of solid fuels, world consumption of petroleum products is about four times greater now than in 1940.

Crude petroleum oil from different oilfields is never exactly identical in composition. *Although* all petroleum is composed essentially of a number of hydrocarbons, they are present in varying proportions in each deposit, and the properties of each deposit have to be evaluated. Samples are subjected to a series of tests in the laboratory, the object of which is largely to determine the correct processing methods to be adopted in each case.

Petroleum is not normally used today in the crude state. The mixture of oils of which it is composed must be separated out into a number of products such as petrol, aviation spirit, kerosene, diesel oils and lubricants, all of which have special purposes. The main method of separation used in refineries is fractional distillation, *although* further processing is normally required to produce marketable petroleum products. The different hydrocarbons present in petroleum have different boiling temperatures, and the fractions can therefore be isolated according to their boiling temperatures. Petrol, for instance, is a mixture of the lower-boiling hydrocarbons, with boiling temperatures ranging from 100° to 400° C. Diesel oils on the other hand have boiling temperatures of upwards of 400° C.

Distillation was originally carried out in batch-stills and, *although* this is still done for special purposes, the development of the pipe-still has revolutionised refinery processes, since it allows continuous vaporisation and rectification of the fractions. The pipe-still consists of a brick-lined furnace, in which is fitted a battery of tubes, through which the crude oil is pumped. The oil is heated, and partial vaporisation occurs. The oil then enters the fractionating tower, where it is distilled by coming into contact with condensed vapour which has previously been evolved from the still. Fractions of different boiling ranges are drawn off at different points in the tower, or, in some plants, in a series of towers, each one distilling successively heavier fractions.

The heavier distillates, such as gas oil, undergo various other processes, of which the most important is known as cracking. In this process, they are heated to a temperature of about 550° C, as a result of which the heavier molecules are broken up, lighter oils such as petrol being produced. Catalytic cracking, in which silicon compounds are used as catalysts to aid the process

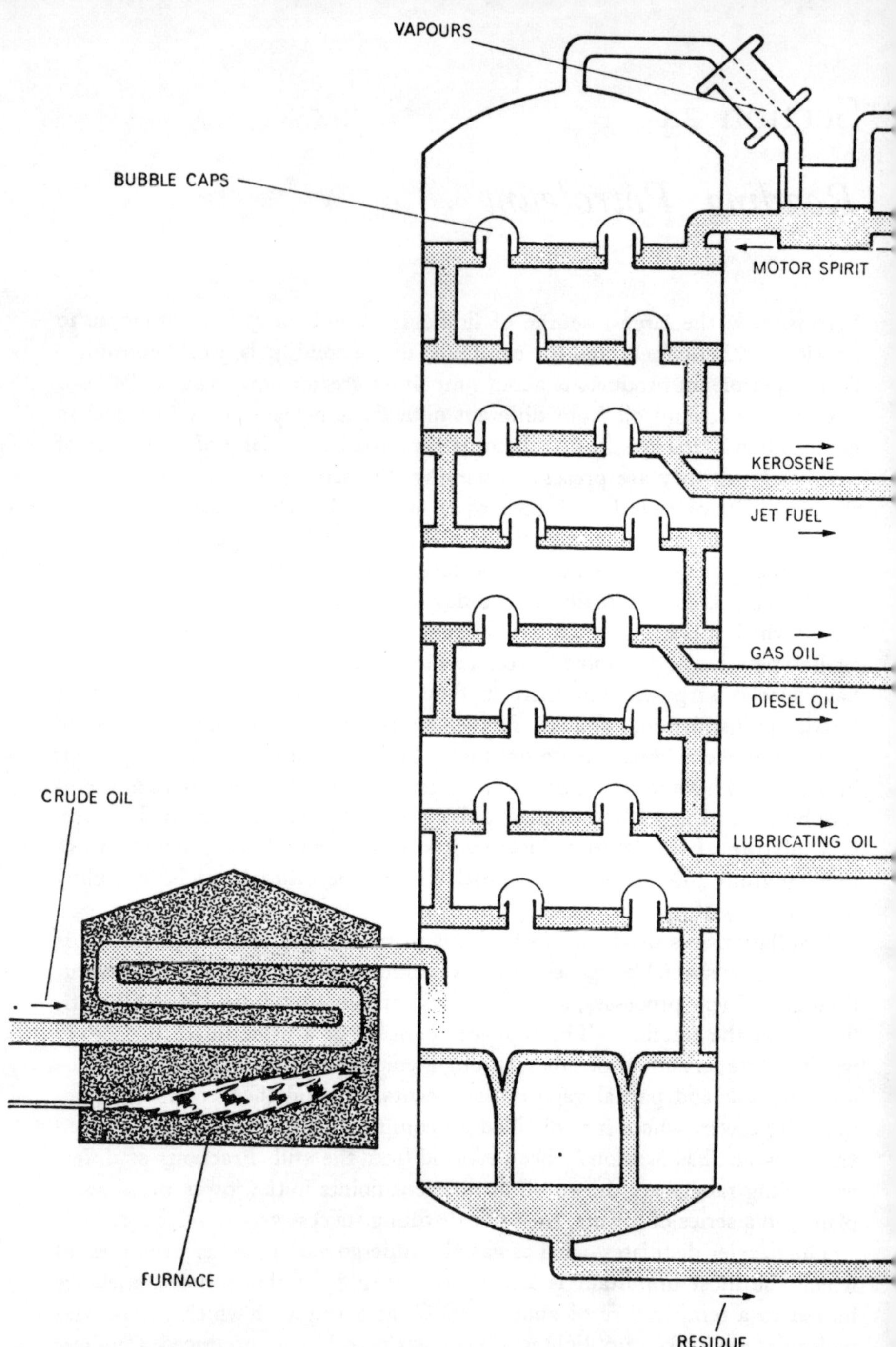

Cross-section of oil distillery

of decomposition, gives higher octane petrols. These are widely used as motor-car fuels, since the high octane value reduces the tendency of the fuel to detonation.

WORD STUDY

Value, Evaluate

The *value* of the property is £500,000. (= worth in money)

These experiments have been of some *value*. (= usefulness)
These experiments have produced some *valuable* data.

The velocity of flow is reduced to a negligible *value*. (= amount, figure)
The calorific *value* of the fuel is determined by experiment.
The temperature does not reach its maximum *value* for some time.
The coefficient of expansion of mercury has a constant *value* at all temperatures.

It is necessary to *evaluate* the results obtained up till now.
The various losses are *evaluated* as a percentage of the total fuel consumption.

Subject, Subjected, Submit, Undergo

1. The tube is immersed in water and is	*subjected to*	rapid heating.
2. Metals tend to creep when they are		stress at high temperatures.
3. Soldering is not suitable for joints		much vibration or heat.
4. The amount of pressure which the material is		affects the finished product.

5. The axial compressor	*is subject to*	some serious disadvantages.
6. This method of working	*suffers from*	certain limitations.

7. Some d.c. machines are	*subject to*	violent fluctuations in load.
8. The walls of the cylinder are	*(liable to)*	cyclical variations in temperature.
9. Compression-ignition engines also are		detonation.

10. The crude oil derived from shale	*is submitted to*	further treatment.
11. The engine	*undergoes*	tests on a test-bed.
12. The heavy distillate		catalytic cracking.

13. Unstable atomic nuclei	*undergo*	a process of decay.
14. Liquid conductors	*suffer*	chemical changes when a current is passed through them.
15. These plans will have to		extensive modification to reduce the cost.

Proceed, Procedure, Process

1. As the expansion of the steam	*proceeds*	its intrinsic energy decreases.
2. If the ignition is not advanced, combustion	*(goes on)*	during the expansion stroke.

3. Research is still *proceeding* on the properties of water and steam.

The *process* of condensation and re-evaporation proceeds throughout the stroke.
The *process* of hammering the steel is more effective than pressing it.
The *process* of fusion involves the supply of additional heat.

The following *procedure* / *technique* should be adopted for testing the machine.

PATTERNS

1. In spite of, Although

Notice these alternative constructions:

a) *But*

It is raining, *but* I am going out for a walk.

b) *Although*

Although it is raining, I am going out for a walk.

c) *In spite of the fact that*

In spite of the fact that it is raining, I am going out for a walk.

d) *In spite of* (or occasionally *despite*)

In spite of the rain, I am going out for a walk.

EXERCISE ONE

Complete these statements:

1. ...... uranium occurs in relatively large quantities, the ores are mostly very low-grade.
2. ...... the widespread occurrence of uranium, the ores are mostly very low-grade.
3. ...... its good performance, the engine is too complicated to be generally adopted.
4. ...... its performance is good, the engine is too complicated to be generally adopted.
5. ...... their small size, locomotive boilers are capable of producing large quantities of steam.
6. ...... they are small, locomotive boilers are capable of producing large quantities of steam.
7. ...... the sand is thoroughly compacted, it still retains a certain amount of air.

8. ...... the thorough compaction of the sand, it still retains a certain amount of air.
9. ...... the good relations which existed between management and labour, there were a few disputes.
10. ...... good relations existed between management and labour, there were a few disputes.

EXERCISE TWO

Complete these statements with *in spite of*, and then alter them for *although* and *in spite of the fact that*.

1. ...... its fairly high resistance, steel wire is sometimes used as a conductor.
2. ...... being superheated, the steam is still slightly wet.
3. ...... the higher capital expenditure involved, the machine may prove more economical in the long run.
4. ...... the basic simplicity of the recovery plant, the radioactivity of the materials makes handling complicated.
5. ...... the allowance made for expansion, stresses were set up in the metal.
6. ...... the remedying of some of the defects by modifications to the engine, it is still not running satisfactorily.
7. ...... the cooling of the gases before they reach the turbine, special heat-resistant metals are still necessary.
8. ...... the widening of the road wherever possible, it is still inadequate for the volume of traffic using it.
9. ...... the expense of multi-stage pumps, they are widely used as they can develop greater heads of liquid.
10. ...... the care which was taken, there were a number of errors in the calculations.

2. Abstract and Generalising Nouns

The scientist and engineer are very largely concerned with phenomena and with processes, and in all technical writing the noun or naming-word has a major function. In particular, you will have noticed the importance of the abstract or generalising word in the scientific style.
Apart from the highly technical terms, there is a large number of abstract words formed from adjectives, verbs or other nouns.
The tables below show some of the more important methods of formation.

NOUN	VERB	ABSTRACT NOUN	EXAMPLES
vapour	vaporise	vaporisation	metal, carbon, oxide, Pasteur,
magnet	magnetise	magnetisation	normal, powder (pulverise),
machine	mechanise	mechanisation	industry.

b) class	classify purify specify putrefy	classification purification specification putrefaction	solid, gas, modify, amplify, rectify, ossify, magnify, liquefy.
c)	moderate propagate insulate	moderation propagation insulation	compensate, generate, operate, oscillate, eliminate, rotate, lubricate, circulate.
d)	combine apply compose	combination application composition	vary, incline, decline, limit, adapt, oppose, propose.
e)	distort connect deposit	distortion connection deposition	insert, adopt, contract, exert, exhaust, subject, project, restrict, extract.
f)	admit convert expand	admission conversion expansion	emit, omit, provide, divide, erode, corrode, compress, depress, include.
g) (Odd formations in *-ion*)	join expel solve	junction expulsion solution	revolve (-ution); dissolve (-ution); absorb (-ption); reduce (-ction); induce (-ction).
h)	move equip achieve	movement equipment achievement	replace, displace, develop, accomplish, attach, arrange.
i)	perform react maintain	performance reactance maintenance	induce (-ctance); continue (-uance); allow, resist, appear.
j)	reverse withdraw dispose	reversal withdrawal disposal	remove (-val); renew; appraise (-sal).
k) waste acre drain		wastage acreage drainage	percent, shrink, mile, leak, ton (-nnage), link, rough, seep.
l) shaft tube gear		shafting (= general) tubing gearing	*pipe, scaffold, panel (-lling), sheet, *plate, *wire, roof, load, *rate, *case, wind. (* lose *e*, as in *tubing*)
m)	forge mill smelt	forging milling smelting	temper, anneal, *machine, heat, drill, survey, *excavate etc. (* lose *e*, as in *forging*)
ADJECTIVE			
n) stable permeable possible		stability permeability possibility	capable, durable, probable, available, machinable, friable, malleable, practicable.
o) porous active humid		porosity activity humidity	viscous, ductile, fragile, grave, mobile, opaque (*opacity*, also *opaqueness*).

EXERCISE

Insert the correct noun form in these statements.

1. The daily (*consume*) of water varies with the season.
2. Nuclear fission results in the (*emit*) of neutrons.
3. The (*extract*) of pure metal from the ore presents some (*complicate*).
4. Transformers are widely used in the (*transmit*) of electrical power.
5. The soil has to undergo (*compact*) before the (*lay*) of the base course.
6. The (*install*) of the new (*equip*) is the (*responsible*) of the manufacturers.
7. The initial (*compress*) of the air is due to a divergent inlet duct.
8. The (*forge*) are machined to size.
9. All the relevant (*inform*) should be detailed in the (*specify*).
10. The maximum temperature of (*operate*) imposes a (*restrict*) on the output.
11. The type of condenser used depends on the (*available*) of ample water in the (*local*).
12. Special (*arrange*) must be made for (*lubricate*) and fuel supply.
13. The (*withdraw*) of the fuel rods is done mechanically.
14. The (*incorporate*) of a number of (*modify*) has brought about an (*improve* in the (*perform*) of the engine.
15. The (*apply*) of a (*volt*) to the grid controls the flow of current.
16. No large (*accumulate*) of scale should be allowed on the boiler tubes.
17. The (*contain*) of radioactive (*emanate*) from the source is imperative.
18. The (*incline*) of the propeller blades is adjustable during flight.
19. The outer (*case*) of the turbine is subjected to fairly low temperatures.
20. One difficulty is the (*susceptible*) of the turbine blades to (*erode*) at high gas velocities.

3. Typical Noun Constructions

The habit of technical writers of using nouns in constructions where we might normally use verbs is illustrated here.

---

a) *Discharge* of the contents of the tank is *effected* / *performed* / *obtained* by a pump.

Note: The normal expression might be: *the contents of the tank are discharged by a pump*. *Discharge* is used as a noun, and a 'neutral' or meaningless verb is substituted.

---

b) The filament is heated by *the application of* a voltage.

Note: The normal expression might be: *the filament is heated by applying a voltage.* The verbal *by applying* is changed to the noun phrase *by the application of.*

---

c) *The testing of* machines by this method entails some loss of power.

Note: This is very economical. The normal expression might be: *if machines are tested by this method, there will be some loss of power*. The 'if-clause' is avoided.

---

d) Considerable lateral pressure is exerted by the concrete *during compaction.*

Note: *During compaction* is usually preferred to *while it is being compacted* (see Section 17 (2)).

EXERCISE ONE

Here are some further examples of the noun constructions. Try to express them in a different way, using verbs instead of nouns.

1. The cooling of the engine is achieved by a thermo-siphoned system.
2. The processing of irradiated uranium must be carried out under extremely radio-active conditions.
3. An increase in the thickness of the lagging will reduce the heat losses.
4. Condensation is reduced by the incorporation of steam jackets round the cylinders.
5. The attainment of hypersonic speeds is now quite common.
6. Transfer of heat from the reactor core is effected by a coolant.
7. Rectification of the current is obtained by means of a commutator.
8. The use of oil in hydraulic systems eliminates problems of corrosion.
9. Compaction of the concrete is done by vibrating machines.
10. An improvement in performance can be achieved by the use of superheated steam.

EXERCISE TWO

Try to change these statements so that a noun is substituted for a verb.

1. If a potential is applied to gas at low pressure, ionisation of the molecules will result.
2. This phenomenon has already been investigated in several laboratories.
3. Supplies to each of the electro-magnets are so timed that each reaches its maximum strength in sequence.
4. Transformers are widely used in transmitting electrical power.
5. These methods will be analysed in a later section of the book.
6. Expansion or contraction of the shaft should be allowed for.
7. The turbine speed is controlled by throttling the steam flow.
8. Efficient burning of the fuel can be assisted by adding certain dopes.
9. If the control is correctly set, the operation will proceed indefinitely without further attention.
10. The temperature can normally be regulated by using a thermo-couple.

Section 25

Reading: Road Foundations

In planning a road, extens*ive* prelimin*ary* surveys must be carried out to determine the precise line of the road, and to work out **how much** earth will require to be moved and **what** quantities of surfac*ing* material will be needed. A second purpose of the surveys will be to take samples of the differ*ent* soils encountered at differ*ent* depths by boring, in order to decide **whether** they are suit*able* for use or **whether** they must be replaced by import*ed* fill. This is of great importance, since vari*ous* types of soil have properties which result in low bear*ing* capacities.

Failures in road surfaces are usually attribut*able* to insuffici*ent* preparation and compaction of the sub-grade – that is, the soil on which the surface of the road is laid. Certain soils, such as clay or peat, are unstable, either because they are largely imperme*able* and hence difficult to drain or because they cannot be properly compacted. It is sometimes poss*ible* to stabilise some soils with cement, but in most cases it will be necess*ary* to excavate the soil to a consider*able* depth and to replace it by a suit*able* granul*ar* soil. The most stable sub-grade soils are gravel or sand, both being readily compact*able* and easy to drain. It is often unnecess*ary* to excavate these soils to a depth of more than three or four inches, and, if suffici*ent* supplies are avail*able* they can be used as fill*ing* material, particularly on embankments, where the soil must be cap*able* of a high degree of compaction.

The stability of a soil is largely depend*ent* on an unchang*ing* moisture-content, and to assist this, adequate drainage is necessary, although in the case of heavy clays no form of drainage is very effect*ive*.

Mechanic*al* excavation is carried out by a variety of machines, including the shovel and drag-line excavator. The choice of plant used will depend on **how** deep a cut is required and also on **how** access*ible* the cut is. After the soil has been excavated to the appropri*ate* depth and filled, it is compacted by a roller until it is firm. Following this, it is common practice to lay a sub-base over the sub-grade soil in order to strengthen it, and to ensure that the traffic load shall be distributed as widely as poss*ible* over the foundations. The sub-base is normally composed of granul*ar* material with good drainage characteristics, and will vary in depth according to the nature of the sub-grade, and also according to **what** thickness of concrete is to be laid above it.

It is essenti*al* that the sub-base should be compacted to a uniform density, since the density of a soil is closely related to its bearing capacity. The com-

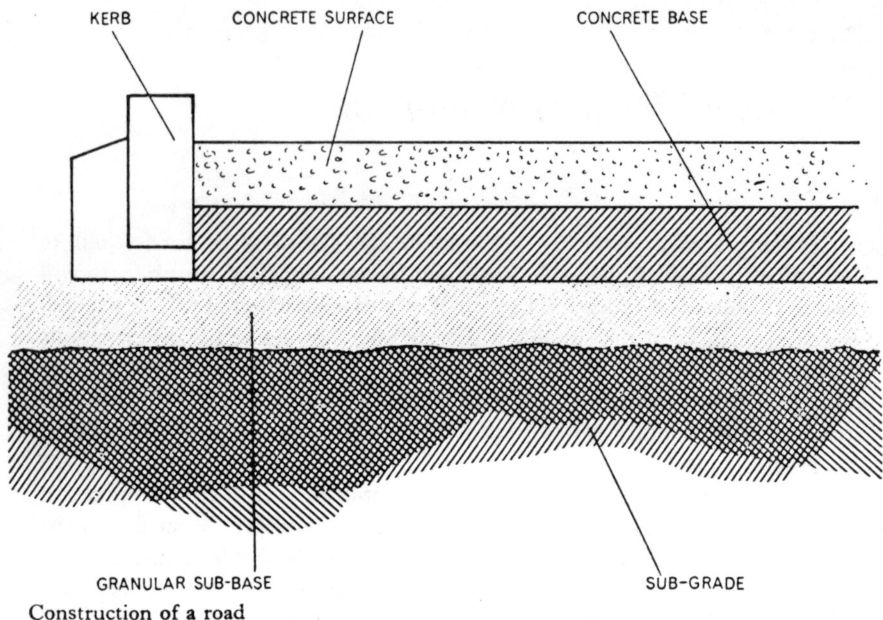

Construction of a road

pact*ed* soil is then covered either with a seal*ing* coat of tar, or with rolls of waterproof paper, the object of which is to prevent liquid cement from the concrete base from seeping into it, thus weakening the lower layers of the concrete and increasing the moisture content of the base.

WORD STUDY

Attribute, Ascribe (= the probable cause)

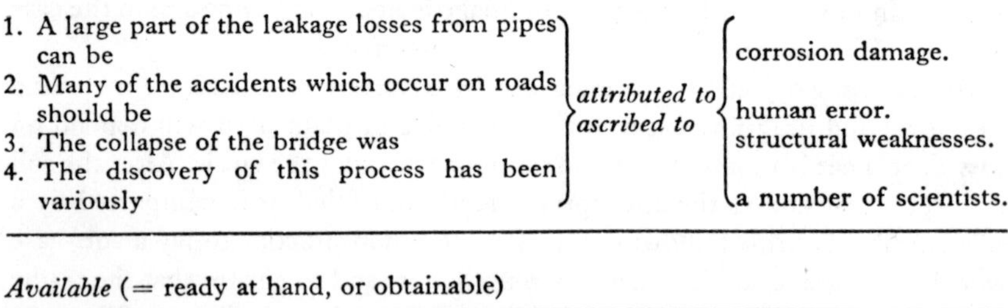

1. A large part of the leakage losses from pipes can be	*attributed to* / *ascribed to*	corrosion damage.
2. Many of the accidents which occur on roads should be		human error.
3. The collapse of the bridge was		structural weaknesses.
4. The discovery of this process has been variously		a number of scientists.

Available (= ready at hand, or obtainable)

1. Large quantities of beryllium will soon be	*available*	for industry.
2. If enough labour is not immediately		, extra workers will be taken on.
3. When sufficient quantities of pure uranium were		the first atomic pile was built.
4. Warm compressed air is therefore		for cabin heating.

Grade (= category); *Graduate*

This uranium ore is too low-*grade* for economic working. (= quality)
The various fuels are *graded* according to their calorific value.

The technical staff is divided into several *grades*. (= level)
The sub-*grade* is the soil layer under the base-course.

The aggregate used for concrete is *graded* according to size. (= size)
The *graded* filter for water contains gravel and sand in carefully selected proportions.

<table>
<tr><td>1. The thermometer is</td><td rowspan="3">graduated
marked</td><td>in degrees Centigrade.</td></tr>
<tr><td>2. The gauge is</td><td>in lb/in² of pressure.</td></tr>
<tr><td>3. The micrometer is</td><td>in hundredths of a millimetre.</td></tr>
</table>

Degree, Extent

The temperature in the furnace was 600 *degrees* Centigrade.

The compass needle moved through an angle of 65 *degrees*.
The tubes are inclined at 45 *degrees* to the horizontal.
The vessel is now in a position 34 *degrees* north of the equator.

A point has three *degrees* of freedom: it can move vertically, horizontally or laterally.

<table>
<tr><td>1. The pressure falls to such a(n)</td><td rowspan="3">degree
extent</td><td>that cavitation may result.</td></tr>
<tr><td>2. The soil is compacted to such a(n)</td><td>that it becomes very stable.</td></tr>
<tr><td>3. These problems can be to some</td><td>overcome by improving the design.</td></tr>
</table>

Bore

The *bore* of an engine cylinder is its internal diameter.

A hole is *bored* into the soil to obtain soil samples. (= a borehole)
Test *borings* are made to discover the character of the soil.

A *bore* is a small tidal wave which comes up a few rivers from the sea.

PATTERNS

1. Introduced Questions

Direct questions with question marks are asked only in speech.
Except in the case of the rhetorical question, which is almost never found in technical writing, written questions are introduced by some word or phrase, and therefore are not really questions at all.
There is no question mark, and there is *no inversion* of the subject and verb.
In technical writing, the introduced question is associated with a very limited number of phrases: here are some examples.

It is necessary to	*examine* *investigate* *estimate* *determine* *discover* *test*	*whether* these results are accurate. *how much* fuel will be consumed.
Information is needed A decision will be taken Research is going on	*as to*	*which* type of fuel is most suitable. *how* the waste can be disposed of.
It is	*doubtful* *not clear* *unknown*	*how* accurate the results are.
The progress of the work will *depend*	*on*	*what* the weather conditions are like. *how* efficient the organisation is.
It is necessary to *decide*	*on*	*which* type of fuel is most suitable. *how* powerful the engine should be.
The type of pump used will vary *according*	*to*	*what* type of liquid is being pumped. *how much* liquid is being pumped.

These statements are usually felt to be rather awkward, and technical writers frequently prefer to avoid them by using noun-statements instead. For example:

It is necessary to examine	the accuracy of these results.
	the quantity of fuel which is consumed.
Information is needed *as to* the most suitable type of fuel.	
The accuracy of these results is doubtful.	
The progress of the work will depend *on* the efficiency of the organisation.	
The type of pump used will vary according *to* the amount of liquid to be pumped.	

EXERCISE

Change these statements, using a noun construction instead of the introduced question.

1. The strength of the concrete pavement largely depends on how well it was compacted after laying.
2. The price of the coal will vary according to how far it has to be transported and how expensive the freight charges are.
3. The delay in production will depend on how extensive the damage to the factory was.
4. The life of a buried pipe will depend on how adequately it can be protected from corrosion.
5. The calorific value of the fuel can be estimated from how much fuel was consumed and what the rise in temperature was.
6. The wetness of the steam largely determines how much condensation will take place in the cylinder.
7. Experts from the company are trying to discover what caused the accident.
8. The thickness of the concrete base will vary according to how stable the sub-grade is and what weight of traffic is likely to pass over it.
9. A firm of consultants was engaged to study how the methods of production could be improved.
10. We can then measure how much air remains in the tube.
11. The efficiency of this turbine would depend on how fast the blades rotate.
12. When construction can begin depends entirely on how soon the surveys of the route are completed.

2. Formation of Adjectives (1)

Apart from the simple adjectives in everyday use, scientists and engineers use a very large number of adjectives which are made up of **verbs** (or verb roots) + a suffix. These adjectives are purely utilitarian, and you will notice that in the three main types (*-able*; *-ed*; *-ing*) they simply take the place of a verbal explanation.
For example:

workable metal = metal *which can be worked.*
worked metal = metal *which has been worked.* (Passive)
working fluid = fluid *which does the work.* (Active)

Here are some of the more important formations.

a) *-able (-ible, -uble)*

This is a very large group; in fact there is no limit to the number of adjectives which can be formed from verbs in this way. Notice that some of the formations are contracted (e.g. *appreciable*); and occasionally the verb form does not exist at all (e.g. *malleable*).

machine	*machinable* steel	*Ex.* fission, recover, service, consider, avoid, govern, accept, suit, (all *-able*); dispense (*-sable*), define (*-nable*), neglect (*negligible*), inflame (*-mmable*), vary (*-iable*), practise (*practicable*), flex- (*ible*).
notice	*noticeable* effect	
control	*controllable* reaction	
handle	*handleable* substance	

b) *-ed*

Practically any verb which can be used in a passive sense can also be used as an adjective by adding *-ed*.

heat	*heated* metal	*Ex.* achieve, obtain, desire, need, filter, machine, *control, expect, *expel, exhaust, refine, immerse, compress, expand, ignite, cool. *(*-lled*)
corrode	*corroded* iron	
extend	*extended* use	
emit	*emitted* rays	

c) *-ing*

compensate	*compensating* jet	*Ex.* communicate, circulate, emanate, change, adjust, vary, rotate, cool, divide, enter, emerge, sustain, burn, lubricate. (Final *e* lost before *-ing*)
conduct	*conducting* medium	
corrode	*corroding* acid	
differ	*differing* amount	

d) *-ive*

This is another very common ending, usually added to a verb-form.

effect	*effective* remedy	*Ex.* conduct, instruct, conclude (*-sive*), connect, impel (*impulsive*), attract, compare (*-ative*). (defect, intense (*-sive*), excess, sense (*-sitive*))
react	*reactive* force	
expand	*expansive* working	
relate	*relative* motion	

e) *-ent* (*-ant*)

converge	*convergent* duct	*Ex.* diverge, consist, resist (*-ant*), prevail (*prevalent*), depend, emerge, differ.
absorb	*absorbent* material	
attend	*attendant* friction	
suffice	*sufficient* power	

EXERCISE

Form the correct adjective by completing the words between brackets.

1. The (*unsuit*) (*excavate*) soil is removed and replaced by a more (*compact*) material.
2. When suspensions of (*abrade*) solids have to be pumped, it is (*advise*) not to use a (*reciprocate*) pump.
3. Now (*combine*) (*mix*) and (*distribute*) plant is (*avail*) for road construction.
4. The (*lump*) bridge is (*adjust*) so as to give the (*desire*) camber to the road.
5. Newly-(*construct*) roads must be made wide enough to satisfy all (*foresee*) traffic requirements.
6. The (*permit*) limits of size for these (*machine*) articles are clearly stated in the (*accompany*) specification.
7. Heat-(*resist*) alloys are required to withstand the (*exceed*) temperatures produced by the burning of the (*combust-*)mixture.
8. (*Extend*) flaps are fitted to the (*trail*) edge of the wing to increase its (*effect*) area, and so make the aircraft more (*control*) at low speeds.
9. Each (*succeed*) stage of the pump receives the water at a greater pressure than the (*precede*) one.
10. The (*expel*) gases provide the (*require*) (*propel*) force to drive the aircraft through the (*surround*) air.

3. Formation of Adjectives (2)

Here are some of the typical adjective formations which are not based on **verbs.** They may be derived from **nouns,** but very often they are added to the roots of Latin or Greek words, which either do not exist in English or exist in a different form. For example:

plast-	*plastic*	(plasticity)
kines-	*kinetic*	(kinesis)
sol-	*solar*	(sun)
fin-	*final*	(end)

a) *-al*

essence	*essential*	*Ex:* detrimental, fundamental, substantial, marginal, axial, radial, horizontal, vertical, experimental, potential, symmetrical, thermal, seasonal.
structure	*structural*	
crisis	*critical*	

b) *-ar*

lamina	*laminar*	*Ex:* popular, polar, solar, nuclear, annular, tubular, circular, cellular, granular.
angle	*angular*	
line	*linear*	

c) *-ic*

	elastic	*Ex:* static, kinetic, automatic, concentric, intrinsic, synthetic, electric, electrolytic, specific, calorific.
	hydraulic	
	sonic	

d) *-ous*

	viscous	*Ex:* fibrous, pervious, calceous, nervous, ambiguous, synonymous, synchronous, analogous, aqueous, gaseous.
resin	*resinous*	
pore	*porous*	

Note: Adjectives used *before* a noun or *at the end of a statement* require no preposition: e.g. the *available* money; the money is *available*.
But in this type of statement, a linking-word is necessary:

The road is *accessible* **to** traffic.
This machine is *identical* **with** the other one.
This substance is *soluble* **in** water.

Other examples are: acceptable *to*, analogous *to*, capable *of*, consistent *with*, compatible *with*, apt *to*, defective *in*, impervious *to*, conditional *on*, inherent *in*, limited *to*, detrimental *to*, responsible *for*, subject *to*, susceptible *to*, available *for*, consequent *upon*, similar *to*, etc.

EXERCISE

Complete these statements with the correct prepositions.

1. These figures are not consistent (......) the results obtained in previous experiments.
2. The motor is designed to run at constant speed, irrespective (......) the load.
3. The metallic sleeves are liable (......) corrosion if they are made of cast-iron.
4. This type of soil is especially susceptible (......) frost damage.
5. Large frictional losses are incompatible (......) high engine efficiency.
6. The volume of the gas will then be directly proportional (......) its absolute temperature.
7. Each operator is responsible (......) the proper maintenance of his machine.

8. Vibration of the work-piece is detrimental (...... the cutting tool.
9. The boiler drum is rather small relative (......) the weight of steam required.
10. The defects inherent (......) this type of machine make it of limited usefulness.

Section 26

Reading: Rigid Pavements

When a vehicle passes over a road, its weight is transmitted through the wheels on to the pavement beneath it. The function of the rigid pavement, as opposed to the flexible tarred pavement, is to distribute the dynamic stresses, and any additional stresses which may be *super*imposed on them through the sub-grade. The maximum stresses occur at the corners and edges of the concrete slabs, and they are therefore sometimes thickened to *counter*act this. The thickness of the concrete base varies considerably, according to the nature of the sub-grade and the anticipated traffic density, being sometimes as much as 14 inches on motorways. On such major roads, where the total width greatly exceeds 15 feet, it is *im*practicable to lay the concrete in a single slab, and the slabs are normally laid in strips with *inter*locking joints.

The cement for the concrete is mixed with fine aggregate, or sand, and coarse aggregate, which may be gravel or crushed stones accurately graded in one or more sizes. The mix varies in its proportions, a 1 : 2 : 4 mix being fairly common, although in some cases a lean concrete (one part of cement to about 10 or 14 parts of aggregate may be used in accordance with the specifications. The mixing is carried out in a batching plant, and water is added to make the cement workable.

Concrete is laid between steel forms, the purpose of the formwork being to retain the concrete in place until it has hardened. The forms may also act as rails on which the vibrating plant can be moved along the roadway. Pavements which are more than seven or eight inches thick are best laid in layers to *en*sure adequate compaction. Where *re*inforcement is used, it is most conveniently placed between the layers. It is now common practice to *re*inforce pavements with steel mesh or with rods. This ensures that any cracking which does occur will be prevented from opening out. The steel is subject to corrosion, and it is normally specified that it should be covered by at least two inches of concrete.

The length of each slab is governed by the need to provide expansion joints, and this will depend partly on the season in which the concrete was laid and partly on the thickness of it. Expansion joints may be **spaced** at regular **intervals** of up to 200 feet, and may require a **gap** of as much as $\frac{3}{4}$ inch between slabs. Since these joints must be watertight to prevent rainwater from draining down into the *sub*-grade, they are filled with some resilient material such as cork, and sealed with a sealing compound. Any tendency of the slab

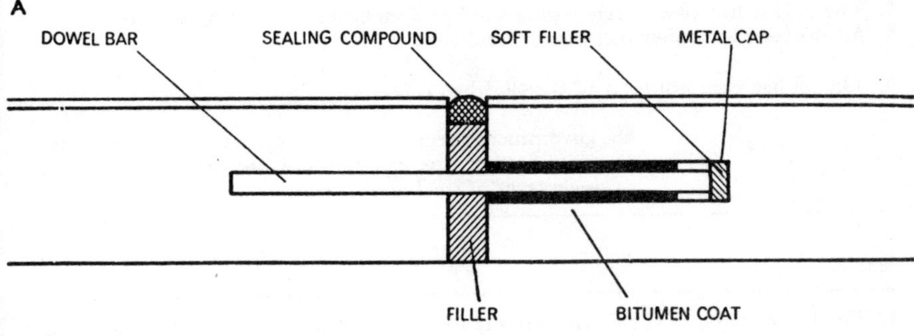

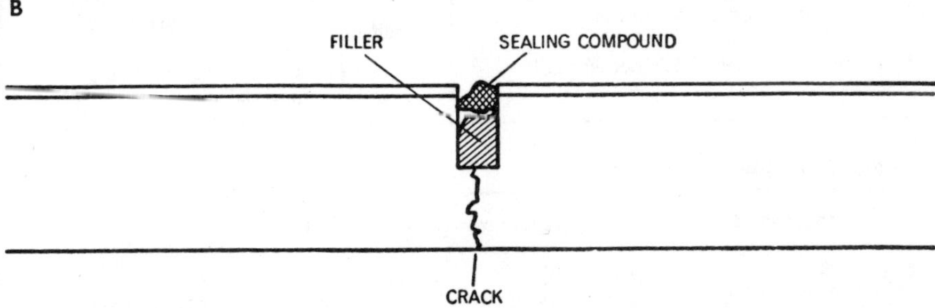

(A) Expansion joint
(B) Contraction joint

to warp or move relative to the next slab is resisted by the use of dowel-bars *em*bedded in the slabs, or by grooving the joints. Contraction joints are perhaps even more important, and aim to control the effects of contraction of the concrete by providing planes of weakness at certain regular **intervals** along the pavement.

Once the surface has been laid, it is compacted by tamping, or by some form of vibrator, and then it is cured. The object of curing is to prevent the concrete from drying out too quickly, and this is achieved by covering the wet concrete with waterproof paper or polythene, or alternatively by spraying on a liquid resin which insulates it from the air.

WORD STUDY

Agree, Accord, Conform, Comply, Consistent

1. The experimental results *agree with* / *accord with* the theoretical calculations.

2. The actual production figures
3. The company's present plans

{ *are in agreement with* / *are in accord with* / *are in conformity with* / *are consistent with* }

{ the estimated figures. / its normal policy. }

4. The engine has given a *consistently* good performance. (= always the same)
5. All the tests have shown *consistent* results.

6. The oil has the *consistency* of treacle when it is cold.

In *accordance* / *compliance* with
- the government's regulations, a fire system has been installed.
- the specification, the concrete has been reinforced with a single layer of steel mesh.

Embed

---

1. The hot junction of the thermo-couple is *embedded* in the metal whose temperature is being measured.
2. One end of the dowel-bar is *embedded* in the end of one slab of concrete.
3. Conducting material is occasionally *embedded* in a matrix of insulating material.

Aggregate (= put together)

---

1. Add together 1, 3, 4, 6: the *aggregate* or *total* or *sum* is 14.

2. *a.* A fine *aggregate* is a quantity of sand graded according to size.
   b. Coarse *aggregate* is a quantity of gravel or stones graded according to size.
   c. The *aggregate* is mixed with cement and water to make concrete.

Course

---

1. He took a *course* in engineering at the University.

2. During the *course* of
   - his studies, he fell ill.
   - construction, at least thirty workmen were killed.

3. The dried-up river *course* can be seen from the air.

4. A *course* of bricks is one layer of bricks in a wall, e.g. a damp-*course*.
5. The base-*course* of a road is the compacted layer under the wearing *course*.

Compact (v and a)

The transistor radio is *compact* enough to fit into one's pocket. (small)
The machine is very *compact* in design, and has no large projection.

The soil is *compacted* to eliminate most of the air voids in it. (pressed)
Compaction of the soil may be carried out with heavy rollers.

A water *seal* is kept in the U-bend of a pipe to prevent back-flow of gas.
Piston rings act as *seals* to prevent combustion gases from entering the crankcase.
Bituminous *seals* are placed on the joints between concrete slabs to prevent the ingress of water.
Mines are *sealed off* with concrete to prevent the spread of fire or flooding.

PATTERNS

1. Some Prefixes

A very large proportion of English words, especially those used in technical writing, came into the language from Greek or Latin or French. We can often learn something of their meaning if we know the meaning of the Latin or Greek or French *prefix*, particularly in the case of verbs. For example:

*ex*pel = push *out*
*circum*vent = go *around*
*in*spire = breathe *in*

But very often the meanings have changed so much that a knowledge of the origin of the word does not help much. In any case, we usually have to learn the word as a *word* in English, because the prefix is not detachable.
But there are also a number of prefixes, which are on the whole detachable, and whose meaning is fairly clear. Some apply mostly to verbs, and others to adjectives or nouns. Here are some of them.

en-, *em-* (forming a verb from a noun or adjective)

Ex: ensure, enrich, enlarge, enable, encrust, entrain, engrain, enclose, encase, encapsule, embody, embrittle, embed, empower, enforce, embank.

inter- (= between or among)

Ex: interlock, interweave, intersperse interconnect, interact, interheat, interlace, interrupt, intercept.
(Nouns: interval, intersection,
Adj: intermediate, intermittent etc.

re- (= again)

Ex: re-use, re-heat, re-circulate, re-charge, re-load, re-soil, re-group, re-align, re-work, re-assemble, re-apply, (reinforce, regenerate, renew, replenish etc.).

counter- (= against, opposite to)

Ex: counteract, counterbalance, countersink, counterweigh.
(Nouns: countershaft, counterpoise, counterweight etc.).

over- (= too much)

Ex: overcharge, overheat, overload, overwind, overstrain, overwork.

over- (= above)

Ex: overhead, overtone, overhaul, overall.

under- (= too little)

Ex: underload, underpay, undersize, underrate, undercompensate.

under- (= below)

Ex: underpin, undercut, undercarriage, underlie, undergrowth.

dis- (= the opposite)

Ex: disconnect, discharge, disjoin, disinfect, disregard, disintegrate, disclose, dissociate, dissolve.

de- (= cause not to be)

Ex: demagnetise, degauss, de-hydrate, de-freeze; decarbonise, de-humidify.

im-, *in-*, *ir-* (= not)

Ex: immature, immiscible, impervious, impure, immoderate, inanimate, incompatible, inactive, inelastic, ineffective, irrespective, irrational, irresponsible.

un- (= not)

Ex: unnecessary, unavailable, unstable, uncontaminated, unspecified, unknown, unlimited, unsaturated.

super- (= above, more than)

Ex: superheat, supercharge, superphosphate, superstructure, superficial, supersonic, supersaturated, superimpose, superpose.

sub- (= beneath, less than)

Ex: substructure, submarine, subsoil, sub-grade, sub-base, sub-surface, substratum, sub-standard.

EXERCISE

Give the opposite of these words by adding the correct prefix, and try to use them in statements.

reversible	controllable	probable	convenient
similar	soluble	variable	economic
permeable	efficient	fertile	distinguishable
available	proportionate	consistent	correct
definable	attainable	limited	compressible.

2. Complex Sentences

You have noticed that in the typical technical sentence there may be a large number of parts, which we call phrases or clauses. The following groups will give some practice in joining the parts together to form a single complex sentence which is long but clear. Remember that there are three particularly common and useful ways of adding parts to a statement:

a) An introductory clause or phrase, before the main part of the statement begins. The sentence is obviously planned in advance.

b) A relative clause, very often with a preposition in front of the word *which*. The word *that* is uncommon, largely because we cannot put a preposition before it.

c) A final clause, which adds more information to the statement which has been made. It is introduced by the *-ing* form of the verb.

EXERCISE

Link each group of facts into one complex sentence with the most appropriate linking word, making any changes that may be necessary.

1. It is not always necessary to reinforce a concrete slab.
   Many major roads employ reinforced concrete.
   Tests show that the reinforcement helps to control cracks.
   The road is thus likely to have a longer life.
2. The nucleus is positively charged.
   The electrons revolve in orbits around the nucleus.
   The electrons are negatively charged.
3. Squirrel-cage motors are frequently used to power cranes.
   A large starting torque is more important for cranes than efficiency.
   The load is not normally continuous.
4. Water is sprayed into the cylinder.
   The steam has been exhausted from the turbine into the cylinder.
   There is a rapid drop in temperature.
   This results in condensation of the vapour.
   The condensation produces a partial vacuum in the cylinder.
5. The concrete is laid.
   Steel formwork is securely fixed in position.
   The function of the formwork is to keep the concrete from spreading.
   The compaction of the concrete takes place.

3. Intervals

a) *In space*

A shaft is supported by bearings *spaced at intervals* along it.
The expansion joints of a concrete road are *spaced at regular intervals* of perhaps 200 feet.
The fuel rods are inserted in the moderator *at intervals*.
The crankshaft of an engine rotates through 360°, and each of the pistons imparts its torque at equal *angular intervals* of say 90°.

A *gap* is left between consecutive rails of a railway to allow for expansion.
There may be a *gap* of $\frac{3}{4}$ inch between the slabs of concrete on a road.
The current sparks across the *gap* between the electrodes of a spark-plug.

A *clearance* space is left between the piston and the cylinder head.
This *clearance* volume is made as small as possible to assist combustion.
The *clearance* ratio is the ratio of the *clearance* volume to the swept volume.
There is a certain *clearance* between the blade-tips and the casing of a turbine, through which steam is liable to leak.
The train passing through the tunnel has a *clearance* of only one foot on either side.

---

b) *In time*

The lighthouse flashes its signal at *intervals* of five seconds. There is one signal *every five seconds.*
The temperature of the water is read *every two minutes*. It is read at *two-minute intervals.*

Combustion of an inflammable mixture is not *instantaneous*. There is a short *interval* between initiation and completion of combustion.
A certain amount of time *elapses* or *passes* between the passing of the spark and the expansion of the gases.

This *delay* is known as the *time lag.*
The current in an inductive circuit *lags* 90° *behind* the voltage applied.

The compression in the cylinders of an engine must be checked *from time to time*. It must be checked *periodically.*
Some power plants are designed to run *continuously,* without stopping. Other plants are designed for *intermittent* use, frequently starting and stopping.

Note: *lag* has a second meaning:

> Steam pipes are *lagged,* or covered with *lagging* of asbestos, etc., to keep the heat in.

Section 27

Reading: Piles for Foundations

When the foundations of a building have to be carried to a considerable depth to provide adequate support for it and to ensure that no undue settlement will occur, it is normal practice to use piles of concrete or steel. Piled foundations are particularly applicable to structures which are to be built over water or on mud, such as wharves and jetties, but also to large concrete structures which impose a very heavy load on their foundations, thereby rendering them liable to total or differential settlement. The carrying capacity of the piles may be due to the frictional resistance of the ground against the sides of the piles, in cases where the strength of the ground does not materially increase with depth; or to the strong bearing layer to which the point of the piles reach, in which case they transmit the load from the soft strata above to the bearing stratum.

The majority of piles are installed by being driven into the ground and displacing the soil through which they pass. Certain soils, however, are difficult to displace by this method, clay being one example, and for this and other reasons an alternative method is adopted, in which the soil is cored out and the hole is then filled with compacted concrete. Such piles are known as *in situ* piles, since they are actually cast in the position in which they are required.

In the case of driven piles, a mechanical pile-driver is required, to hold the pile firmly while it is being driven into the ground by blows from a hammer moving up and down the frame. The frame in some machines can be adjusted so that the pile is driven either vertically downwards or at the required rake. The amount of penetration with each blow will vary with the force of the impact and the resistance of the ground. The piles are liable to be damaged by the repeated blows of a hammer which may weigh as much as eight tons, and the heads must therefore be protected by a helmet of cast steel, packed with hardwood or some similar material.

Steel piles, commonly in the form of H-beams, have a greater strength-weight ratio than concrete piles, and are capable of being driven through hard material with less risk of damage. Extra lengths may be butt-welded on to the driven sections to increase their length. Where concrete piles are used, they are pre-cast except for those cast *in situ*, and this involves difficult handling and transportation problems, since they are very heavy and may be as much as 100 feet in length. Partly for this reason, driven concrete piles usually require reinforcement, whereas for the *in situ* piles this is not normally essential, as

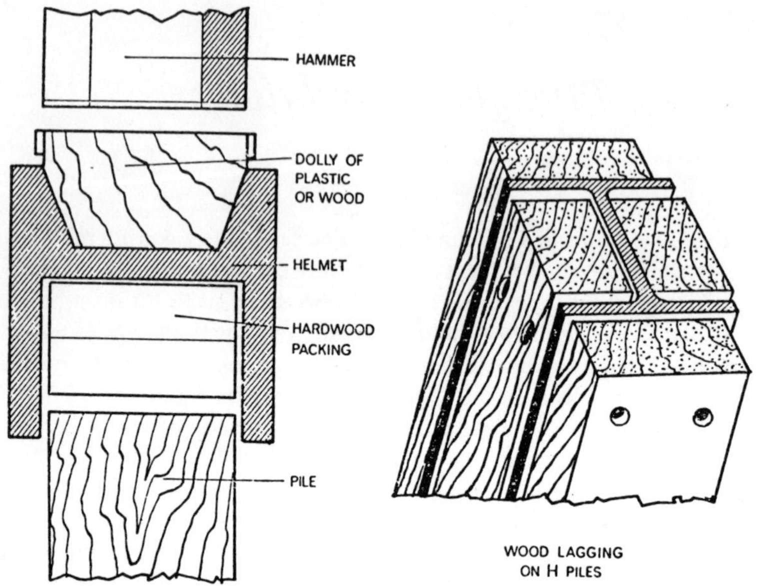

WOOD LAGGING ON H PILES

Pile-driver with hammer

they are subject to no handling stresses and are not hammered into the ground. When the pile has been driven to the required depth, the reinforcement bars must be exposed at the top by breaking out the concrete, and they are then tied in to the rest of the foundations.

WORD STUDY

Expose

1. When the plate of the light-meter is	*exposed*	to light, electrons are emitted.
2. The vegetable matter of the tree is		to the air, and begins to decay.
3. Workers in nuclear power plants must not be		to excessive doses of radiation.
4. The mild steel core of the bar is		when the hardened case is machined off.
5. The total cooling surface which is		to the air is increased by the use of fins.
6. As a result of the neglect of all safety rules, the workers were		to considerable danger.

Bear, Bearing

1. These results *bear out* the theory put forward by Smith. (= support, agree)

2. *a*. The rotating shaft *bears on* a thrust block. (= pushes against)
   b. The two pieces of metal *bear on* each other.

3. *a.* The shaft is carried on *bearings* spaced at regular intervals.
   b. The use of roller *bearings* reduces the amount of friction.

4. *a.* The *bearing* capacity of the pile is about 25 tons. (= carrying)
   b. The *bearing* stratum of rock lies at a depth of 50 feet.

5. *a.* The aircraft is flying on a *bearing* of 270°.
   b. The lighthouse *bears* 10° to port of the ship.

Pile

The atomic reactor is also called the atomic *pile*. The *pile* building is the building in which the reactor is housed.

Concrete *piles* are driven into the ground to support the bridge.
A great deal of *piling* will be necessary on this peaty soil.

The threads or fibres which stand out of a carpet or piece of cloth are called the *pile* of the carpet or cloth.

Rake

The concrete pile is driven in at a *rake* of 1 in 2. It is driven in at a certain angle to the vertical.
Raking piles are often used for jetties and light bridges.
The top edge of a cutting tool is *raked* back at a certain angle so that it clears the work piece which is being cut.

The coal in the furnace has to be *raked* at intervals to clear away the ash.

Displace

An object immersed in water *displaces* a weight of water equal to its own weight.
The movement of the piston down the cylinder *displaces* a certain amount of steam at each stroke.

PATTERNS

1. That, Those

Look at these statements.

The first task was *that of* surveying the route.
Roads built here are narrower than *those* built in Germany.

The words *that* and *those* are used instead of repeating the words *the task* and *roads*. This structure is very common in writing, but not very common in speech. When we are speaking we often shorten the statement by leaving out the repeated subject altogether.

Roads built here are narrower than in Germany.

This is not always accurate or clear, and technical writers usually avoid the shortening by using *that* or *those*.

EXERCISE

Here are some statements which involve a repeated subject. Read them through and then change them to the pattern shown above.

1. The most difficult problem was the problem of controlling the chain reaction.
2. The most suitable types of soil are the soils which can be easily drained and which are also easily compacted.
3. The resistance of a metallic conductor is usually less than the resistance of an electrolyte.
4. The heat removal capacity of liquid metal coolants is less than the heat removal capacity of water.
5. The capacities of a.c. machines are not limited, as the capacities of d.c. machines are.
6. Cylinders should never be charged with a gas other than the gas for which they were intended.
7. Breeder reactors are reactors which produce more fissile material than they consume.
8. Specific gravity is defined as the ratio of the density of a substance to the density of water.

2. Phrasal Verbs

Colloquial English uses a very large number of **verb + adverb** units which we call Phrasal Verbs (e.g. *look + over*; *throw + out* etc.). Some have a literal meaning, some a metaphorical meaning, and some have both meanings.
Many of these tend to be used also when *speaking* about technical things, but when *writing* about technical things, engineers and scientists often prefer a more formal verb, either for dignity or for precision.
There is generally no need for a following adverb, because the formal verb includes the adverbial idea in its prefix (e.g. *ab-*, *ap-*, *circ-*, *com-*, *cor-*, *de-*, *ex-*, *ob-*, *per-*, *pro-*, *re-*, *sus-*, *trans-*, etc.).

EXERCISE

Read the following statements as they stand, and then find more formal verbs in place of the phrasal verbs which are in *italics*.

1. Hand compaction of the concrete may be *carried out* by wooden tampers with handles at either end.
2. A number of tests have been *thought out* to *find out* the moisture content of the soil.
3. The magnetic field appears to *go round and round.*
4. A heated body *gives off* energy in the form of electro-magnetic waves.
5. These windings on the generator *make up* for the flux distortions in the main field.

6. During radioactive decay, alpha or beta particles are *thrown out of* the isotope.
7. The control rods are *taken out of* the reactor core by remote control.
8. A hovercraft is *held up* by a cushion of air *squirted out* of nozzles underneath it.
9. Air may be *dragged along* by the moving fluid and cause an air-lock in the pipes.
10. The furnace *eats up* fuel at the rate of three tons per hour.
11. The governor may *swing to and fro* if it is too sensitive.
12. The soil must be *dug out* down to the level of hard rock.
13. It is not possible to *tell in advance* what the results of the experiment will be.
14. The petrol/air mixture is *sucked into* the cylinder by the piston.
15. The condensate is *carried along* in pipes back to the boiler.
16. Much of this heat can be *got back*, instead of being allowed to go to waste.
17. After inspection, the plugs were *put back in their places*.
18. The company *set up* a new factory in the industrial area.
19. The speed should not be allowed to *go beyond* the rated limits.
20. The nylon thread is *pushed out* through a number of holes in a special machine.
21. A certain amount of vapour is *given off* from the hot metal.
22. A secondary winding is *put on top of* the primary winding in the armature.
23. The balloon is *blown up* with hydrogen from these cylinders.
24. The concrete is *carried across* from the mixing plant to the site in lorries.
25. The heat of combustion is *kept in* by the use of firebrick linings.

3. Phrasal Verbs (cont.)

Here are some examples of phrasal verbs which are commonly used both in speech and in writing. There is in most of these cases no formal verb which can readily be substituted.

---

1. In this chapter we shall *deal with* different fuel oils.
2. The terminal voltage *falls off* as the load increases.
3. The current in the conductor *sets up* a magnetic field.
4. The fire in the engine *sets off* a series of explosions.
5. The fly-wheel *gives up* some of its stored kinetic energy.
6. Sulphuretted hydrogen *gives off* a peculiar smell.
7. The motor is quickly *run up* to normal speed.
8. When this type of battery *runs down*, it cannot be re-charged.
9. The aircraft will *run out of* fuel in another hour.
10. The stretch on the belt must be *taken up* or it will slip.
11. He *took over* the management of the factory on his father's death.
12. The aircraft will *take off* at ten o'clock.
13. The ship will stop at Cherbourg to *take on* passengers and mail.
14. A film of oil is put between the metal surfaces, so that they do not *bear on* each other.

15. The supply to the motor is suddenly *cut off*.
16. The insulation is *cut back* to expose the wire conductor.
17. The boiler has to be *shut down* for inspection and repair.
18. The metal bar is *cut down* to the right size.
19. The metal is allowed to *cool off* slowly.
20. This line of enquiry is promising and should be *followed up*.
21. If the engine is allowed to run without oil it will *seize up*.
22. The rain-water is *run off* by means of ditches at the side of the road.
23. The building was *jacked up* with powerful hydraulic jacks.
24. The waterproof paper is *spread out* on the compacted base of the road.
25. The excess steam is *blown off* through the valve.
26. The temperature is *kept down* by providing a large cooling surface.
27. The gases are *forced out* through the exhaust valve.
28. The crew *cast off* the ship's mooring lines as it leaves the dock.
29. The two ends of the tunnel *link up* in the middle.
30. The rivet-holes are *opened out* to the correct size with a drill.
31. The weld should be *smoothed up* after it has been made.
32. The tool is *fed in* until it just touches the work-piece.

Section 28

Reading: Suspension Bridges

Suspension bridges are frequently constructed in preference to other types of bridge, especially where relatively light traffic has to be carried over long spans, since they are more economical in material and are extremely strong. There are in existence suspension bridges with main spans of more than 3000 feet, the entire weight of the deck being supported from above by cables (usually only two or four in number) suspended between two towers at either side of the river.

The cables are composed of thousands of wires, made of high-tensile steel, which are galvanised to resist corrosion. Two or three hundred of these wires, each of about 0·19 inch in diameter, are clamped together *to form* a single strand, and the whole cable may consist of a considerable number of such strands compacted and bound together with wire. In constructing the cable, two distinct methods may be adopted. The wires may either be twisted into strands, the strands then sometimes being twisted round a central strand *to form* the completed cable, or they may be spun parallel to each other, and clamped together at intervals. This latter method obviously involves a much longer spinning operation, since each wire or small group of wires must be spun and adjusted to the correct sag individually, whereas the strands of twisted wire can be erected as units, provided that they are not so heavy as to be unmanageable. However, on bridges with very long spans, there are certain advantages in the parallel wire method of spinning the cable.

The cables are normally made continuous through the tops of the towers, down through side towers, where these exist, and thence into the anchorage. They bear on specially constructed saddles on the towers, which are shaped to accommodate them, the saddles being either fixed so that the cables may slide over them, or mounted on rollers so that they move with any movement of the cables. In view of the enormous pull exerted by the heavy cables, their ends must be secured in firm anchorages, and unless they can be embedded in sound natural rock, constructions of masonry or concrete must be provided strong enough to withstand the severe pressures put upon them. The cable strands are normally looped round strand-shoes, which are in turn connected by chains to an anchor-plate embedded in the base of the anchorage.

At intervals along the main span, cast-steel cable-bands are attached to the cables, gripping them firmly and excluding moisture from them, and from these bands suspenders of wire-rope or chains hang down. Since these sus-

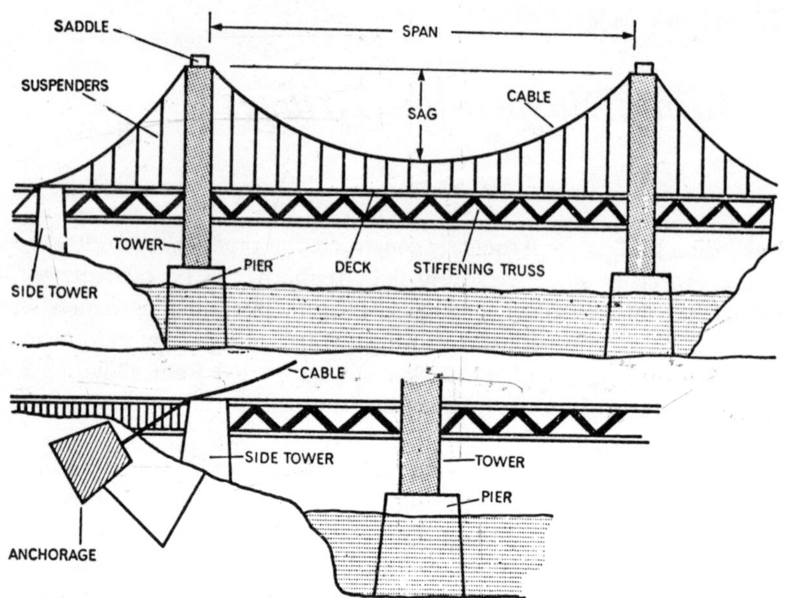

Suspension bridge and anchorage

penders have to take the weight of the deck to which they are attached, they must have a high tensile strength. One advantage of using the braced-chain suspenders is that they largely dispense with the need for a system of stiffening, being themselves rigid. This stiffening is necessary to resist deformations of the deck of the bridge due to moving traffic loads and also to resist lateral pressures from wind. In the case of wire-rope suspenders, the stiffening must be provided by trusses constructed at the level of the deck, the depth of the truss varying with the length of the span.

WORD STUDY

Load

1. This truck carries a maximum *load* of five tons.
   The un*laden* weight of the truck is eight tons.
   The goods are *loaded* into the truck by a fork-lift.
   The tools are *loaded* into the automatic lathe by hand.
   The *loading* of the automatic lathe is carried out manually.

2. This aircraft carries a very large pay-*load* for its size.
   The bridge cables carry the *dead load* of the deck and suspenders, plus the *live load* of the traffic moving over the deck.
   The wire undergoes a *breaking load* test to determine its ultimate tensile strength.

3. The turbine runs at constant speed under steady *load.*
   The machines should be tested under normal *load* conditions.
   Cranes and hoists carry only an intermittent *load.*
   Electricity generating plant is designed to run at continuous *load.*
   The *load* is the amount of work which is performed by an engine or motor.

Adjust (= make slight alterations)

The amount of sag in each wire is *adjusted* with the aid of a guide rope.
The brush pressure on the commutator can be *adjusted* by *adjusting* the springs on the brushes.
The loading on the governor spring is *adjustable* with nuts.

Modify (= make important alterations)

It should be possible to *modify* the ordinary cathode-ray tube to take colour transmissions.
The engine can be *modified* to burn gas instead of petrol.
The normal process of decomposition is *modified* when the air supply is limited.
A number of *modifications* have been incorporated in the new model.

Transform (= completely alter)

Electrical power is *transformed* into mechanical power in the motor.
Reactors can be used to *transform* fertile material into fissionable material.
The *transformer* is used to step up or down the voltage applied to it.

Adapt (= alter for a different purpose)

All living creatures have to *adapt* themselves to their environment.
The aircraft has been *adapted* to carry passengers instead of cargo.
This motor has been *adapted* to work on a different voltage.
An *adapter* has been fitted to enable the device to work with any type of plug.

PATTERNS

1. Infinitive of Result

This is a peculiar construction of only limited use. The *to + infinitive* is used to indicate the result of the action previously stated, and is used with only a few verbs, of which the commonest are *form* and *produce.*

The wires are bound together *to form* a single strand.

The idea here is one of *result* rather than *purpose.* '. . . with the result that a single strand is formed'.

EXERCISE

Link these statements in the same way.

1. The anions unite with the copper of the plate. New copper sulphate is produced.
2. Hydrogen and oxygen combine chemically. They form the molecule H_2O.
3. The unstable isotopes undergo radioactive decay. Other isotopes are formed as a result.
4. The sand and gravel are mixed in suitable proportions. This makes a satisfactory aggregate.
5. The three companies have decided to merge. This will result in a very powerful industrial group being formed.
6. The wax former is melted out. This leaves the hollow electro-formed component.
7. Another ten feet of concrete was added to the wall. This made a total thickness of 25 feet.
8. Two thousand more workers were taken on. This gave a total labour force of 8000 at the height of the operation.
9. A number of piles are driven into the ground. They form a solid foundation for the piers.
10. The cable is suspended between the towers of the bridge. A parabolic curve is formed.
11. Air is ejected through nozzles underneath the hovercraft. A cushion of air is produced on which the craft rides.
12. The lengths of rail are welded together. A continuous rail is thus formed.

2. Phrasal Verbs (cont.)

Here are some further examples of the *phrasal verbs* frequently used in colloquial speech.
There are of course many hundreds of these *Verb + Adverb* constructions in English. But the ones which are illustrated here have a *formal verb* equivalent, which is commonly used in technical and scientific writing. They are an essential part of the scientific style, and should be learned.
Notice that the majority of them are *one-word* equivalents. That is, they are *verb and adverb* in one.

e.g. *take in* = *absorb*

But they may still require a preposition when followed by a noun.

e.g. *draw out of* = *extract from*

EXERCISE

Read these statements as they are written. Then substitute a formal verb for the phrase in *italic* print.

1. The heat *coming out of* a body can be measured by a pyrometer.
2. Large areas of land in Holland have been *won back* from the sea by dykes
3. Most synthetic fibres do not easily *take in* moisture.
4. Multi-stage pumps are *made up* of several impellers on one shaft.
5. New methods of construction have gradually been *brought out* through long years of experience and testing.
6. A number of modifications were *built into* the machine.
7. Tests were *carried out* on many specimens of soil.
8. The emission of neutrons always *goes with* nuclear fission.
9. The concrete is *stirred up* continuously while it is being transported.
10. The spokes of a wheel *spread out* in all directions from the centre.
11. The lever must be *pushed down* to start the motor.
12. The turbine blades are liable to be *worn down.*
13. The two towers were *put up* in less than a year.
14. At very high speeds the resistance of the air *takes on* a much greater importance.
15. The machines can easily be *taken to pieces* and *put together again* after they have been *looked at.*
16. The compaction should be *spread out* all through the area of the concrete.
17. It should be possible to *find out* the necessary thickness of the concrete from the formulae.
18. The whole weight of the deck is *held up* by the four cables.
19. The railway lines seem to *go further apart* as they *come towards* the observer.
20. The light is *spread out* by dust particles in the air.
21. Work on the bridge was *started again* after the strike was over.
22. The aircraft is *driven forward* by thrust from the airscrews.
23. The unprotected pipes are being *eaten away* by exposure to the air.
24. The cold water *goes round and round* inside the tubes of the condenser.
25. High speed steel *keeps up* its hardness well, even at high temperatures.

3. Verbs (cont.)

We have seen that there are many formal verbs commonly used in technical writing which are the equivalent of the normal *phrasal verbs* of speech.
There are large numbers of formal verbs apart from this. They may be used because they are more *dignified* (build = *construct*); or because they are more *accurate* (increase = *augment*); or, and this often happens, because they are more *convenient* (turn into vapour = *evaporate*). They can often sum up something that would take quite a few other words to express clearly and accurately, and this is a great advantage.
There are a few typical endings to these verbs. For example:

-en: weaken, hasten, toughen. (See Section 1)
-ise: normalise, metallise, energise.
-ate: approximate, integrate, accelerate.
-fy: rectify, nullify, electrify, purify.

But many others do not have any recognisable endings. You will notice that very often they are equivalent to:

$$\left.\begin{matrix} \textit{make} \\ \textit{become} \\ \textit{turn} \end{matrix}\right\} + \text{Noun} + \text{Adjective}$$

EXERCISE

Read these statements as they stand, and then substitute a suitable verb for the parts in *italics*.

1. Reinforcement of the concrete will *make* the effect of cracking *as small as possible.*
2. Regular maintenance and lubrication will *give* the engine a *longer* life.
3. The ends of the cable are *fixed firmly and safely* in concrete foundations.
4. The bar of metal will *get shorter* as it cools.
5. One way of *making* the soil *stable* is to inject cement into it.
6. It is first necessary to *take the air out of* the vessel by means of an air-pump.
7. The hydrogen *sticks* to the copper electrodes in the form of small bubbles.
8. The motorway will gradually be *made longer* until eventually it runs from north to south through the country.
9. It should soon be possible to *make changes in* the cathode-ray tube, so as to lower the cost.
10. This work was formerly done manually, but it is now *carried out by machines.*
11. The acid is *made weaker* by the addition of water.
12. The formwork for the concrete is specially designed to *make* its erection and removal *easy.*
13. *More and more* carbon *collects* round the spark plug.
14. The tube is *marked off at intervals* in degrees Fahrenheit.
15. The radio signals are *made weaker* as the distance from the transmitter increases.

16. The petrol is *turned into a spray* by mixing it with air and injecting it through a small nozzle.
17. The volume of noise from the efflux *gets less* as the velocity of the gas stream is reduced.
18. The condensed steam then *falls under the influence of gravity* to the bottom of the condenser.
19. The special properties of this alloy are now being *made use of* in industry.
20. The valve has the effect of *making* the voltage *greater*.
21. When its temperature is reduced beyond a certain point, the gas will *turn to liquid*.
22. The beam of light passes through lenses, which *make* the image *larger*.
23. The electrodes are *put under the surface of* the liquid in the vessel.
24. When joining two shafts together, care must be taken to *make certain* that they are properly *in line with each other*.
25. An automatic timing device *makes* the spark *come later* at slow engine speeds, and *makes* it *come earlier* at higher speeds.
26. A beam of light entering water from air is *bent* towards the normal.
27. The image seen through the convex lens is *turned upside down*.
28. The water is *made slightly acid* by the addition of a little sulphuric acid.
29. A 300-ohm resistor is *put* into the circuit *instead of* the 3000-ohm resistor.
30. Guard rings are fitted in the photo-electric cell to *get rid of* current leaks.

REVISION (SECTIONS 22–28)

Read these statements, choosing the correct word rom the alternatives in brackets.

1. Soil surveys are (*performed, effected, conducted*) in order to (*determine, realise, resolve*) the bearing (*capacity, ability, capability*) of the soil at any point. The (*datum, data*) which (*is, are*) obtained will (*effect, affect*) the planning of the road to be built, since (*unsuitable, unsuited*) soils will be (*avoided, eliminated, obstructed*) wherever it is (*practical, practicable, unpractical*) to do so.
2. Colour television is not (*liable, likely, possible*) to (*introduce, be introduced*) here until a high (*grade, percentage, degree*) of perfection has been (*accomplished, won, achieved*), and until a simple (*manner, method*) has been (*devised, adopted, contrived*) of (*adapting, adopting, diverting*) an ordinary receiver to take colour (*transmissions, emissions*).
3. In a (*work, job, undertaking*) such as the (*erection, construction*) of a motorway, a large (*number, amount*) of excavating and road-building (*equipment, equipments*) (*is, are*) required, which (*is, are*) normally (*assembled, accumulated*) at convenient (*situations, sites*) ready for use.
4. (*It, There*) has been a (*tendency, liability, trend*) for industry to be (*as-

sembled, *concentrated*) in a single region, instead of (*to be*, *being*) (*distributed*, *dispersed*, *diffused*) evenly over the (*whole*, *all*) country. As a result, the (*remains*, *residue*, *remainder*) of the country is much poorer, and (*works*, *jobs*, *employments*) are difficult to find.

5. On main roads which are (*subject*, *subjected*, *susceptible*) to heavy traffic loads, the surface is (*liable*, *likely*, *apt*) to (*damage*, *damages*) unless the loads (*impressed*, *imposed*, *sustained*) by the (*traffic*, *traffics*) (*is*, *are*) adequately distributed through the concrete.
6. The power (*achieved*, *generated*, *developed*) by a piston engine in an aircraft (*increases*, *decreases*) (*with*, *as*) an increase in height. The volume of (*air*, *the air*) taken in is (*consistent*, *constant*) at all heights, but its weight decreases (*as*, *with*) the pressure falls. This (*loss*, *lack*, *failure*) of power can be (*overcome*, *counteracted*, *reacted*) by supercharging the engine.
7. The four (*phase*, *act*, *stroke*) cycle can be (*exchanged*, *converted*, *converged*) into a two (*phase*, *act*, *stroke*) cycle by (*admitting*, *impelling*, *evolving*) the fresh charge under pressure in such a way (*as*, *that*) the exhaust gases are expelled (*as*, *while*, *during*) the piston reaches the end of the working (*phase*, *act*, *stroke*).
8. Various methods (*for*, *of*) stabilising the soil beneath a road surface have been (*designed*, *evolved*, *devised*) to (*prevent*, *protect*, *obviate*) it from (*failure*, *error*, *defect*). One (*such*, *of such*) method is grouting, which (*consists of*, *comprises*) injecting cement into it, the cement (*acts*, *acting*) (*as*, *for*) a binder to hold the soil (*articles*, *particles*, *atoms*) together.
9. A high (*grade*, *degree*, *level*) of accuracy is demanded in the (*machining*, *working*) of these electronic (*components*, *constituents*).
10. (*Assumed*, *Assuming*, *Considering*) that the demand for power (*continues*, *goes on*) to (*rise*, *increase*) at the current (*rate*, *speed*, *level*), it will not be long (*until*, *before*, *when*) traditional (*sources*, *mines*, *supplies*) become inadequate.

Key to the Exercises

Exercises to which a key is not given can be answered correctly in a number of ways.

page

6. 1 include 2 content 3 composition 4 consists 5 constituents . . . include 6 comprises 7 is composed 8 include 9 constituent 10 comprises 11 content 12 constituent 13 is composed/made up of 14 contain 15 components 16 consists of 17 component 18 comprise 19 contains 20 include
10. 1 caused . . . to 2 enables . . . to 3 enables . . . to 4 causes . . . to 5 caused . . . to 6 enables/allows . . . to 7 caused . . . to 8 caused . . . to 9 allows/permits . . . to 10 enables . . . to 11 caused . . . to 12 causes . . . to 13 causes . . . to 14 caused . . . to 15 permits/allows . . . to
11. 1 (far) less than/not so great as; (far) greater than 2 as much/as high a percentage . . . as 3 weighs less/is lighter than, etc.
16. 1 will (certainty)/can, may (possibility) 2 will 3 will 4 can/may be obtained 5 will (certainty)/may (possibility) 6 can 7 can/may 8 may 9 will 10 can 11 will 12 may/can (no difference) 13 will 14 will 15 will 16 will; will 17 can 18 will (certainty)/may (possibility) 19 can/may be fed 20 will
18. 1 protect 2 prevented/kept 3 prevented/kept 4 keep/kept 5 prevents 6 protect; prevents/keeps 7 protection; reduce 8 avoid 9 prevents/keeps 10 keeps 11 prevents/keeps 12 obviates 13 keeps 14 prevention 15 avoids 16 reduces/eliminates
23. 1 depends/is dependent on 2 depends on 3 depending on/according to 4 depend on 5 depends/is dependent on 6 depending on/according to 7 irrespective of 8 depends/is dependent on 9 depends/is dependent on 10 irrespective of 11 rely on 12 depend/be dependent on 13 depends on 14 depending on 15 depends on
28. This type of metal can be cast . . . 2 The ore is smelted . . . and reduced 3 Many operations can be carried out 4 The two metal plates are clamped 5 Millions of tons 6 Several new products 7 Production will be started 8 Heat for welding can be 9 An electric current is passed 10 A vee-shaped weld is normally 11 Heavy . . . is not/No heavy . . . is 12 The cross-slide is allowed 13 The appropriate gear is selected 14 These supports are called 15 Damage to the shaft will be 16 The metal surfaces will be 17 A thin grease can be 18 The characteristics of steel can be 19 The steel must be 20 Care must be taken not to
30. (Bracket shows meaning 1, 2 or 3 in table) 1 (3) 2 should be made (1) 3 should not be permitted (1) 4 should be tempered (1) 5 (3) 6 should be applied (1) 7 (2) 8 should be written (1) 9 should be reduced (3) 10 should be allowed (1) 11 (1) 12 (2) 13 (2) 14 should be kept (1) 15 (3)
34. (*by* . . . is required in all sentences) 1 is being built; was built; will be built 2 is/was/will be generated 3 are/were/will be given 4 is/was/will be powered 5 is/was/will be caused 6 are/were/will be produced 7 are/were/will be caused 8 be replaced 9 is/was/will be carried along 10 is/was/will be absorbed 11 is/was/will be provided 12 be controlled 13 is/was/will be refracted 14 is/was formed 15 be accepted 16 is/will be produced 17 is/was/will be absorbed 18 is/was/will be gripped firmly 19 is/was/will be provided 20 was caused
36. 1 enough 2 sufficiently 3 (not) enough/(in)adequate/(in)sufficient 4 too 5 exceeds/is greater than/in excess of 6 adequate; excess 7 deficient in 8 too; for 9 too; to 10 too; inadequate/insufficient 11 exceed 12 exceeds/is greater than/in excess of 13 excessive 14 excessively 15 adequate 16

page

enough/sufficient/adequate 17 too; to 18 too; or 19 too great/excessive 20 excessive

37. *Ex. 5* A test-tube should be filled . . . and heated . . . The tube should be supported . . . and allowed . . . The temperature should be taken . . . The water should be stirred (*or* A glass rod should be used to stir) . . . The readings obtained (*or* you obtain) should be recorded and plotted . . . This should be repeated . . . The solid should be allowed . . . The liquid should be heated . . . (then) the tube should be fixed . . . and allowed . . . The results should be recorded . . . and plotted.

Ex. 6 Thoroughly clean . . . Do not leave (*or* Leave no) . . . Heat the ends . . . Use an . . . Apply a . . . Press the . . . Take care . . . Then smooth off . . .

42. *Ex. 2* 1 Water-tubes are fitted in a boiler to/so as to/in order to absorb . . . *or* for the purpose of/with the object of/etc. absorbing . . .

43. 1 necessitate 2 needs/requires 3 necessary/essential; to be 4 needs/requires 5 obviate 6 necessitate 7 dispense 8 for; to be 9 with the need for 10 is necessary/essential; required/requisite 11 needs/requires; necessitates 12 required/requisite/necessary 13 makes necessary/necessitates 14 dispensed/done away with 15 required 16 needs/requires 17 requisite; essential

43. *Revision* 1 for; body; consists of; of; contains; amount; heated; expands; rises; depending 2 high; generated; this, material; able; withstand; prevent; with; means; conserved 3 is; composed; for; a number; highly 4 rather; than; This; employment; machinery; of cutting; than; by 5 offers; number; over; temperature; fairly; irrespective; wide; under; greater 6 most; adopted; On; at; point; normal 7 liable; chemical; action; protected; way; means; achieve; coat; known 8 machine; work; machined; high; feed; means; driven; accommodated 9 adequate; for; too; fall; enable; complete 10 intensely; electric; across; to be welded; between 11 rise; cause; increase; prevent; relieve; letting 12 few; resources; on; raw; for them 13 experiments; ago; has; made; lack; terminated; object; achieved 14 constructed; bring; first of all; prevent; ensure; enable; power 15 devoted; carrying; research; into; properties; material; papers; journals; aroused

49. *Ex. 1* 1–13 by . . . ing 6 By using/By the use of

50. *Ex. 2* 1 by 2 by means of 3 by/by means of 4 by 5 with 6 by 7 with 8 by 9 with 10 by 11 with/by means of 12 by/with

51. 1 are 2 may be 3 should be 4 is/may be 5 are 6 may be 7 is/may be 8 need not 9 does not form 10 will/may 11 may be 12 is not

52. 1 supply of air 2 containing water 3 of 4 using mercury 5 made of 6 of the 7 made of 8 valve made to stop the passage 9 water for feeding (supplying) the boiler 10 containing/to contain 11 containing 12 for rolling 13 conducting power 14 design of the head of a cylinder 15 of the type which works by 16 in or for a/the 17 of the gears 18 used for injecting 19 of the kind which locks 20 in 21 using 22 of 23 having a 24 c. under which a 25 p. of the t. of power 26 p. for extracting from c. 27 o. of p. from the g. 28 l. from the cylinder by c. 29 system of l. by feeding by g. 30 d. for the i. of b. of this type

56. 1 As soon as 2 As 3 Before 4 As soon as 5 As 6 Before 7 As 8 Until 9 After 10 As 11 When 12 Before 13 Before 14 until 15 As 16 As

62. (Alternatives shown in table are possible.) 1 Before mixing 2 While rising, the piston carries 3 When landing 4 After passing 5 In rotating 6 On reaching 7 In cooling 8 When rotating 9 Prior to entering 10 On leaving 11 While travelling 12 Before becoming 13 . . . on exceeding 14 After transmitting 15 . . . before being 16 In rotating 17 On passing 18 After being heated 19 While entering 20 Before being

65. 1 progressive 2 previously 3 series 4 progressively 5 succession 6 initial 7 previous/preceding 8 subsequently 9 series 10 initial 11 successive 12 progressively 13 succeeded 14 series 15 alternate

page

69. 1 When/As soon as 2 As 3 As/While 4 Before 5 When/Once 6 As 7 By the time 8 After 9 Before 10 When 11 Until/Before 12 When 13 As 14 . . . until 15 When 16 By the time 17 By the time 18 As soon as

71. *Ex. 2* 1 alternative 2 either; or 3 else/alternatively 4 Either; or; whether; or 5 else/alternatively

77. 1 tubes filled 2 area exposed 3 work done . . . heat received 4 power demanded 5 research being carried out 6 steam extracted 7 torque exerted 8 process adopted 9 Generators not required 10 steel obtained

83. *Ex. 1* 1 where 2 at which 3 through which 4 in which 5 for which 6 with which 7 with which 8 during which 9 through which 10 of which 11 on which 12 of which 13 of which 14 of/about which 15 where 16 of which 17 of which 18 where 19 at which 20 whereby

84. *Ex. 2* 1 sphere into which steam 2 in which (where) 3 spring the tension of which 4 for which 5 into which 6 all of which 7 soil over which the road surface was laid was 8 prism through which the light passes 9 purpose of which 10 station in which plutonium is produced is

93. *Ex. 2* 1 decreases with 2 increases with 3 varies with 4 vary with/according to 5 varies with/according to 6 decreases with 7 varies with 8 decreases with 9 increases with 10 increases with 11 varies with 12 decreases with 13 increases with 14 varies with 15 increases with

93. *Revision* 1 equipped; involved; outlay; hand; dispensed with; fewer; operate; machine 2 rate; transfer; providing; Thereby; area; available; greatly; diffused 3 has been; progressive; last; installation; machines; succession; made; introduced 4 While; deflected; original; in; deflected; exerts; force; causes; rotate; 5 fire; sequence; downward; transmitted; movement; way; much 6 conditions; cylinder; conducive; efficient; largely; achieved 7 For; have tried; discover; of; force 8 in; acquires; conduction; until; to 9 induced; ignited; gap; spreads; whole 10 On; engine; faster; consequently; raised; force; thereby; effect; operating 11 In; allow; great; over/in; Unless; would; inadequate 12 cycle; compressing; extremely; consequent; sufficiently; injected; to ignite; spontaneously 13 cost; equipping; against; likely; effected; efficient 14 function; applied; work; prevention; during 15 generated; as; rate; achieved; draught

99. 1 so; that 2 so; as to 3 such an; that 4 so; that 5 so; as to 6 so; that 7 such; that 8 so; that 9 so; as to 10 Such; that 11 so; that 12 such a; that 13 such a; that 14 so; that 15 so much; that 16 such a; as to

100. 1 The engineers designing the motorway had 2 rotating 3 expanding 4 containing 5 weakening 6 transmitting 7 coming 8 lying 9 lining 10 lying 11 leaking 12 having 13 having 14 leading 15 having 16 falling 17 enabling 18 emanating 19 installing 20 standing 21 striking 22 entering 23 passing 24 containing 25 spanning

101. (Brackets refer to numbered section above) 1 (3) 2 (2) 3 (3) 4 (1) 5 (1) 6 (1) 7 (2) 8 (1) 9 (2) 10 (3) 11 (1) 12 (2) 13 (1) 14 (1 except) 15 (1)

106. *Ex. 1* 1 increases; will automatically come 2 fails; will operate 3 contains; will be converted 4 will be admitted; is fissioned 5 will rise; is increased 6 is superheated; will be 7 is fitted 8 is passed; will be set up 9 act; will remain 10 will result; are shielded 11 will be experienced; falls 12 will be; stretches 13 reaches; will ignite 14 are not diluted; will be 15 is properly designed
Ex. 2 1 If the neutron flux increases 2 If . . . is not 3 fails 4 falls 5 prove 6 are allowed 7 rises 8 is not removed

107. *Ex. 1* 1 (a) 2 (a)(b – only if) 3 (a)(b – only if) 4 (a)(b) 5 (a)(b) 6 (a) 7 (a)(b – only if) 8 (a) 9 (a) 10 (a)(b) 11 (a) 12 (a) only

114. *Ex. 1* 1 so designed that . . ./designed in such a way that . . . 2 Stored in such a way that . . . etc.

115. *Ex. 2* 1 *or* designed in such a way as to/so designed as to, etc. 2 Stored in such a way as to prevent contamination, etc.

page

115. 1 When 2 During 3 Once 4 If 5 During 6 When 7 When 8 If/When 9 Before 10 When; if/once 11 On/During 12 When 13 When; if 14 When 15 If/When 16 If 17 If/When 18 On/During 19 After 20 If/When 21 Once/When 22 After 23 When/If 24 When/Once 25 If

121. 1 has been proved 2 has already been photographed 3 have been largely overcome 4 have had 5 has just begun 6 have since died 7 has been exhausted 8 have been made 9 has recently invited 10 has been designed 11 have been exhausted 12 have not yet been completed 13 has been taken 14 has spent 15 has expanded 16 have been used 17 has proved 18 have been carefully considered; has/have been found; has been awarded 19 has been heated 20 was founded; has expanded; has done 21 has been made 22 has suffered 23 have been made; has necessitated 24 has condensed 25 was built; has become; has ever known

122. 1–10 so . . . ed *or* thus . . . ed

123. In the case of polonium; in the case of such; In the case of gamma; cases where workers; in some/certain cases severe; In no case may; used in every case/in all cases; in many cases to view; in certain/some cases heavy; in some cases as much; In other cases a maze; in cases where the level; In the case of a nuclear

127. 1 It is undesirable to 2 It is not difficult to pump 3 It is necessary/essential to eliminate 4 It is usual to 5 It is impracticable to carry out 6 It is preferable to 7 It is advantageous to work 8 It is inadvisable (etc.) to use 9 It is now possible to 10 It is common (practice) to 11 It is advisable to 12 It proves necessary to maintain 13 It is necessary/essential to temper 14 It is possible to 15 It is instructive to look

128. 1 as such 2 is expressed as 3 acts as 4 as 5 is usually expressed as 6 as such 7 are known/referred to as 8 is sometimes referred to as 9 as 10 as 11 considered/regarded as 12 is usually known/referred to as 13 as 14 may be used as 15 as such

133. 1 It can be shown/that 2 can be proved 3 will be appreciated 4 is assumed 5 is obvious 6 is clear 7 can be demonstrated 8 will be seen 9 is hoped 10 is known 11 should be noted 12 is assumed 13 is possible 14 is known 15 is desirable

135. 1 identical 2 like 3 like 4 as 5 in 6 with 7 like/similar to 8 as; was 9 as 10 as 11 like 12 as; are 13 as 14 like 15 as

140. 1 would have 2 were not lubricated 3 would be able 4 would have been cancelled 5 would be unable 6 had risen 7 were; would be 8 would contaminate 9 had not been sealed 10 had not been planned

142. 1 are different/differ from; in 2 is different/differs from; in 3 unlike 4 distinguish/differentiate/make a distinction between 5 unlike 6 as against/compared with 7 is different/differs from: in that 8 Unlike 9 as against/etc.

143. *Revision* 1 associated; dissipates; fairly; number; decay; level; disposed 2 plants; liable; exposed; doses; counteract; taken; protective 3 through; offers; resistance; various; devised; this; entirely; eliminated 4 contains; channels; inserted/introduced; elements; whose; function; regulate; rate 5 involves; provision; maintaining; discharged; retains; sustained 6 filament; an evacuated; applied; generated; emitted; impinge; alternating; applied 7 extended; accommodate; except for; installed; in case 8 with; last; except for; stage; capable; delivering; than 9 During; have been; a; greatly; facilitated; work; has; unemployed. 10 the case; engine; dispensed with; effected; raising; temperature; where; injected 11 supplies; current; circuit; actuated; in; with; thus; current; flow; secondary 12 products; include; including; such as 13 attain, entails; research; Unless; little; made 14 properties; substitutes; range; affected; as; as; conduct; as 15 source; mineral; operations; for; scale; expanded; had been

148. (A = addition; E = explanation) 1 each being driven A 2 the oil then draining

A 3 being one A 4 being essential E 5 being converted A 6 being restricted E 7 being conveyed A 8 being the fertile A 9 each being connected A 10 forming a film E 11 passing over A 12 being passed E 13 being negatively E 14 being deposited A 15 being assumed A 16 being as follows A 17 being then A 18 having passed E

149. 1 such as to 2 such that 3 s. that 4 s. as to 5 s. that 6 s. that 7 s. that 8 s. that 9 s. as to 10 s. that 11 s. that 12 s. that 13 s. that 14 s. as to 15 s. that

154. 1 thus causing 2 thereby raising 3 thus increasing 4 thus lowering 5 thus increasing production 6 thus/thereby preventing 7 thus/thereby accelerating 8 thus giving 9 thus/thereby hastening 10 thus bringing

155. 1 in that/inasmuch as 2 in that/inasmuch as 3 in 4 in that/in so far as/inasmuch as 5 in that/inasmuch as 6 in 7 in that/inasmuch as 8 in 9 in that/inasmuch as 10 in that/in so far as/inasmuch as 11 in that, etc. 12 in 13 in that, etc. 14 in that, etc.

160. *Ex. 1* 1 (b)(c) 2 (d) 3 (d) 4 (b)(c) 5 (d) 6 (b)(c) 7 (b)(c) 8 (d) 9 (d) 10 (b)(c)

161. *Ex. 2* With *In spite of*, no change. With *Although* and *In spite of the fact that:* 1 it has 2 it is 3 a higher . . . is involved 4 the recovery plant is basically simple 5 allowance had been made 6 some of the defects have been remedied 7 the gases are cooled 8 the road has been widened 9 multi-stage pumps are expensive 10 great care was taken

163. 1 consumption 2 emission 3 extraction; complications 4 transmission 5 compaction; laying 6 installation; equipment; responsibility 7 compression 8 forgings 9 information; specification 10 operation; restriction 11 availability; locality 12 arrangements; lubrication 13 withdrawal 14 incorporation; modifications; improvement; performance 15 application; voltage 16 accumulation 17 containment; emanation(s) 18 inclination 19 casing 20 susceptibility; erosion

164. *Ex. 1* 1 is cooled by 2 must be processed 3 If . . . is increased 4 Steam jackets . . . reduce 5 Hypersonic . . . are quite often/commonly attained 6 Heat is transferred 7 The current is rectified 8 Problems . . . are eliminated by using 9 is compacted 10 Performance can be improved

Ex. 2 1 The application . . . results in/produces 2 Investigation . . . made/undertaken 3 The timing . . . is so arranged that 4 The use . . . is common/widespread 5 The analysis . . . will appear/be undertaken/etc. 6 Allowance should be made 7 Control . . . is effected/etc. 8 The addition . . . will assist/etc. 9 Correct setting . . . ensures/etc. that 10 Regulation . . . can be effected *or* The use . . .

169. 1 depends on the thoroughness/etc. of the compaction 2 according to the distance it has to be transported and freight charges 3 the extent of 4 extent/degree to which 5 quantity . . . rise 6 extent to which 7 cause 8 stability . . . weight 9 possible improvement 10 amount/quantity/volume 11 speed of rotation 12 date of completion/speed with which

171. 1 unsuitable; excavated; compactable 2 abrasive; advisable; reciprocating 3 combined; mixing; distributing; available 4 tamping; adjustable; desired 5 constructed; foreseeable 6 permitted; machined; accompanying 7 resistant; excessive; combustible 8 Extending; trailing; effective; controllable 9 successive; preceding 10 expelled; required; propulsive; surrounding

172. 1 with 2 of 3 to 4 to 5 with 6 to 7 for 8 to 9 to 10 in

178.

ir	un	im	in
dis	in	in	un
im	in	in	in/un
un	dis	in	in
in	un	un	in/un

page

184. 1 was that of 2 are those which 3 than that of 4 than that of 5 as those of/as are those of 6 than that for 7 are those which 8 to that of

184. (Only one equivalent is given but alternatives exist in a number of cases) 1 achieved 2 devised; discover 3 rotate 4 emits 5 compensate 6 ejected from 7 removed from 8 sustained; expelled from 9 entrained 10 consumes 11 oscillate 12 excavated 13 foretell 14 induced into 15 conveyed 16 recovered 17 replaced 18 established 19 exceed 20 extruded 21 emitted 22 superimposed on 23 inflated 24 transported 25 retained

190 1 to produce 2 to form 3 to form 4 to make/form 5 to form 6 to leave 7 to make 8 to give 9 to form 10 to form 11 to produce 12 to form

191. 1 emanating from 2 reclaimed 3 absorb 4 composed 5 introduced 6 incorporated in 7 performed 8 accompanies 9 agitated 10 radiate 11 depressed 12 abraded 13 erected 14 assumes 15 dismantled; reassembled; examined 16 distributed 17 discover 18 supported 19 diverge; approach 20 diffused 21 resumed 22 propelled 23 corroded 24 circulates 25 maintains

192. 1 minimise 2 prolong 3 anchored 4 contract 5 stabilising 6 evacuate 7 adheres 8 extended 9 modify 10 mechanised 11 diluted 12 facilitate 13 accumulates 14 graduated 15 weakened 16 atomised 17 diminishes 18 gravitates 19 exploited 20 increasing 21 liquefy 22 magnify 23 immersed in 24 ensure; aligned 25 retards; advances 26 refracted 27 inverted 28 acidulated 29 substituted in . . . for 30 eliminate

193. *Revision* 1 conducted; determine; capacity; data; are; affect; unsuitable; avoided; practicable 2 likely; be introduced; degree; achieved; method; devised; adapting; transmissions 3 an undertaking; construction; amount; equipment; is; is; assembled; sites 4 There; tendency; concentrated; being; dispersed; whole; remainder; jobs 5 subjected; liable; damage; imposed; traffic; are 6 developed; decreases; with; air; constant; as; loss; counteracted 7 stroke; converted; stroke; admitting; that; as; stroke 8 of; evolved; protect; failure; such; consists of; acting as; particles 9 degree; machining; components 10 Assuming; continues; rise; rate; before; sources

Index of Words

The references are to the Sections in which the words can be found. Numbers in heavy print indicate that illustrations of the word, or explanations of its meaning, are given. Technical words are not included in this list.